Welcome to
THE

THESE HANDY, ACCESSIBLE BOOKS are designed to be the perfect travel companions. Whether you're traveling within a restricted budget or feeling the urge to splurge, you will find all you need to know to create the ideal vacation for yourself and your family.

These travel-friendly books present the latest information on hotel accommodations, restaurants, shopping, and transportation, as well as money-saving tips and strategies to beat the crowds and avoid the lines. Also included are detailed descriptions that help you make those tough decisions on which attractions to include in your travel itinerary.

Use these books to help you plan your vacation and then take them along with you for quick and easy reference. You can read them cover to cover or simply pick out the information you need. Let the *Everything® Travel Guides* pave the way for your fun-filled and exciting adventures!

 TRAVEL TIP

Quick, handy tips

⊕ HOT SPOT

Places not to be missed

☰FAST FACT

Important sound bytes of information

THE
EVERYTHING®
— Travel Guides —

Dear Reader,

You're about to visit The Disneyland Resort, a theme park that continues to be called "The happiest place on Earth!" While this California-based Disney theme park resort isn't as large as The Walt Disney World Resort in Orlando, with the opening of Disney's California Adventure, it's certainly an incredibly popular vacation destination that's well worth the trip.

The rides, shows, attractions, and parades at the Disney theme parks are like nothing you'll find elsewhere. Combine this with the other nearby theme parks and tourist attractions, such as Universal Studios Hollywood, Knott's Berry Farm, Six Flags Magic Mountain, SeaWorld, LegoLand, and everything there is to see and do in the Los Angeles area, and you're in for an incredible vacation!

Since the tragedy of September 11th, you'll find security at the major airports to be tighter than ever. Plus, it's now necessary to pass through metal detectors and have your bags searched as you enter into the various theme parks. Don't allow this, however, to get in your way of having a wonderful time. With a little extra planning on your part, you'll be able to save time and money without compromising the fun of your vacation.

Use this book to help preplan your vacation and make it easier to figure out how you'll spend your time (and money) once you're in the Los Angeles area. You'll find this book is filled with time and money saving tips!

Well, here's to you having a wonderful Los Angeles vacation! When you get home, please feel free to email me at *jr7777@aol.com*, or visit my Web site at *www.JasonRich.com*, and let me know how you enjoyed your trip!

Sincerely,

THE

EVERYTHING®

TRAVEL GUIDE TO
THE DISNEYLAND RESORT®, CALIFORNIA ADVENTURE®, UNIVERSAL STUDIOS®, AND THE ANAHEIM AREA

A complete guide to the best
hotels, restaurants, parks,
and must-see attractions

Jason Rich

Adams Media Corporation
Avon, Massachusetts

Publishing Director: Gary M. Krebs
Managing Editor: Kate McBride
Copy Chief: Laura MacLaughlin
Acquisitions Editor: Allison Carpenter Yoder
Development Editors: Lesley Bolton,
                    Michael Paydos
Production Editor: Khrysti Nazzaro

Production Director: Susan Beale
Production Manager: Michelle Roy Kelly
Series Designer: Daria Perreault
Cover Design: Paul Beatrice, Frank Rivera
Layout and Graphics: Brooke Camfield,
Colleen Cunningham, Rachael Eiben
Michelle Roy Kelly, Daria Perreault

An Everything® Series Book.
Everything® and everything.com® are registered trademarks of F+W Publications, Inc.

Published by Adams Media, an F+W Publications Company
57 Littlefield Street, Avon, MA 02322 U.S.A.
www.adamsmedia.com

ISBN: 1-58062-742-0
Printed in the United States of America.

J I H G F E D C B

Library of Congress Cataloging-in-Publication Data
Rich, Jason.
The everything travel guide to the Disneyland Resort, California
Adventure, Universal Studios, and the Anaheim area / Jason Rich.
    p.   cm.   (An everything series book)
                Includes index.
            ISBN 1-58062-742-0
1. Amusement parks—California—Guidebooks. 2. Disneyland (Calif.)—Guidebooks.
      3. Anaheim (Calif.)—Guidebooks. I. Title. II. Everything series.
GV1853.3.C2 R53   2002
917.94'96—dc21   2002008431

This publication is designed to provide accurate and authoritative information with regard to the subject matter covered. It is sold with the understanding that the publisher is not engaged in rendering legal, accounting, or other professional advice. If legal advice or other expert assistance is required, the services of a competent professional person should be sought.
            —From a *Declaration of Principles* jointly adopted by a Committee of the
            American Bar Association and a Committee of Publishers and Associations

The following are registered trademarks of The Walt Disney Company: California Adventure, Disneyland Resort, Main Street, U.S.A.

Although the author has taken care to ensure that this book accurately sets forth information as of the time it was prepared, prices, practices, and policies at Anaheim attractions may change at any time, and may be different from the information provided here.

Universal Studios is a registered trademark of Universal Studios, Inc.

Cover Illustrations by Barry Littmann.
Cartography by Creative Force, Inc.

This book is available at quantity discounts for bulk purchases.
For information, call 1-800-872-5627.

Visit the entire Everything® series at everything.com

Contents

Acknowledgments

Thanks to everyone at Adams Media for making this book a reality. Thanks also to Mark, Ellen, Sandy, Emily, Ferras, and my family for all of their love and support.

Introduction

So, you're about to embark on a vacation to Los Angeles. This book describes the major attractions and theme parks in and near Los Angeles County, Anaheim (where The Disneyland Resort is located), and nearby San Diego. As you'll quickly discover, there's a lot to see and do, so be prepared for an exciting and memorable adventure!

The theme parks featured in this book are family-oriented attractions. In other words, much of what you'll find within the parks is suitable for people of all ages—kids, teens, adults, and senior citizens alike. In order to cater to entire families, the theme parks offer a wide range of rides, shows, attractions, and activities. Some attractions cater to specific age groups, while others are for the whole family.

Every year, millions of people visit the various California theme parks and have a wonderful time. Unless you're planning to spend several weeks and an absolute fortune, there's no possible way you'll be able to experience everything that the Anaheim, Los Angeles County, and San Diego areas have to offer. So, you'll have to make some decisions about which theme parks you want to visit, which attractions you want to experience, what shows and parades you want to see, and where you want to dine.

This book is designed to help you make those decisions. Here you will find detailed descriptions of all the activities and attractions at The Disneyland Resort, Disney's California Adventure, Downtown Disney, Knott's Southern California Resort, Six Flags Magic Mountain, and Universal Studios Hollywood, as well as other attractions in Anaheim, Los Angeles County, and nearby San Diego such as SeaWorld, the San Diego Zoo, the San Diego Wild Animal Park, and LEGOLAND California. This book also provides all sorts of tips and suggestions on how you can save time and money while making the most of your vacation.

This book is 100 percent "unofficial," which means that it is in no way authorized or sanctioned by The Walt Disney Company, Universal Studios Florida, SeaWorld, or any other theme park, attraction, travel agency, hotel chain, restaurant, or airline. Thus, this book can tell it as it is and offer you money-saving advice that you won't find in any other travel guides or vacation-planning books.

To help you choose which theme park rides, shows, and attractions are most worth experiencing, this book offers a star-based rating system for each activity. The ratings are based on the age group each attraction will most appeal to. For each ride, you'll see a chart listing several age groups, plus a one- (★) to three- (★★★) star rating.

Thus, if a rating chart for an attraction has three stars for each age group, the attraction is suitable for the entire family—so don't miss it. If a specific ride, for example, receives three stars but only for one age group, then the ride is best suited for that specific age group. An N.S. rating indicates that the attraction is not suited for that age group. The following brief summary describes how each ride, show, and attraction is rated within this book:

One star (★): Rides and attractions that earned just one star aren't worth waiting for and can be skipped, especially if your time is limited.

Two stars (★★): Rides and attractions that earned two stars are good, but they don't fall into the must-see category.

Three stars (★★★): The rides and attractions that earned three stars are definitely worth seeing and should not be missed, even if there's a significant wait.

N.S.: This denotes rides and attractions that are "Not Suitable" for a specific age group.

Keep in mind that these ratings are only recommendations. If you have a mature nine-year-old child, he or she may very well enjoy a ride, show, or attraction that's shown to be suitable for an eleven- to fifteen-year-old. As a parent, that's a judgment call you'll need to make based on the information provided within this book and after seeing the ride, show, or attraction for yourself.

Well, your Southern California vacation planning is about to begin! Get those travel reservations made, pack your bags, and get ready to go! The more time and effort you put into planning your vacation before you leave home, the more fun you'll have once you arrive. By preplanning your tentative itinerary, you'll know how to better manage your time and money, and you'll have a plan that involves experiencing exactly what you want to once you arrive in Los Angeles, Anaheim, or San Diego.

Greater Anaheim Metro Area

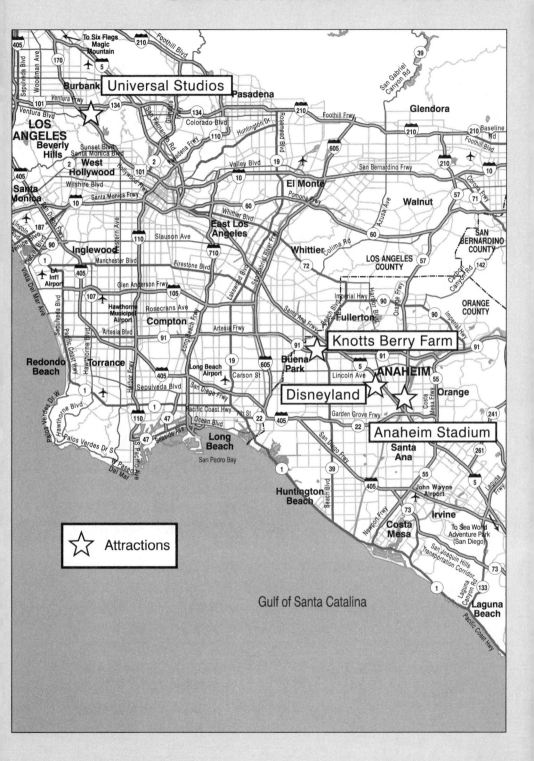

Disneyland Theme Park

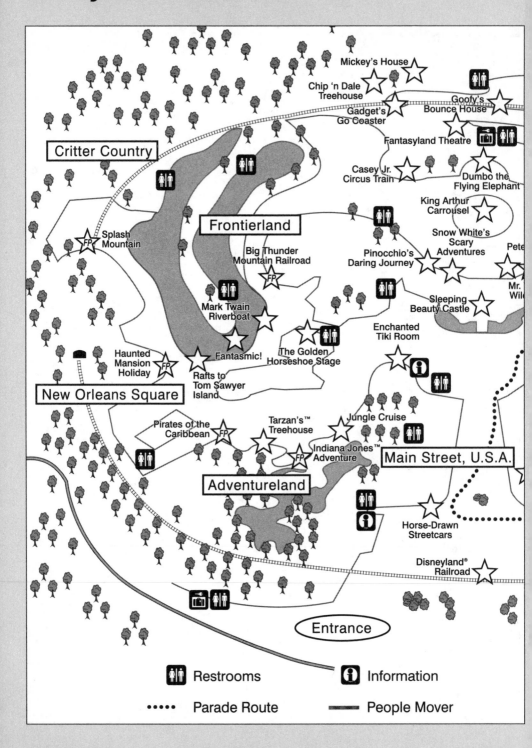

Mickey's House

Chip 'n Dale Treehouse

Gadget's Go Coaster

Goofy's Bounce House

Fantasyland Theatre

Critter Country

Casey Jr. Circus Train

Dumbo the Flying Elephant

King Arthur Carrousel

Frontierland

Snow White's Scary Adventures

Splash Mountain

Big Thunder Mountain Railroad

Pinocchio's Daring Journey

Pete...

Mr. Wild

Mark Twain Riverboat

Sleeping Beauty Castle

Enchanted Tiki Room

Fantasmic!

The Golden Horseshoe Stage

Haunted Mansion Holiday

New Orleans Square

Rafts to Tom Sawyer Island

Tarzan's™ Treehouse

Jungle Cruise

Pirates of the Caribbean

Indiana Jones™ Adventure

Main Street, U.S.A.

Adventureland

Horse-Drawn Streetcars

Disneyland® Railroad

Entrance

👥 Restrooms   ℹ Information

••••• Parade Route   ━━ People Mover

2

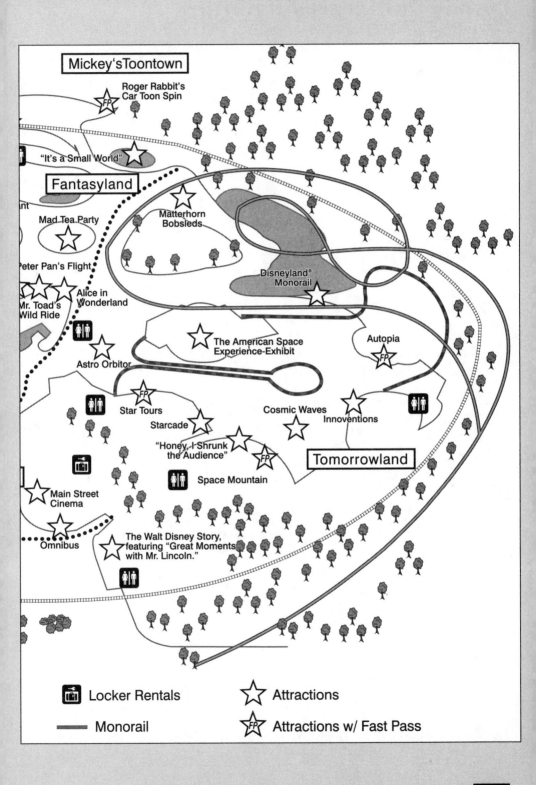

Disney California Adventure

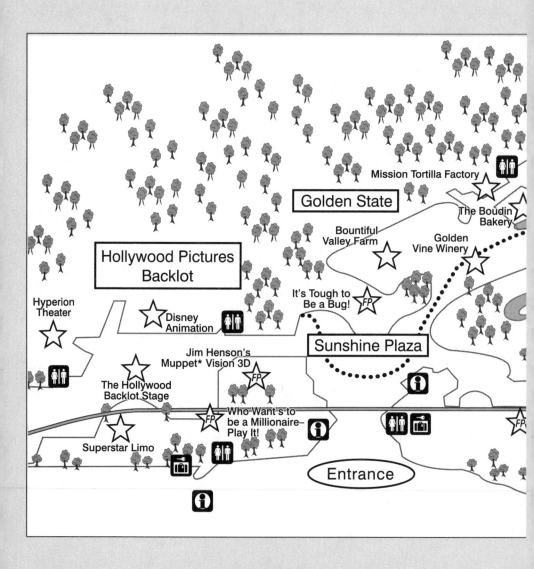

Mission Tortilla Factory

Golden State

The Boudin Bakery

Bountiful Valley Farm

Golden Vine Winery

Hollywood Pictures Backlot

It's Tough to Be a Bug!

Hyperion Theater

Disney Animation

Sunshine Plaza

Jim Henson's Muppet* Vision 3D

The Hollywood Backlot Stage

Who Want's to be a Millionaire– Play It!

Superstar Limo

Entrance

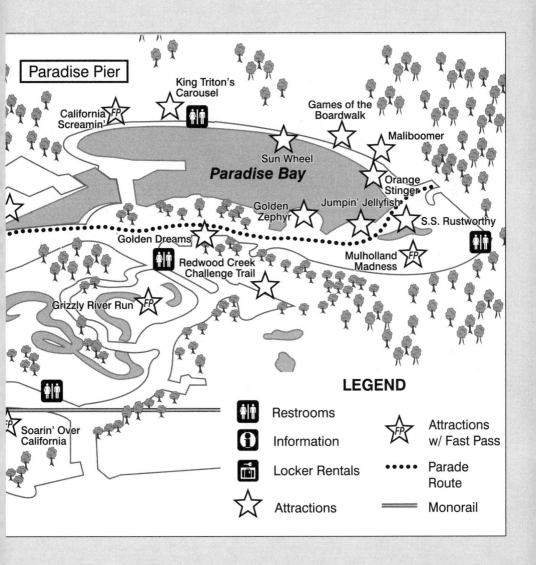

Paradise Pier

King Triton's Carousel

California Screamin' *FP*

Games of the Boardwalk

Maliboomer

Sun Wheel

Paradise Bay

Orange Stinger

Golden Zephyr

Jumpin' Jellyfish

S.S. Rustworthy

Golden Dreams

Redwood Creek Challenge Trail

Mulholland Madness *FP*

Grizzly River Run *FP*

Soarin' Over California

LEGEND

🚻 Restrooms		⭐ *FP*	Attractions w/ Fast Pass
ℹ️ Information		•••••	Parade Route
🧳 Locker Rentals		══	Monorail
⭐ Attractions			

Six Flags Magic Mountain

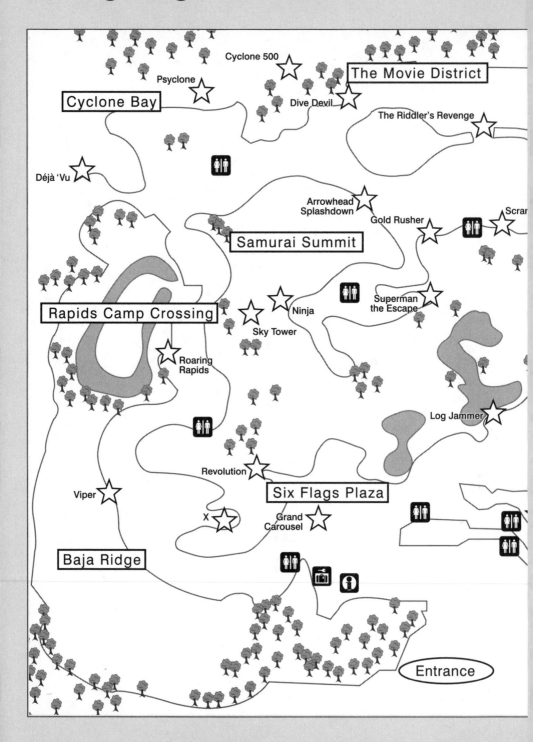

Cyclone 500

The Movie District

Psyclone

Cyclone Bay

Dive Devil

The Riddler's Revenge

Déjà 'Vu

Arrowhead
Splashdown

Gold Rusher

Scrar

Samurai Summit

Superman
the Escape

Rapids Camp Crossing

Ninja

Sky Tower

Roaring
Rapids

Log Jammer

Revolution

Six Flags Plaza

Viper

X

Grand
Carousel

Baja Ridge

Entrance

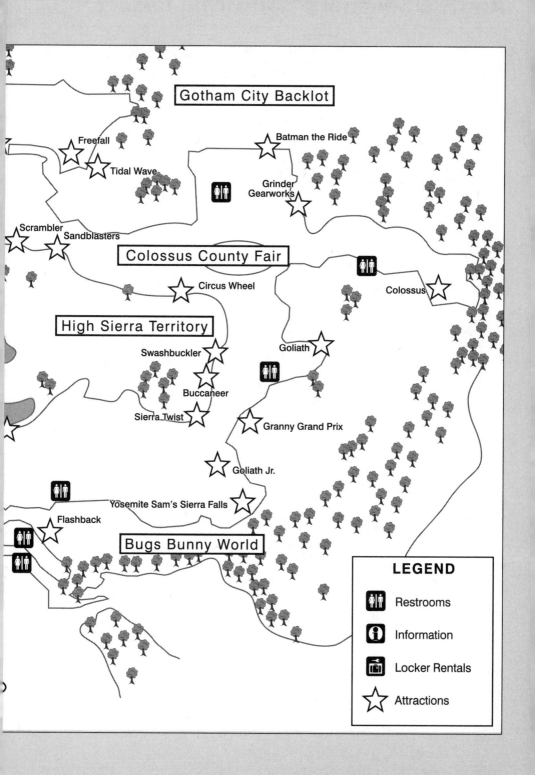

Gotham City Backlot

Freefall

Batman the Ride

Tidal Wave

Grinder Gearworks

Scrambler

Sandblasters

Colossus County Fair

Circus Wheel

Colossus

High Sierra Territory

Swashbuckler

Goliath

Buccaneer

Sierra Twist

Granny Grand Prix

Goliath Jr.

Yosemite Sam's Sierra Falls

Flashback

Bugs Bunny World

LEGEND

Restrooms

Information

Locker Rentals

Attractions

Knott's Southern California Resort

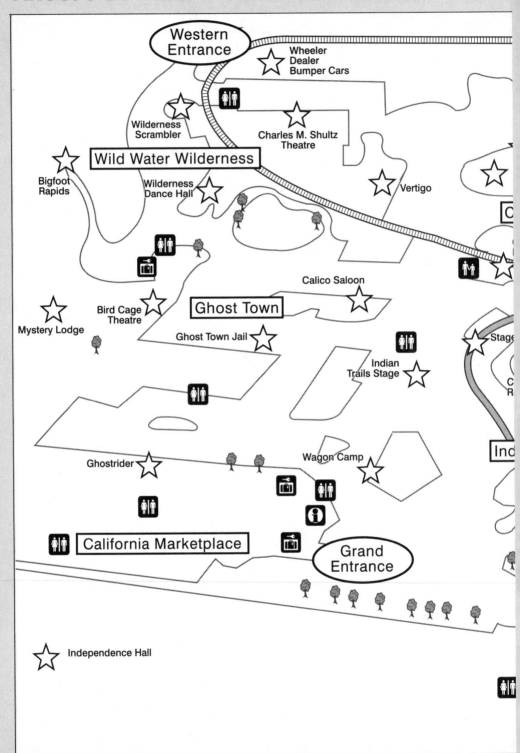

Western Entrance

Wheeler Dealer Bumper Cars

Wilderness Scrambler

Charles M. Shultz Theatre

Wild Water Wilderness

Bigfoot Rapids

Wilderness Dance Hall

Vertigo

Calico Saloon

Ghost Town

Mystery Lodge

Bird Cage Theatre

Ghost Town Jail

Indian Trails Stage

Stage

Ghostrider

Wagon Camp

California Marketplace

Grand Entrance

Ind

Independence Hall

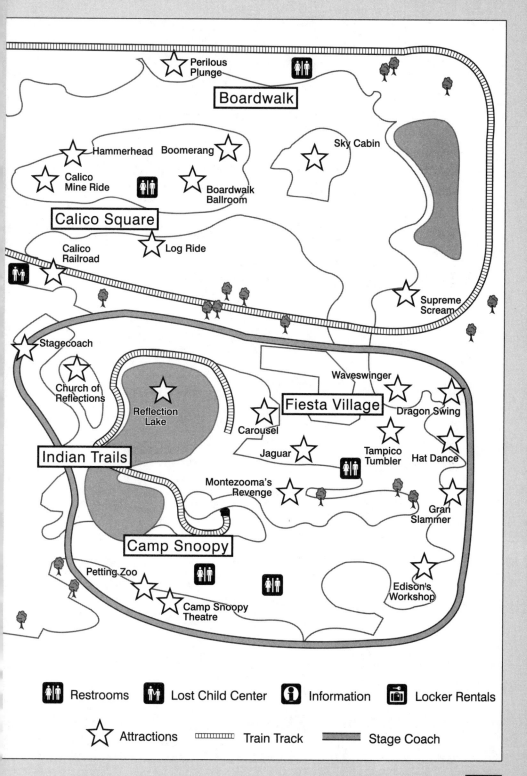

Perilous Plunge

Boardwalk

Sky Cabin

Hammerhead   Boomerang

Calico Mine Ride

Boardwalk Ballroom

Calico Square

Calico Railroad

Log Ride

Supreme Scream

Stagecoach

Waveswinger

Church of Reflections

Reflection Lake

Fiesta Village

Dragon Swing

Carousel

Indian Trails

Jaguar

Tampico Tumbler

Hat Dance

Montezooma's Revenge

Gran Slammer

Camp Snoopy

Petting Zoo

Edison's Workshop

Camp Snoopy Theatre

👫 Restrooms   👪 Lost Child Center   ℹ️ Information   🛅 Locker Rentals

⭐ Attractions   ▭▭▭ Train Track   ▬▬▬ Stage Coach

9

LEGOLAND

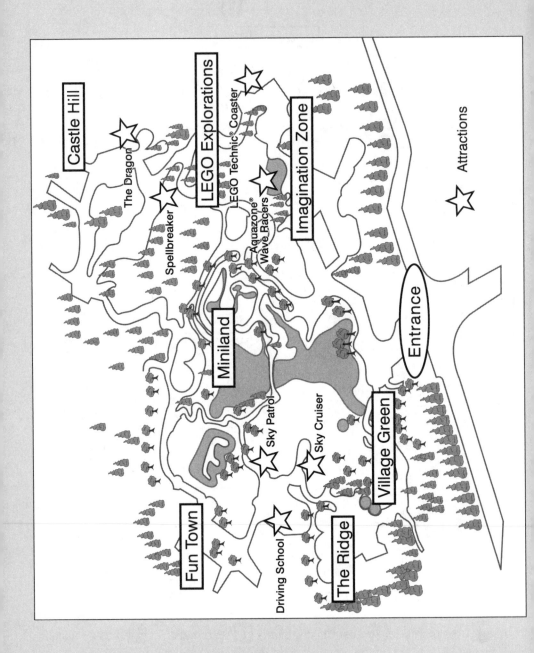

Sea World Adventure Park

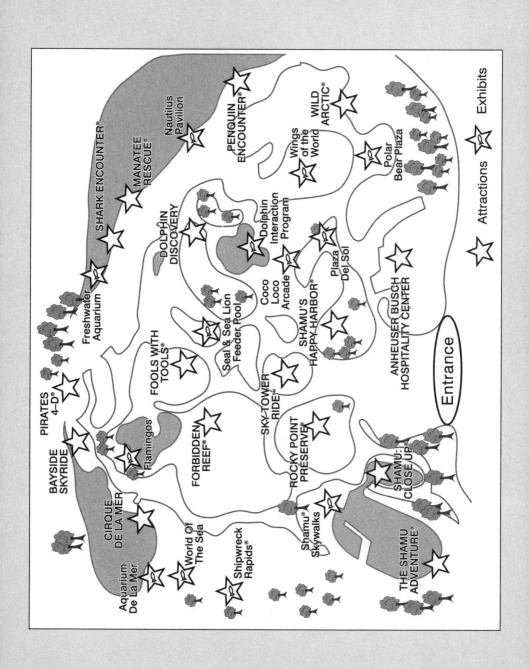

CHAPTER 1

Disneyland: Yesterday, Today, and Tomorrow

ALTHOUGH THERE ARE DOZENS of tourist attractions in Southern California, none is more popular than the Disneyland theme park, especially among young people. Here, you can interact with your favorite Disney characters, experience rides and attractions based on classic Disney movies and T.V. shows, and witness shows, parades, and other spectacles that offer an entertainment experience that only Disney can provide.

Disney's Dream

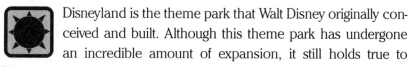 Disneyland is the theme park that Walt Disney originally conceived and built. Although this theme park has undergone an incredible amount of expansion, it still holds true to Disney's dream. Now, as you plan your own trip, you're about to experience what hundreds of millions of people already have—the magic of Disneyland. Yet, no matter how many people pass through the gates of this incredible place, each person takes away a unique experience and set of memories.

Walt Disney, his brother Roy Oliver Disney, and their fellow "Imagineers" and animators were the creative geniuses behind Mickey Mouse and all of the Disney animated characters. Walt and Roy founded Disney Brothers Studios in 1923. Soon thereafter, they became the creative force behind dozens of full-length animated and live-action movies, T.V. shows, and, of course, the theme parks.

Dubbed "The Happiest Place on Earth," Disneyland was the first of the Disney theme parks. Located in Anaheim, California, it opened to the public on July 17, 1955, with eighteen major attractions. The original cost to build Disneyland was about $17 million. Some of the individual attractions added to the park since then have cost considerably more than that. Over the years, Disneyland has grown into a thriving, 430-acre resort, complete with two major theme parks, three upscale resort hotels, and the dozens of shops and restaurants that comprise Downtown Disney. The Disneyland theme park alone now contains more than sixty major attractions.

≡ FAST FACT

At the grand opening of the Disneyland theme park in 1955, Walt Disney said these words: "To all who come to this happy place: welcome. Disneyland is your land. Here age relives fond memories of the past . . . and here youth may savor the challenge and promise of the future. Disneyland is dedicated to the ideals, the dreams and the hard facts which have created America . . . with the hope that it will be a source of joy and inspiration to all the world."

Since Disneyland's opening, the magical experience has touched over 450 million people of all ages and from all over the world. On a typical peak-season day, upward of 65,000 guests will pass through the park's main entrance. Back in the 1940s and early 1950s, when Walt and his team were dreaming up this theme park, who would have thought that what was then a 180-acre orange grove in Anaheim would soon be transformed into a tourist destination to be enjoyed for generations?

Disneyland Lands

 The original Disneyland theme park is divided into several areas, known as lands. Each land has an entirely different theme inspired by America's past, present, or future. For Walt Disney, each land had its own set of inspirations. For example, Fantasyland stemmed from Walt's goal of making dreams come true for young visitors. The initial inspiration is said to have come from the now-famous song lyrics, "When You Wish upon a Star." Walt once stated, "What youngster has not dreamed of flying with Peter Pan over moonlit London, or tumbling into Alice's nonsensical Wonderland? In Fantasyland, these classic stories of everyone's youth have become realities for youngsters—of all ages—to participate in."

☰FAST FACT

Located in Anaheim, California, less than one hour's drive from downtown Los Angeles and about ninety minutes from San Diego, The Disneyland Resort is a vacation destination that people come to from across the state, around the country, and all over the world.

While Frontierland, Adventureland, and Main Street, U.S.A., for example, look back at America's exciting past, Tomorrowland depicts a positive look toward our future. Walt once stated, "Tomorrow can be a wonderful age. Our scientists today are opening the doors of the Space Age to achievements that will benefit our children and generations to come. The Tomorrowland attractions have been designed to give you an opportunity to participate in adventures that are a living blueprint of our future." Even today, the Innoventions attraction within Tomorrowland (formerly the Carousel of Progress attraction) is a showcase of cutting-edge technology that has and will impact all of our lives.

Since 1955, Disneyland has undergone many changes. It continues to be a state-of-the-art theme park, yet the rich history of this magical place remains intact. Many of the original attractions created by Walt Disney and his team of Imagineers are still in place, while countless others have expanded upon Walt's dream, decades after his death.

The Hidden Mickeys

 "It all started with the mouse!" That's a popular saying among the thousands of employees at The Walt Disney Company, and it's a statement that's very true. Mickey Mouse is, without a doubt, the best-known cartoon character on the planet. He's also the corporate icon for one of the most powerful entertainment companies in the world, as well as the face behind the world's most popular Disney theme parks.

Mickey Mouse was certainly a major inspiration behind the creation of Disneyland. In fact, this famous mouse can be seen everywhere you look. Throughout the park, built into the rides, attractions, landscaping, and other structures are countless "Hidden Mickeys," an ongoing tribute to the mouse that started it all.

TRAVEL TIP

If someone you're traveling with is celebrating his or her birthday on the day of your visit, go to City Hall within the Disneyland Park and tell a cast member. The birthday boy or girl will be given a free personalized sticker to wear. Throughout the day, the person wearing it will be wished a happy birthday by cast members, and will be treated extra nicely.

According to the unofficial Hidden Mickey Web site (⌨ *www.hiddenmickeys.org*), "Hidden Mickeys started out as inside jokes among the Walt Disney Imagineers. A Hidden Mickey is an image of Mickey Mouse concealed in the design of a Disney attraction." As you explore The Disneyland Resort, keep your eyes peeled for these Hidden Mickeys; they're everywhere! This is a fun, family-oriented activity. Who can spot the most Hidden Mickeys each day?

Guided Disneyland Tours

 If you're interested in the rich history of Disneyland and the countless stories behind the theme park and resort, consider taking the two-hour **A Walk in Walt's Footsteps** tour. This guided walking tour of the park brings you on a journey into the past, through the life and times of Walter Elias Disney.

Along the way, you'll learn fascinating facts about Walt's original vision and discover how he brought his dream to life. You'll also get a peek at areas of the park that most guests aren't allowed to explore. The cost of this enjoyable tour is $16 for adults and $14 for kids; however, it's definitely something that adult Disney fans will appreciate more.

The four-hour **Welcome to Disneyland** guided tour takes small groups of people for a detailed look at the landmarks and history. This tour is definitely more enjoyable for adults. The price of the tour is $16 for adults and $14 for kids.

≡ FAST FACT

After Walt's death on December 15, 1966, the magic continued as Roy O. Disney took over for his brother. Later, Roy Edward Disney (Roy O. Disney's son and Walt's nephew) took charge of the Disney empire. These days, Roy E. Disney is vice chairman of the Walt Disney Company, which is run by Michael Eisner (chairman and CEO).

For the ultimate upclose and totally personalized tour of Disneyland, consider a **Premiere Tour,** which is a private tour of the theme park. This tour, which can accommodate up to ten people, lasts a minimum of four hours. The cost is $75 per hour, and there is a four-hour minimum.

All Disneyland tours are offered daily and are given by highly knowledgeable Disneyland cast members. Departure times vary, so call ✆ (714) 781-7290 for details, or drop into City Hall, located at the end of Main Street, U.S.A. All tour prices are in addition to admission. Use an American Express credit card to pay for any of the tours, and you'll be offered special discounts. If you're a Disney fan, any or all of these tours are highly recommended.

Commemorate Your Visit

 The Walk of Magical Memories is an ongoing tribute to Disneyland's guests. It's a walkway comprised of thousands of 10-inch hexagonal bricks that are imprinted with the names of guests who wish to commemorate their visit to Disneyland in a lasting way.

For a onetime fee of $150, a brick can be personalized with up to three lines of text (sixteen characters per line). Each brick includes a special number so you can locate it easily when you return in the years to come.

Special bricks are available to commemorate weddings and anniversaries, or you can have Mickey's head or Mickey's hands as the graphic imprinted along with the text on your brick. There are several limitations as to what text can be imprinted on the bricks, however. The Walt Disney Company plans to leave the bricks in place for at least ten years.

 TRAVEL TIP

To sponsor a brick, drop by the Disney's Walk of Magical Memories kiosk, located near the entrance to Disneyland, or call ☎(800) 760-3566 for an application/order form.

Sponsoring a brick along Disney's Walk of Magical Memories is an excellent way to remember your vacation. You'll receive a special certificate that includes a replica of the imprinted brick, along with information and a map on how to locate your brick during your next visit. This is an excellent way to commemorate a special event, such as a honeymoon, anniversary, family trip, birthday, or simply your vacation to Disneyland.

Since the brick you sponsor will remain at the park, for an additional $30 you can take home a scaled-down, wooden replica. These replicas can be hung on a wall or placed on a table or desk.

When to Experience the Magic

 During The Disneyland Resort's peak summer season (and during major holidays), you could be sharing your vacation with 40,000 to 65,000 other visitors. Throughout the year, Saturday is the theme park's busiest day of the week. Around noon, the park is usually the most crowded. On Sundays and during the week, the park is less crowded. However, the drawback to visiting on a weekday is that the parades and shows happen less frequently, and sometimes not at all.

As soon as you arrive, pick up a copy of *Disneyland Today* and/or the *Souvenir Map and Guide to Disney's California Adventure*. These colorful booklets, which are given out at the main entrances of the respective parks, contain the times for all parades and shows, describe the times and places to meet the Disney characters, and offer a detailed map of the park with all of the major attractions, restaurants, and amenities (restrooms, public phones, ATMs, etc.).

If it's raining, you can count on much smaller crowds than usual. Bring along rain gear (avoid umbrellas), or pick up one of the plastic Mickey Mouse rain ponchos sold throughout the park on rainy days. Expect all parades, outdoor shows, and even a few outdoor rides to be canceled or closed on rainy days. Much of the park (including most of the attractions) will, however, be open and the lines will be far shorter.

For the shortest lines, visit the Disney theme parks on any weekday in the off-season. If you happen to visit on a busy day, go against the crowds. For example, in the morning, most people race toward the most popular rides and attractions; then they stake out a prime viewing spot for a parade up to two or three hours before show time. Most of the park's most popular parades happen twice each afternoon or evening. The best time to visit all of the most popular attractions—such as the Indiana Jones Adventure, Splash Mountain, Space Mountain, Star Tours, or the Matterhorn—is during the first parade. You can catch the second showing of the parade when the crowds are greatly reduced. Likewise, when most people break for lunch or dinner, many of the lines for attractions are shorter.

 TRAVEL TIP

At any time, you can find out exactly what the lines are like for every attraction by visiting the Information Desk/Wait Board located near Central Plaza (a.k.a. "The Hub") at the end of Main Street, U.S.A. near the Walt Disney and Mickey Mouse statue. A second Information Desk/Wait Board can be found in Tomorrowland.

The Best of Times

Here are the best dates to visit Disneyland:

- Early January through Presidents' Week
- The end of Presidents' Week through one week before Easter
- Two weeks after Easter Sunday through the week of Memorial Day
- After the week of Labor Day through the week before Columbus Day
- Just after Thanksgiving through the week before Christmas

The Worst of Times

The busiest times of the year for Disneyland include:

- Every Saturday throughout the year
- Sundays during the summer and holiday weekends

- Presidents' Week
- The week before and after Easter Sunday
- The start of summer through Labor Day weekend
- Thanksgiving weekend
- Christmas Day through New Year's Day

TRAVEL TIP

If you're planning your Disney vacation during one of these busy periods, book your reservations as early as possible, especially if you hope to stay at The Disneyland Hotel or one of the other Disney-owned hotels. If your first choice for accommodations is already booked solid, make alternate reservations, but keep checking back with your first choice. Last-minute cancellations are common.

CHAPTER 2

Preparing for Your Vacation

TO MAKE YOUR VACATION to Southern California and/or The Disneyland Resort the best it can possibly be, you'll want to invest some time before you depart to plan your trip. This chapter will help you make travel reservations and save money in the process.

Vacation-Planning Strategies

 As you plan your California vacation, and while you're at the various theme parks and tourist attractions, keep the following travel tips in mind:

1. Don't overspend! The theme park business is extremely profitable in part because the parks are designed to encourage people to buy souvenirs and make other spontaneous purchases that weren't in the original vacation budget. Remember to set aside money in your budget to purchase extras and souvenirs, and then stick to it!

2. Always wear comfortable shoes. No matter which theme park you visit, you'll be doing a lot of walking. One of the most common injuries at the Disney theme parks is blistered feet because people don't wear comfortable shoes or sneakers to the various parks. Also, be sure to pack a

second pair of comfortable shoes, in case the first pair gets wet (due to rain or water attractions and rides). In addition to comfort, your shoes should be dry.

3. Especially on hot and sunny days, drink plenty of fluids and apply plenty of sunblock to all exposed skin. Make sure children are also well protected from the sun. Wearing sunglasses and a hat (with a visor) are excellent ways of protecting your face and head. Even on overcast days, the California sun can cause serious sunburn.

4. During family vacations, people need to get away from each other, so don't be afraid to split up for a few hours a day to indulge your own interests. Especially if you're traveling with a large group, you'll find that everyone's vacation will be more enjoyable if some time is spent apart each day.

5. During the vacation-planning stages, get input from everyone, including the kids, regarding the types of activities you want to participate in. Make sure everyone has at least some say in how to spend your vacation in order to ensure that everyone has a great time.

6. Pace yourself at the theme parks! Get plenty of rest and, especially if you're traveling with kids, plan to take short breaks throughout the day. Don't overextend yourself or you'll wind up too tired to enjoy yourself after the second or third day of your vacation.

7. Let your imagination run wild; be sure to relax and have fun!

8. Make reservations early. Especially during the peak travel seasons, hotel accommodations, dining availability, private golf/tennis lesson availability, and show tickets (when applicable) fill up quickly.

Driving to Disneyland

If you decide that driving to Disneyland is your best option, there are some things you will want to keep in mind before heading out. First of all, are you going to drive your own or borrowed vehicle, or would you rather rent a car for the trip? Regardless of the vehicle you choose to drive, you will need to know where you're going.

Driving Directions

The Disneyland Resort (in Anaheim, California) is located about 30 miles south of downtown Los Angeles. Considering that Los Angeles's traffic can be an absolute nightmare, plan on a sixty- to ninety-minute drive. Remember that odd-numbered freeways travel north/south, and even-numbered freeways travel east/west.

- If you're approaching Disneyland from the south on the Santa Ana Freeway (I-5), exit at Ball Road. Turn right at the end of the exit ramp (onto Ball Road) and travel west. Turn left onto Disneyland Drive and follow the signs to the parking area.
- When approaching Disneyland from the north on I-5, exit at Katella Avenue; then travel west on Harbor Boulevard by turning right. Look for the Disneyland signs.
- When traveling eastbound or westbound on the 22 Freeway, exit at Harbor Boulevard North. Travel north on Harbor Boulevard for about 2 miles, and follow the Disneyland signs.

 **TRAVEL TIP**

Traffic in the Los Angeles area is typically heavy and somewhat unpredictable. For an up-to-date traffic report, call the Disneyland Traffic Advisory Hotline at ☎(714) 781-4400.

If you're worried about getting lost, Hertz offers the NeverLost feature in some of its rental cars. Using the Global Positioning System, the NeverLost unit identifies exactly where you are at any time, and then shows and tells you how to get to wherever you want to go. If you're new to Southern California, this is an excellent add-on for a rental car. The additional cost is about $5 per day. If you don't want to incur the added cost of the NeverLost system, remember that most car rental agencies provide computer-generated driving directions and maps, free of charge, from the airport to virtually any location in California, including all of the popular hotels and attractions.

Reserving a Rental Car

Just as in making airline reservations, there are several tricks to use when reserving a rental car that will help you get the lowest rate possible. For starters, reserve the car as far in advance as possible (seven days, minimum) and try to get the weekly rate. Most rental car companies will apply their weekly rates to five-, six-, or seven-day rentals.

Especially in tourist areas, like Los Angeles and Anaheim, rental car companies constantly run special promotions. Be sure to ask about them, and look in your local newspaper and in your favorite magazines for ads, as well. In addition, many companies provide a discount to AAA members.

Some popular credit cards also have special promotional deals with major rental car companies, so check with your card's customer service department. (The number is listed on the back of the card.) While you're on the phone, ask if your credit card automatically provides rental car insurance if you use that card to pay for the rental. American Express, Diner's Club, and virtually all Visa and MasterCard credit cards (issued as part of an airline's frequent flier program) automatically offer this insurance.

If you think you've found an awesome rate, reserve the car but continue to shop around. Call three or four other companies and see if they'll beat the deal you've been offered. Many travelers believe that the best-known companies are the most expensive, but that isn't always the case. You'll often be pleasantly surprised to discover that majors like Hertz, Avis, and National offer highly competitive rates once you take advantage of their special promotional deals, airline frequent flier discounts, and AAA member discount.

When making a reservation, make sure unlimited mileage is included in the price. Some companies charge by the mile, in addition to the daily rental fee, so make sure you understand what's included in the price you're being quoted. Extremely low daily or weekly rental rates often do not include unlimited mileage, and once you travel above the allowed miles, you're charged a hefty fee per mile.

 TRAVEL TIP

If you're a member of any airline's frequent flier program, you can often receive a rental car discount from promotional partners of that airline. Check your monthly frequent flier statement from the airline for information about special rental car offers.

Rental Car Companies

The following rental car companies are located in the Southern California area. If you are renting a car outside Southern California, check your local yellow pages for companies in your area.

A-One Rent-A-Car: (310) 417-1656
AAA Rent-A-Car: (310) 348-1111
ABC Rent-A-Car: (310) 641-4399
Access Rent-A-Car: (310) 641-8001
Adventure Rent-A-Car: (310) 670-3100
Airport Rent-A-Car: (800) 445-4375
Alamo Rent-A-Car: (310) 649-2245
All International Rent-A-Car: (310) 337-7201
Allstate Car Rental: (800) 245-4555
Ariana Rent-A-Car: (800) 426-0333
Avis Rent-A-Car: (310) 342-9208
Beverly Hills Rent-A-Car: (310) 646-4574
Budget Rent-A-Car: (310) 642-4555

Costless Car Rental: ✆(800) 770-0606

Discovery Rent-A-Car: ✆(310) 412-9506

Dollar Rent-A-Car: ✆(310) 412-9506

Enterprise Rent-A-Car: ✆(310) 215-6856

Exotic Car Rental: ✆(626) 583-1500

Fox Rent-A-Car: ✆(888) 332-4369

Global Rent-A-Car: ✆(800) 554-5059

Hertz Rent-A-Car: ✆(310) 568-3434

Hertz #1 Gold Club: ✆(800) CAR-GOLD

Internet Rent-A-Car: ✆(310) 670-1749

LAX Rent-A-Car: ✆(800) 641-0075

Los Angeles Rent-A-Car: ✆(619) 537-5914

Lucky Rent-A-Car: ✆(800) 400-4736

Marathon Rent-A-Car: ✆(800) 446-3737

Mega Rent A Car, Inc.: ✆(310) 646-1313

Midway Car Rental: ✆(310) 646-1496

National Car Rental: ✆(909) 937-7555

Red and Blue Rent-A-Car: ✆(310) 672-0225

Resort Rent-A-Car: ✆(310) 645-2100

Rex Rent-A-Car: ✆(800) 667-0787

Ritz Rent-A-Car: ✆(800) 641-3222

Rocket Rent-A-Car: ✆(310) 674-4600

Sakura Rent-A-Car: ✆(310) 645-9696

Sunrise Rent A Car: ✆(310) 649-5354

Sunset Rent-A-Car: ✆(310) 649-3983

Thrifty Car Rental: ✆(310) 645-1880

U-Save Auto Rental: ✆(310) 649-5806

United Rent-A-Car: ✆(310) 645-1515

Do You Need Insurance?

No matter what hourly, daily, or weekly rate you're quoted by the rental car companies, these rates do not include the various types of insurance offered, nor do they include tax. What most travelers don't know, however, is that they do not need all of the optional insurance, because their own regular insurance policies, as well as the travel insurance provided free of charge by some credit card companies, offer more than adequate protection.

Prior to renting a car, call the customer service number for your auto insurance company, as well as your homeowner's insurance company. Ask if rental car insurance is automatically offered under your existing policy. If so, you probably don't need any of the insurance offered by the rental car companies. If you rely on your existing insurance, however, and you're forced to make a claim as a result of an accident in the rental car, your regular insurance rates could go up. One benefit of purchasing the optional insurance from the rental car companies is that your existing policies won't be affected if you have to make a claim (assuming any damage or injury claims are under the limit of the insurance you purchase).

TRAVEL TIP

Purchasing all of the insurance options offered by the rental car companies can more than double the quoted rate.

Optional Insurance Plans

Rental car companies offer a variety of optional insurance plans. The renter's financial responsibility for loss of or damage to the rental car varies by state. According to Hertz's literature, "The customer is responsible for loss of or damage to the car, up to its full value regardless of who is at fault, due to collision, rollover, and, in many instances, a limited number of other causes as specified in the rental agreement. The customer is generally not responsible for damage to the car resulting from acts of nature and accidental fire, provided the car is used in accordance with all terms and conditions of the rental agreement."

Collision Damage Waiver (CDW), or Loss Damage Waiver (LDW), is not insurance. According to Hertz's literature, it "is an option available for an additional daily charge which, when offered and accepted, waives or reduces the customer's responsibility for loss of or damage to the rental car, provided the car is used in accordance with all terms and conditions of the rental agreement. CDW or LDW charges apply to each full day or partial rental day, CDW and/or LDW may not be available at some locations, and the charge varies by location and by car group/class."

To increase protection, Hertz offers a Liability Insurance Supplement (LIS), "an optional supplement which will increase the limits of liability protection to a combined total of $1,000,000 (one million U.S. dollars)."

Another optional service offered by Hertz and most other rental car companies is Personal Accident Insurance (PAI). According to Hertz's literature, PAI covers the renter's accidental death and medical expenses resulting from bodily injury. Total indemnity for any one accident is limited to $225,000 (U.S. dollars). Benefits are payable in addition to any other coverage for which the customer is eligible. The renter is covered for the duration of the rental, if he or she is inside or outside the vehicle, as follows:

> Loss of life for $175,000
> Medical up to $2,500
> Ambulance up to $250

Passengers are only covered while entering, occupying, or leaving the Hertz vehicle as follows (most other rental car companies offer similar benefits, but be sure to ask):

> Loss of life for $175,000
> Medical up to $2,500
> Ambulance up to $250

Personal Effects Coverage (PEC) is another optional service offered by the rental car companies. According to Hertz's literature, "PEC provides protection for loss of or damage to covered personal effects of the renter and their immediate family traveling with the renter and residing with the renter. Some exclusions apply. The maximum coverage per person is $600.00 (U.S. dollars) with a total of $1,800.00 (U.S. dollars)."

▐█▌ TRAVEL TIP

Hertz offers Combined Personal Accident Insurance/Personal Effects Coverage for a single fee of approximately $5 per day. They are not sold separately. Once again, check with the rental car company you choose for details about the insurance options offered and the additional costs and benefits associated with them.

Special Services

Most rental car companies will provide child safety seats, either free of charge or for a small daily fee, but they must be reserved in advance. This service will save you the hassle of having to bring your own seat(s) with you.

Many companies offer cellular phone rentals as well; however, the rates are extremely high. If you have a handheld or trans-portable cellular phone that you can bring with you, you're better off paying the roaming charges than the high daily rental and per-minute service fees associated with renting a cellular phone.

When you pick up the rental car, ask about the company's policy for additional drivers. Typically, unless you complete additional paperwork, only the person whose name appears on the rental agreement is legally permitted to drive the car. Some rental car companies charge to add additional names to the rental contract, allowing for multiple drivers. The following people are often exempt from additional driver charges (but check with the company): the renter's employer or regular fellow employee when on company business; the renter's spouse; the renter's mate, life companion, significant other, or live-in; and disabled renters who have completed a special form.

 **TRAVEL TIP**

> If you're a nonsmoker, be sure to ask for a nonsmoking vehicle when you make your reservation. Otherwise, you could get stuck with a car that reeks of smoke.

Questions and Tips

First, ask if you're required to return the car with a full tank of gas, or if you're paying for the gas in advance. If you're required to return the car with a full tank of gas and you fail to do so (which many people do), you'll be billed at up to three times the going rate per gallon of gas needed to fill the tank. Before returning the car, find a low-priced gas station and fill the tank with basic unleaded gasoline (the cheapest stuff you can find).

If you pick up the car at 3:00 P.M., you usually must return the car before 3:00 P.M. on the day your rental agreement ends, or you'll automatically be billed for additional hours at a high rate. When you pick up the car, ask what time the car must be returned by to ensure you won't be billed overtime hours, and ask what the overtime rate is.

If you have rented a car from an airport location, plan on arriving at the airport about ninety minutes (or even two hours) before your scheduled flight time to return the rental. You will most likely be returning your car several miles from the actual airport, and you'll need to allow ample time to return the car, take the complimentary shuttle bus to your airline terminal, check in, check your bags, and get to the actual gate. It's a common problem for travelers to miss their flight because they didn't allow enough time to return their rental car, so plan accordingly.

As soon as you pick up your car, and before you leave the rental car company's parking lot, make sure there is nothing obviously wrong with the vehicle. If there's a problem, report it immediately.

Before getting behind the wheel, make sure you're totally awake and alert and that you have detailed driving directions for reaching your destination. If you have flown in and are too tired to be driving, take a taxi or shuttle bus to your hotel and pick up your rental car later in the day or on the following day. Just remember to call the rental car company and mention your change of plans to avoid being charged.

TRAVEL TIP

If you get stuck on the road, call the rental car company and report your situation. They'll provide free assistance, often including towing services, and you'll often be given a replacement rental car.

Flying to California

 As a general rule, book your flight as far in advance as possible. Many airlines offer the best prices if you book and pay for your tickets twenty-one days in advance. You can, however, also obtain good fares if you make your reservations (and pay for your airline tickets) fourteen or even seven days early. When making your travel plans, try to have the most flexible schedule possible. If your schedule permits staying a Saturday night, you'll almost always get a better airfare.

All of the airlines listed in this section (and possibly a few others) offer competitive rates and travel packages to the Los Angeles International Airport (LAX), so be sure to shop around for the best airfares and flights. Keep in mind, with discounted or special airfares, the tickets are not refundable, and there is a fee to change the travel date(s). The change fee is usually between $100 and $150, plus the price difference in the airfare itself. To avoid this change fee, most airlines allow you to fly standby; however, this does not guarantee you a seat on a specific flight. If you're traveling with a family and the flight you're trying to get onto is crowded, the chances of getting your whole family on the same flight are slim, especially during peak travel periods.

If you use frequent flier miles to book your airline ticket(s) to Los Angeles, keep in mind that seats may be difficult to reserve during peak travel periods, so make your reservations early. The advantage of using a frequent flier ticket is that it's free, plus most airlines allow you to change your travel plans at the last minute, with no penalties or fees.

Always ask the airline reservation representative for the lowest airfare available. After an airfare is quoted to you, ask again if it is the best deal. Next, ask if there are flights to and from Los Angeles at around the same times as the ones quoted to you that would make the airfare less expensive. You won't often be quoted the absolute lowest prices the first time you ask. Also, check the travel section of your local newspaper for advertised special fares and promotions. You can make a reservation that will be held for twenty-four hours without having to pay for the ticket, so make an unpaid reservation and then call additional airlines to shop around.

▌ TRAVEL TIP

Red-eye flights that leave Los Angeles between 10:00 P.M. and midnight and return to the East Coast the following morning are almost always the cheapest return flights available. Although most people hate flying all night, you can save up to several hundred dollars.

Shopping for the Best Fares

There are several alternatives available to you when it comes to shopping around for the best airfare. You can go to the airport, visit an airline ticket counter, or call an airline and book your travel.

You can also surf the Internet and visit the various travel-related Web sites, such as ✎ Travelocity.com, ✎ Priceline.com, ✎ LastMinuteTravel.com, or ✎ Orbitz.com (described later in this chapter).

Another alternative is to call a travel agent and have them do the busywork for you. Travel agents have computer systems that allow them to search for flight availability on all airlines at once. Most travel agents will be happy to work with you over the telephone, so it's not necessary to take time out of your busy schedule to visit their office.

When choosing a travel agent, find someone who is highly recommended by someone you trust. Travel agents can be extremely helpful and save you money, but some will quote you higher priced airfares, since they're receiving a commission from the airline based on the price of the ticket(s) they sell. AAA and American Express both have highly reputable travel agencies that offer their services either in-person or by telephone to members.

Finally, you might want to look into package deals offered by the various airlines. Many packages include airfare, hotel, rental car, and perhaps meals or show tickets. Most airlines have a separate Vacation Package reservation department.

As you choose the actual times of your flights, if you plan on sleeping during the flight and you book an early-morning or late-night departure, beware. When it comes to tourism, the Los Angeles airport is one of the busiest in the world. With all the tourists and family travelers, those cute babies and adorable young children can wind up screaming and crying throughout the flight, especially as the air pressure during landing and takeoff affects their ears.

🧳 TRAVEL TIP

Consider using public transportation to get to the airport in your home city. The cheapest option is to have a friend or family member drop you off and pick you up when you return. Another option is to use a door-to-door shuttle bus service, which is almost always cheaper than a taxi, limo, or town car service.

If the noise of young kids (or of the airplane's engines) bothers you, invest in a pair of earplugs before your trip. The cost will be under $2 per pair. You can also purchase high-tech noise-canceling headphones from Bose Corporation that connect to a portable CD or tape player (or the airplane's audio system); however, the cost of these headsets is somewhat high.

The Los Angeles International Airport

Los Angeles International Airport (LAX) is ranked third in the world for number of passengers handled, and its popularity shows no sign of decreasing. In 2000, more than 67.3 million people traveled through LAX.

The following domestic airlines fly to and from this international airport. (Airlines are subject to change.) Not all of these airlines will service your home city, so call the airline to inquire about flight availability. To learn more about LAX and the international airlines that service it, visit the Los Angeles World Airports' Web site at *www.lawa.org* and click on the LAX link.

Here is a list of the domestic airlines that service LAX:

Air Canada: (800) 776-3000 or *www.aircanada.ca/index.html*
America West Airlines: (800) 2-FLY-AWA or
www.americawest.com
American Airlines: (800) 433-7300 or *www.aa.com*
American Eagle: (800) 433-7300 or *www.aa.com*
Continental: (800) 525-0280 or *www.continental.com*
Delta Airlines/Delta Express: (800) 221-1212 or
www.delta-air.com
Frontier Airlines: (800) 432-1359 or *www.flyfrontier.com*
Hawaiian Air: (800) 367-5320 or *www.hawaiianair.com*
Horizon Air/Alaska Air: (800) 547-9308 or *www.alaska-air.com*
Miami Air: (305) 871-8001 or *www.miamiair.com*
Midwest Express: (800) 452-2022 or *www.midwestexpress.com*
Northwest Airlines: (800) 225-2525 or *www.nwa.com*
Southwest: (800) I-FLY-SWA or *www.southwest.com*

Spirit Airlines: ✆(800) 772-7117 or 🖰 www.spiritair.com

Sun County Airlines: ✆(800) 359-5786

TWA: ✆(800) 892-2746 or 🖰 www.twa.com

United: ✆(800) 241-6522 or 🖰 www.ual.com

United Express: ✆(800) 453-9417 or 🖰 www.ual.com

United Shuttle: ✆(800) 748-8853 or 🖰 www.ual.com

US Airways Trip Packages: ✆(800) 455-0123 or
🖰 www.usairways.com

US Airways: ✆(800) 428-4322 or 🖰 www.usairways.com

Vanguard Airlines: ✆(800) 826-4827 or 🖰 www.flyvanguard.com

Virgin Atlantic: ✆(800) 862-8621 or 🖰 www.virgin-atlantic.com

A handful of other airlines also operate charter flights to and from LAX and other major U.S. cities and foreign countries.

🧳 TRAVEL TIP

If you're planning to meet people in Los Angeles or want others to be able to determine when you'll actually arrive, be sure to give them the name of the airline, the flight number, and your departure date and time.

Airport Security Information

Be sure to arrive at the airport at least ninety minutes before your scheduled departure time and have your driver's license, military ID, or passport ready to show multiple times at various security checkpoints.

The following items cannot be taken past the security checkpoint at any airport, nor can they be kept in a carry-on bag taken onto an airplane. The majority of these items, however, can be packed in your checked luggage.

- Aerosol cans (i.e., hairspray)
- Baseball bats
- Box cutters

- Carpet knives
- Corkscrews
- Cutting instruments
- Golf clubs
- Hockey sticks
- Ice picks
- Knitting/crochet needles
- Knives of any size
- Pepper spray
- Pool cues
- Scissors of any size
- Ski poles
- Straight razors

 TRAVEL TIP

If you're booking your airline reservations directly with an airline, be sure to check that airline's Web site for special "online only" fares and specials.

To and from LAX

From LAX, there are several nonstop shuttle van services to the Disneyland area. SuperShuttle's fleet of blue vans provides inexpensive door-to-door service from your airline terminal to whatever hotel you're staying at near Disneyland. You'll probably have to share your van with up to three other parties, but taking the SuperShuttle is typically more convenient than using a scheduled bus service and far cheaper than taking a taxi or limo service. The per-person cost between LAX and any Disneyland-area hotel is $14 per person each way. To make a **SuperShuttle** reservation, call ☎ (800) 554-3146 or ☎ (310) 782-6600. If you're traveling with young children, this may not be the best option. Remember, you'll be traveling with up to three other parties and making multiple stops before reaching your hotel, which could add an extra hour or more to your travel time. If you're traveling with four or more adults, using a town car, taxi, or private van service may be more cost effective and convenient.

Another alternative is the **Airport Bus,** which offers service from all LAX and John Wayne Airport terminals directly to Disneyland and nearby hotels. For information or to make a reservation, call ✆ (800) 772-5299.

Door-to-door taxi service is also available from several licensed companies; however, this mode of transportation is costly. Expect to pay about $35 each way between John Wayne Airport and Disneyland, and $75 each way between LAX and Disneyland.

To schedule taxi service, call **Yellow Cab of Orange County** at ✆ (714) 535-2211 or **West Coast Taxi Cab** at ✆ (714) 547-8000. You can also pick up a taxi at either LAX or the John Wayne Airport without a reservation. See the ground transportation information desk at either airport for more details.

 **TRAVEL TIP**

> If you live in a city with multiple airports, or you live between two cities that both have airports, price your airline tickets going to and from each airport. Airlines often offer special deals and promotions from some airports and not from others.

To and from John Wayne Airport

Located in Orange County, California, about 15 miles from The Disneyland Resort, **John Wayne Airport,** at ✆ (949) 252-5200 or ✍ *www.ocair.com*, is smaller than LAX and is serviced by fewer airlines. However, if you're traveling to The Disneyland Resort (Anaheim), as opposed to the Los Angeles area, it is a more convenient airport to fly into and out of.

The following domestic airlines service the John Wayne Airport:

Alaska Airlines: ✆ (800) 426-0333
Aloha Airlines: ✆ (800) 367-5250
America West Airlines: ✆ (800) 235-9292

American Airlines: ☎(800) 433-7300
Continental Airlines: ☎(800) 525-0280
Delta Airlines: ☎ (800) 221-1212
Northwest Airlines: ☎(800) 225-2525
Southwest Airlines: ☎(800) 435-9792
TWA: ☎(800) 221-2000
United Airlines: ☎(800) 241-6522
US Airways: ☎(800) 428-4322

The following rental car companies have branches located at the John Wayne Airport:

Alamo Rent-A-Car: ☎(800) 327-9633
Avis Rent-A-Car: ☎(800) 230-4898
Budget Rent-A-Car: ☎(800) 221-1203
Enterprise Rent-A-Car: ☎(800) 736-8222
Hertz: ☎(800) 654-3131
National Car Rental: ☎(800) 227-7368

═FAST FACT

American Taxi—call ☎(888) 482-9466—services the John Wayne Airport. You can meet the taxi at the Ground Transportation Center on the lower level of the main terminal. This service offers both cars and vans. Ask about flat fees to predetermined destinations. Otherwise, meter rates are $2.30, plus $2.10 per mile.

Taking the Train

The closest **Amtrak** train station is located about 2 miles from The Disneyland Resort. To get information about taking an Amtrak train from anywhere in the country to Disneyland, call ☎ (800) USA-RAIL or go online at ✍ *www.amtrak.com*. Train service is also available from Los Angeles and San Diego.

Amtrak offers travel discounts to all students and veterans, as well as to AAA and AARP members who present their membership card when purchasing a ticket. You can also buy Amtrak tickets from many travel agents, by visiting any Amtrak ticket office, or by calling Amtrak directly and using a major credit card.

Busing to Anaheim

 Greyhound's Anaheim bus depot (located at ▢ 100 West Winston Road) is located about one mile from The Disneyland Resort. From this bus stop, you can get a taxi to Disneyland. From downtown Los Angeles and San Diego, direct bus service to Disneyland is also available, although these buses make multiple stops along the way. For bus schedules or additional information, call **Greyhound** at ✆(714) 999-1256 or ✆(800) 231-2222.

The following scheduled buses provide service from LAX to various parts of Los Angeles and some surrounding regions. These buses pick up passengers on the Lower/Arrival Level islands in front of each terminal under the sign Buses & Long Distance Vans.

- **Airport Bus:** Travels to Pasadena, about 28 miles northeast of LAX; to Anaheim, about 32 miles southeast of LAX; and to Buena Park, approximately 28 miles southeast of LAX
- **Metropolitan Express:** Travels to downtown Los Angeles and to Union Station, about 19 miles northeast of LAX

Your Travel Budget

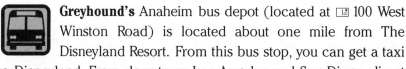 As you begin to plan your trip, it's important to establish a basic travel budget for yourself and to stick to that budget. Once you reach your destination, you'll no doubt be tempted to dine at fancy restaurants, buy extravagant souvenirs, and participate in costly activities. So, when you create your budget, make allowances for these unplanned splurges.

The first step in planning a budget is to figure out how much money you have to spend on your upcoming vacation. Next, determine how many people you'll be traveling with (and paying for), how many days you'll be away, and what you want your travel itinerary to include.

Use this form to help you approximate the cost of your trip to The Disneyland Resort/Southern California in advance. Planning your schedule/itinerary before you leave and setting budgetary spending limits will help you enjoy your vacation without going into unexpected debt or spending outside of your budget.

BUDGET CHECKLIST		
Expense	**Calculation**	**Totals**
Adult airfare	$ _____ per ticket × $ _____ (# of adults)	$ _____
Child airfare	$ _____ per ticket × $ _____ (# of children)	$ _____
Rental car	$ _____ per day/week × $ _____ (# of days/weeks)	$ _____
Insurance/gas	$ _____ per day × $ _____ (# of days)	$ _____
Transportation (taxi, bus, etc.)	$ _____ per trip × $ _____ (# of people) × $ _____ (# of trips)	$ _____
Hotel/motel	$ _____ per night × $ _____ (# of rooms) × $ _____ (# of nights)	$ _____
Adult Disney ticket	$ _____ per ticket × $ _____ (# of people) × $ _____ (# of days)	$ _____
Child Disney ticket	$ _____ per ticket × $ _____ (# of people) × $ _____ (# of days)	$ _____
Adult Universal Studios ticket	$ _____ per ticket × $ _____ (# of people) × $ _____ (# of days)	$ _____

BUDGET CHECKLIST (continued)

Expense	Calculation	Totals
Child Universal Studios ticket	$ _____ per ticket × $ _____ (# of people) × $ _____ (# of days)	$ _____
Other attraction	$ _____ per ticket × $ _____ (# of people) × $ _____ (# of days)	$ _____
Other attraction	$ _____ per ticket × $ _____ (# of people) × $ _____ (# of days)	$ _____
Adult nighttime entertainment	$ _____ per person × $ _____ (# of nights)	$ _____
Child nighttime entertainment	$ _____ per person × $ _____ (# of nights)	$ _____
Show/movie	$ _____ per person × $ _____ (# of shows)	$ _____
Total meal budget	$ _____ per person × $ _____ (# of meals) × $ _____ (# of days)	$ _____
Snack/drink budget	$ _____ per person × $ _____ (# of days)	$ _____
Souvenir budget	$ _____ per person	$ _____
Child care	$ _____ per hour × $ _____ (# of hours) × $ _____ (# of children)	$ _____
Kennel costs	$ _____ per day × $ _____ (# of days) × $ _____ (# of pets)	$ _____
Airport parking	$ _____ per day × $ _____ (# of days)	$ _____
Other	_____	$ _____
Other	_____	$ _____
Other	_____	$ _____
Approximate Vacation Expenses Total:		$ _____

Once you've priced out everything, the total price of your planned vacation should be within your proposed budget. Before making your reservations, however, shop around for money-saving deals and/or packages. Finding a coupon or a deal that'll save you $50 on a hotel, for example, is money that can be used for souvenirs or kept in your bank account.

Also, you can save money by not eating at the theme parks. Instead of having a fancy (and sometimes costly) breakfast at your Disney-owned hotel every morning, consider experiencing that breakfast once, then eating at the nearby Denny's to save some money. Obviously, there's something very special (especially for kids) about eating Mickey Mouse–shaped waffles with the Disney characters roaming the dining room and meeting guests. However, it probably doesn't need to be experienced every morning.

⊕ HOT SPOT

The Denny's located across the street from The Disneyland Resort offers good, inexpensive food, twenty-four hours a day. It's a great place to stop for lunch or dinner. Because of its location, however, this restaurant tends to be very crowded during peak breakfast time, so be prepared to wait up to thirty minutes.

If this isn't your first trip to The Disneyland Resort, you can save a lot of money by staying at a non-Disney-owned hotel/motel that's close to the theme parks. Although you won't experience the legendary Disney service or the perks associated with staying at a Disney-owned hotel, the financial savings will add up quickly.

Unless your budget is unlimited, chances are, once you get to Southern California, you will not be able to afford to do absolutely everything you'd like to during one trip. Thus, you'll want to use this book (and your firsthand experience) to determine which activities you'd most enjoy and focus on those to start off with.

Using a Travel Agent

 Using a full-service travel agency to plan your trip and make your reservations will save you a lot of time but not necessarily a lot of money. Most travel agents specialize in corporate travel or high-priced vacations and earn their income by taking a commission of the total price of the trip they coordinate for you. So, unless you have an established relationship with a travel agent, they're not always apt to find you the lowest possible rates. Of course, there are plenty of exceptions.

If you don't already have a reliable travel agent, consider asking a friend or relative for a recommendation instead of just opening up the yellow pages. Make sure the travel agent you choose specializes in planning family vacations and is familiar with Southern California and Anaheim.

Booking Your Vacation Online

 If you have some time to plan your vacation, and you have access to the Internet, you can save an absolute fortune by planning and booking your travel arrangements online. Using the Web and a major credit card, you can reserve and pay for airfare, hotels, and rental cars.

Use Your Options

When using the Internet to plan and book your own travel, you have three primary options:

1. You can visit the Web site of the specific airline, hotel chain, and/or rental car company. For example, to book your airfare on **US Airways**, you'd visit ✐ *www.usairways.com*. Often, each airline offers discounted online-only fares and specials that cannot be obtained anywhere else. The drawback to using an airline's Web site is that in order to shop for the best fares, you need to visit the Web sites of multiple airlines.

2. You can use the services of an online travel-related Web site, such as **Travelocity** (✎ *www.travelocity.com*), **Expedia** (✎ *www.expedia.com*), **Orbitz** (✎ *www.orbitz.com*), or **Yahoo! Travel** (✎ *http://travel.yahoo.com*). These services allow you to quickly search the major airlines for the best flights and fares. You'll also find great deals on hotels, rental cars, and travel packages. When using one of these services, the more time you spend exploring them, the better your chances of saving a lot of money. Once you know when you want to travel, try searching for better fares by altering your travel dates slightly. Sometimes, leaving a day earlier or later can save you money. You can also try looking up various airport combinations. For example, if you're flying from New York's LaGuardia to LAX, you can also check out flights departing from Kennedy Airport and New Jersey's Newark Airport. See if you can save money by flying into John Wayne Airport (Orange County) or Burbank Airport as well. Checking each variable takes only seconds using one of these online travel services.

3. If you have a somewhat flexible travel schedule, you can save between 50 and 80 percent of airfares, hotels, and rental cars using a service such as **Priceline.com** (✎ *www.priceline.com*), **Last Minute Travel** (✎ *www.lastminutetravel.com*), or **Travel Hub** (✎ *www.travelhub.com/airfares*).

Saving a Fortune Using Priceline.com

Priceline.com, ✆ (800) 774-2354, can save you an absolute fortune when booking any type of travel. The catch is, while you can choose what dates you want to fly, you cannot choose your departure times or airlines. Likewise, when booking a hotel, you can choose the quality of the hotel (between one and four stars) and the approximate location (e.g., Anaheim, near Disneyland), but you can't choose a specific hotel chain or exact location. With rental cars, you can choose rental dates and the class of car, but not the rental car company you'll be using. However, Priceline only works with the nation's top five rental car companies.

If you're willing to make these concessions, you can name your own price for what you're looking for. After researching the best possible airfare you can find, you can typically make an offer to Priceline for between 40 percent and 70 percent of that best published fare, and receive your airline tickets for that discounted price.

 **TRAVEL TIP**

> Once you make an offer, if Priceline is able to find the airfare, hotel, or rental car you're looking for at the price you offered, you must make the purchase. You cannot change travel arrangements made through Priceline, nor can you get a refund.

According to Priceline, "We work with the best in the business—the names you know and trust—to bring you savings you won't find anywhere else. Our name-brand partners are willing to give you their best prices because you agree to be flexible with the brand and the specific itinerary or product that you want to buy. It's a simple concept, but by 'shielding the brand' from you until your price is accepted, our partners can now offer you prices not available to the general public. Our brand-name partners will accept your price based on their availability at the time you Name Your Own Price. Of course, this requires some flexibility on your part, but this is what allows you to save up to 40% on brand-name products every day. For each of our products, you tell us exactly what you're looking for and how much you want to pay, and then agree to be flexible with what we find for you. For example, if you use Priceline to purchase round-trip airline tickets you can save up to 40% over the lowest published fares for the dates and cities of your choice. In return, the exact airline and flight times are not disclosed to you until after your tickets are purchased."

Once you visit Priceline.com, the whole process takes about thirty minutes and you must have a major credit card. When booking airline travel through Priceline, the chances of having your offer accepted improve greatly if you say yes to any or all of the following options (you will be prompted for each):

- You're willing to fly from one of several airports in your area (you'll be given specific options). For example, if you live in New York, you'll be asked to select from LaGuardia Airport, Kennedy Airport, and/or Newark Airport.
- You're willing to fly into any of several airports (you'll be given specific options).
- Your departure and/or return dates are flexible (you can provide specific dates).
- You're willing to accept flights with up to two connections each way.
- You're willing to fly in nonjet aircraft (operated by a major airline).
- You're willing to fly during off-peak hours (typically red-eye flights).

Assuming you have flexibility in your travel schedule and you're willing to cope with the concessions you're forced to make when using Priceline, there are some amazing travel deals to be had, especially if you're booking your trip last minute (with no seven- or fourteen-day advance purchase and/or no Saturday night stay). This service is 100 percent legitimate and well worth checking out!

TRAVEL TIP

If you're planning to book your airfare, hotel, and rental car through Priceline, do three separate transactions, starting with your airfare. For people who book their airfares through Priceline, the company typically offers special "Insider Rates" for hotels and rental cars.

Vacation Packages and Other Discounts

 A variety of organizations offer discounts and travel packages to The Disneyland Resort and Southern California (Los Angeles). A travel package may consist of any or all of the following: airfare, hotel accommodations, meals, rental car, and admission to one or more theme parks. Using the budget checklist in this chapter, calculate what it will cost you to plan your own vacation; then compare those rates with those offered by comparable travel packages from an airline or one of the following travel organizations.

In addition to contacting the various airlines directly about individual airfares or travel packages, contact organizations such as the **American Automobile Association's travel department—** ✆ (800) 222-7448 or ✉ *www.aaa.com*—or **AARP**—✆ (800) 424-3410 or ✉ *www.aarp.org.*

Two travel agencies that offer an assortment of different travel packages for people interested in The Disneyland Resort are **American Express Travel**—✆ (800) 346-3607 or ✉ *www.itn.net*—and **Walt Disney Travel Company**—✆ (800) 225-2024 or ✉ *www.disneyland.com.*

The Disney Club

The Disney Club—✆ (800) 654-6347 or ✉ *www.disneyclub.com*— is a program sponsored by the Walt Disney Company that offers its members discounts on theme park tickets, Disney merchandise, and Disney-owned/operated hotel accommodations. There's an annual membership fee of $35. This program should not be confused with The Disney Vacation Club (which offers timeshares) or The Walt Disney Travel Company (which is a full-service travel agency).

If you're planning a trip to The Disneyland Resort and plan to stay at a Disney-owned hotel, eat in Disney-owned restaurants, buy Disney merchandise, or visit the theme parks, not only will you recoup the annual membership fee, but you'll most likely save considerable money on your purchases. The discount also applies to purchases from The Disney Stores as well as the Disney Store Catalog and DisneyStore.com.

The Entertainment Book

Entertainment Books—☏ (800) 933-2605 or ✎ *www.entertainment .com*—offer 50 percent off and two-for-one discounts at your favorite places for dining, shopping, attractions, sports, and services like dry cleaning and movie rentals. Entertainment Books also include discounts at hotels and other travel services.

The Entertainment Ultimate Hotel & Travel, Dining Advantage, and National Value directories offer deep discounts toward worldwide hotels, travel, dining, retail, and services. The travel and hotel directories contain helpful amenity icons, so you can choose the hotel that best meets your needs. The pages of these directories also include bonus value savings on airlines, cruises, car rentals, and attractions.

The 2002 Entertainment Book, which covers Orange County (Anaheim), is priced at $40. It offers discounts and money-saving coupons for more than 464 area restaurants, over 5,000 hotels (nationwide), and special deals from rental car companies and various retail stores and tourist attractions. The Los Angeles edition of the Entertainment Book is priced at $35.

 **TRAVEL TIP**

The Entertainment Book is an extremely useful resource for finding restaurants in the Anaheim area. The book typically offers sample menus as well as money-saving offers.

CHAPTER 3

Packing for Your Vacation

CHANCES ARE you want to have an absolutely incredible vacation, right? Well, to help ensure that this will be the case, invest the necessary time preparing for your trip. In addition to carefully planning an itinerary and prebooking all of your travel, you'll also want to ensure that you pack all of the belongings and wardrobe items you'll need while traveling.

The California Climate

 Throughout the year, the weather in Southern California is generally pretty comfortable; however, in the winter months, it tends to get pretty chilly at night, so dress accordingly. Average temperatures at Disneyland throughout the year are:

Month	Average High (°F)	Average Low (°F)
January	65	44
February	67	45
March	68	46
April	70	50
May	72	53
June	77	56
July	82	61

August	83	60
September	81	59
October	77	55
November	73	50
December	67	46

💼 TRAVEL TIP

To find out the current weather in Southern California (Anaheim), be sure to watch the Weather Channel, check the weather map in *USA Today*, or visit the Disneyland Web site at ✍ *www.disneyland.com*.

Theme Park Attire

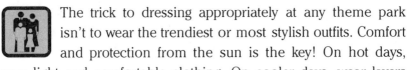 The trick to dressing appropriately at any theme park isn't to wear the trendiest or most stylish outfits. Comfort and protection from the sun is the key! On hot days, wear light and comfortable clothing. On cooler days, wear layers that can be removed and that aren't too bulky. (You can always store clothing items in the lockers available at the theme parks.)

A hat and sunglasses are always a must. Even if the skies are overcast, it's still possible to get sunburned, so make sure that you use powerful sunblock on all exposed skin area. This is particularly important with children.

If you're traveling with kids or plan to experience rides where you get wet, bring along an extra change of clothes and store them in a locker or in your car until they're needed. Ideally, you'll want to keep your hands as free as possible, so try to avoid heavy purses, backpacks, and shoulder bags. Waist packs are an excellent solution for storing smaller items, such as wallets, glasses, keys, and small cameras.

Rainy Days

On rainy days, many people are inclined to bring an umbrella to the theme parks. This is a bad idea. Navigating the crowds in theme parks is particularly difficult with an open umbrella. You're better off wearing a waterproof hat, raincoat, or one of the plastic rain ponchos sold at the theme parks for about $5 each.

Before getting dressed, find out what the weather will be like for the day and dress accordingly, keeping in mind that the temperature may drop at night.

Comfortable Walking Shoes

As you'd expect, medical emergencies periodically take place at The Disneyland Resort and other popular tourist destinations. While the first-aid personnel at the Disney theme parks, for example, are highly trained and can handle virtually any medical situation, the most common problem is blisters.

To avoid blisters, wear comfortable walking shoes. You're going to be doing a lot of walking and your vacation will be much more enjoyable if your feet don't hurt! Be sure to pack at least two pairs of comfortable walking shoes and plenty of socks. If the weather is bad or you go on the park's water rides, you'll want a pair of clean, dry shoes to change into.

 **TRAVEL TIP**

Due to heightened security measures, all bags you carry into a theme park will be searched by security personnel, so plan accordingly.

While sneakers are ideal foot attire for theme parks, some of the most comfortable walking shoes you'll find anywhere in the world are manufactured by **Ecco** (✍ *www.ecco.com*) and are available nationwide at upscale shoe stores, such as the **Walking Company** (✍ *http://walkingco.store.yahoo.com*). These shoes aren't cheap. A pair of men's Ecco Track Low Boot walking shoes, for example, cost about $189, but they are designed to protect your feet and be stylish, water-resistant, and extremely comfortable in a wide range of weather conditions.

Choosing the Best Luggage

Knowing what you want to bring with you to California is the first step, but choosing your luggage and then actually packing your bags can be a challenging and somewhat confusing task. In this section, Chad Mellen, vice president of marketing for Tumi Luggage, Inc., offers his advice for purchasing or choosing your luggage and packing.

How Will You Use the Luggage?

If you don't yet own luggage that's suitable for airplane travel, the first step is to determine how you'll be using your luggage. The actual pieces of luggage a business traveler might purchase are very different from the luggage a family going on vacation would use. "A family that takes just one trip per year doesn't need to spend as much on their luggage as an individual or family that travels often," says Mellen. "No matter who you are, you should purchase good quality luggage. Luggage that will be checked at the airport, as opposed to being carried on an airplane, needs to be extremely durable. Some luggage is specifically designed to keep clothing, such as suits and dresses, wrinkle free, while other luggage pieces are designed to hold a lot of casual clothing."

Quality and Layout

When you go shopping for new luggage, Mellen suggests looking at the quality of the fabric or the leather. "Tumi luggage is manufactured using Napa leather, which is wonderfully soft, yet incredibly strong, or Tru-Ballistic nylon, which was originally developed for the military for use in bulletproof vests. The Tru-Ballistic Nylon is pretty indestructible, and when you realize what your bags go through once you check them at the airport, you'll appreciate the strength of this material. The outer covering of bags tends to go through a lot of wear and tear. Some less expensive luggage materials simply can't hold up to repeat abuse, which means it'll have to be fixed or replaced much sooner. No matter what style or brand of luggage you purchase, choosing luggage manufactured with durable fabric is critical," adds Mellen. Ballistic nylon, used to manufacture many soft-body pieces of luggage, is water-resistant, usually puncture proof, and much easier to carry and store.

▐█▌ TRAVEL TIP

Don't forget to examine the handle system on the luggage. Look for handles that are strong, comfortable, and durable.

"Likewise, if you're buying luggage with wheels, it's important to evaluate the quality of those wheels. Do they spin smoothly? Do they wobble? Tumi, for example, uses the same wheels used on in-line skates, so they have a minimum of friction. This is important when you're dragging 30 to 60 pounds of luggage behind you through the airport, which sometimes requires walking over one-half mile along crowded airport concourses."

Overall, luggage needs to be strong and lightweight. All of the stitching should be tight, with no visible loose threads. Another thing to look for when choosing luggage is to examine how well it's laid out. Mellen adds, "Are the compartments where you'd want to put them? Do the compartments provide added efficiency? Also, is all of the space in the bag usable for packing? Can any of the pockets be accessed from the outside? You should be able to open the bag and say to yourself, 'Wow, this bag was laid out well and will be able to hold all of the belongings I plan on traveling with.'"

Shop Around

When shopping for luggage, Mellen suggests visiting a specialty luggage store or a major department store that carries many luggage styles from different manufacturers. "You want to purchase luggage from a retailer that will fix or replace your luggage if it gets damaged or has a manufacturer's defect. If you don't buy from a reputable dealer, they probably won't try to help you get your luggage fixed or replaced, no matter whom it was manufactured by. The most important thing to do is test-drive the luggage at the retailer before you buy it. If it's on wheels, fill up a sample bag and walk around the store with it to see how it feels," says Mellen. A final thing to look at when purchasing luggage is the manufacturer's warranty.

≡FAST FACT

These days, the materials and fabrics used to manufacture soft-body luggage is as durable, if not more durable, than hard-body luggage. In addition, thanks to expandable compartments, most soft-body luggage is much lighter weight and can often hold more than the same size hard-body luggage or suitcases.

Protect Your Possessions

Since many pieces of luggage look alike, and most bags come in standard solid colors, like black, it's a good idea to make your bag look a bit different when you check it at the airport. Just so the wrong person doesn't accidentally grab your bag off the baggage claim conveyor belt, tie a brightly colored ribbon around the handle. Also, make sure you have a well-attached luggage tag on each bag. The tag should list your full contact information (some people use a work address and phone number for security reasons). In addition to having this information on a luggage tag on the outside of the bag, it's also an excellent idea to include the same information inside the bag, so if your bag gets lost, and the luggage tag falls off, the person who finds it can still contact you.

Mellen advises travelers to avoid using the paper luggage tags supplied by the airlines. These tags fall off too easily. "Many luggage companies, including Tumi, will monogram your luggage. This is another way to make your bags more easily identifiable," he explains. "If you're traveling to Los Angeles from outside of the U.S. or you're traveling overseas, make a photocopy of your passport and place it inside your luggage, near the top."

Once your bag is packed, it's always a good idea to use the locks that come with the suitcase or bag, not so much to prevent theft as to ensure that the bag won't accidentally open while in transit. "Once a bag is checked at the airline, there really isn't anything a traveler can do to protect their bags from receiving physical abuse. The only thing a traveler can do is buy the best made luggage they can find or afford. Incidents of baggage theft are minimal, but travelers should never pack jewelry, computer equipment, cameras, or other valuables in the luggage that will be checked at the airport. These items should be carried onto the plane in a carry-on bag," says Mellen.

 **TRAVEL TIP**

If your luggage is damaged or lost by the airline, it's critical to make your claim in person before leaving the airport. Should a problem arise, visit your airline's lost baggage counter located near the baggage claim area.

Luggage for Families

For families traveling together, the best pieces of luggage to purchase are large, soft-body suitcases that are on wheels. Mellen recommends families use large packing cases or duffle bags on wheels. Tumi's Wheel-A-Way Suiter Packing Case, for example, measures 22" × 29" × 12" and holds plenty of clothing. Using two of these bags, a family of four can easily pack clothing for a week or longer.

Another excellent piece of luggage to consider is a large duffle bag on wheels. These types of bags aren't great for fancy suits or dresses, but they can hold a tremendous amount of casual clothing (and other items), and they're easy to carry or roll around an airport. Each traveler can also pack a carry-on bag, which should have both a handle and a shoulder strap for convenience.

An Investment

Luggage may not be an item that you'll use often, but consider it an investment that you want to last for many years. Thus, by spending a bit more to purchase quality suitcases, your chances of having the luggage that falls apart while you're on a trip are minimized. Finally, be sure to look for luggage that offers features that add convenience and ease of mobility, such as wheels, handles, shoulder straps, compartments, and so on.

To find out more about **Tumi Luggage**, visit a specialty luggage retailer or major department store, or call ✆ (800) 322-TUMI. In addition to Tumi, dozens of different manufacturers offer luggage in a wide range of colors and styles and at a variety of prices.

 TRAVEL TIP

Keep in mind that quality varies greatly among manufacturers. Although two bags from different manufacturers might look similar, their overall quality level and price might be very different. So, examine each bag before you purchase it.

What to Carry with You

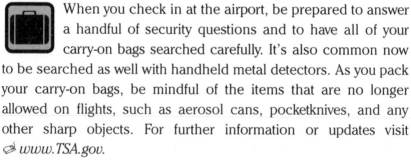 When you check in at the airport, be prepared to answer a handful of security questions and to have all of your carry-on bags searched carefully. It's also common now to be searched as well with handheld metal detectors. As you pack your carry-on bags, be mindful of the items that are no longer allowed on flights, such as aerosol cans, pocketknives, and any other sharp objects. For further information or updates visit ✎ *www.TSA.gov.*

In addition to a higher level of security at the airports, you'll also notice heavy security at theme parks and tourist attractions. For example, at the entrance to every major California theme park, guests are now required to pass through a metal detector and are subject to being searched by security personnel. On busy days, this could delay your entrance into the park by up to thirty minutes, depending on the crowds.

As you embark on your vacation, be prepared to deal with the enhanced security measures in a calm and patient manner. By following the posted rules and regulations, you'll keep any additional stress and hassle associated with travel to a minimum.

All airlines have changed their policies regarding carry-on luggage. This term describes what you physically carry onto the airplane and store either under your seat or in the overhead compartment. Virtually all airlines allow only one or two carry-on bags (including a purse or laptop case) per passenger, and the size requirements for each bag continue to change. The following list gives basic guidelines for some of the major airlines in terms of what they allow to be taken onto the plane.

Airline	Carry-on Bag Size (inches)
American	9 × 13 × 23
Continental	45 linear inches
Delta	9 × 14 × 22
Northwest	9 × 14 × 22
Southwest	10 × 16 × 24
TWA	10 × 16 × 24
United	9 × 14 × 22
USAir	10 × 16 × 24 (overhead); 8 × 16 × 21 (under the seat)

Although guidelines for carry-on bags are changing as new security measures are implemented and tested by the various airlines and airports, the following guidelines from US Airways are pretty consistent with the rest of the airline industry.

According to US Airways:

Customers are limited to one piece of carry-on baggage plus one personal item. Pets and duty-free items are considered carry-on baggage. Personal items include a purse, briefcase, laptop computer, diaper bag, camera bag, or backpack.

Carry-on baggage cannot exceed 40 pounds or exceed the following dimensions: valet—4" × 23½" × 45"; overhead stowage—10" × 16" × 24"; under seat stowage—8" × 16" × 21". All carry-on baggage must be properly stowed in the overhead bin or underneath the seat. Customers are now being permitted to carry on nail clippers, safety razors (including disposable razors), syringes (with proper documentation), tweezers, walking canes, and umbrellas.

Whether traveling by airplane, bus, or train, here are some suggestions for what you might want to bring in your carry-on bag instead of in your regular luggage. (Some of the items, such as your cash, credit cards, and ID, should be kept on your person, in a wallet, for example):

- ☐ Airline tickets and printed itinerary
- ☐ Book(s) and/or magazine(s) to read
- ☐ Camera, camcorder
- ☐ Cash, credit cards, traveler's checks, personal checkbook
- ☐ Cellular phone, pager, or other personal electronics (Keep in mind, these devices typically cannot be used onboard an airplane.)
- ☐ Change of clothing, depending on the length of your flight (Also, it never hurts to have a change of clothing just in case you spill something on yourself or your checked luggage gets lost and you need something to change into when you arrival at your destination.)
- ☐ Eyeglasses/contact lenses
- ☐ Jewelry and other valuables
- ☐ Laptop computer
- ☐ Photo identification (license, passport, military ID)
- ☐ Planner, personal calendar, or personal digital assistant
- ☐ Prescription and nonprescription medications (Airlines will not supply pain relievers, such as aspirin, to passengers.)

☐ Snacks or food

☐ Toys, coloring items, and other items to entertain the kids

⟹FAST FACT

Aside from Tumi, other popular luggage manufacturers include Atlantic, American Tourister, Andiamo, Biggs & Riley, Dakota Metro, Hartmann, Kipling, Samsonite, and Travelpro. Visit any major department store or specialty luggage store to see the luggage products offered by these and other manufacturers.

Packing Tips from the Pros

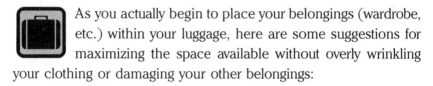 As you actually begin to place your belongings (wardrobe, etc.) within your luggage, here are some suggestions for maximizing the space available without overly wrinkling your clothing or damaging your other belongings:

- Never pack and check at the airport any items that you absolutely must have when you get off the plane, such as prescription medications.
- If you're planning to pack fancy clothing, use a garment bag or a suitcase with a special compartment designed for formal suits and dresses.
- Instead of folding casual clothing items, roll them up and place them in your luggage.
- Place shampoos, perfume bottles, toothpaste, mouthwash, and other fluid items that might leak or that could be damaged in plastic bags.
- While packing your luggage, make a list of each bag's contents and leave the list at home. If your bag gets lost or stolen, having a list of missing items will help you get reimbursed by the airline or insurance company.
- Once your bags are packed and you're ready to leave, keep your bags with you at all times until they are safely checked

with the airline at a designated baggage check-in location, such as the airline's ticket counter.

- All of your travel documents (airline tickets, etc.) should be kept in a pocket or in a carry-on bag while you're traveling.
- Before you start packing, call your hotel to see if self-service laundry facilities are offered. If you're willing to do laundry on vacation, you can pack fewer clothing items.
- Make sure you have ID tags on the outside of your luggage and inside as well.

TRAVEL TIP

During the fall and winter months, Southern California and Orange County are generally comfortable, but be prepared for cold evenings and for the possibility of rain. It is conceivable that the temperature could drop into the mid-40s in the evening.

As you choose what clothing to pack, make sure you bring along one or two sweatshirts/sweaters, a lightweight and/or medium-weight jacket (preferably one that's waterproof), and at least two pairs of extremely comfortable walking shoes. You'll definitely be doing a lot of walking when visiting the various theme parks and attractions in Southern California. If one pair of shoes gets wet, you'll want to be able to change into another dry pair. The importance of wearing comfortable shoes can't be emphasized enough!

Although everyone has his or her own preferences when packing for a trip, here's a checklist of what you might want to include in your suitcase(s) or carry-on(s):

- ☐ Airline tickets and travel itinerary (including airline, hotel, and car rental reservation confirmation numbers); also pack copies of tickets and the itinerary
- ☐ Aspirin or nonaspirin pain relievers

- ☐ Baby care products (if applicable)
- ☐ Bathing suit
- ☐ Belt
- ☐ Book/magazine to read on the plane and at the pool
- ☐ Camcorder and accessories
- ☐ Camera, film, and batteries
- ☐ Cash (carry and use traveler's checks instead of large sums of cash when traveling)
- ☐ Casual evening dress
- ☐ Comfortable walking shoes/sneakers (2 pairs)
- ☐ Credit cards, AAA and/or AARP membership card, Magic Kingdom Club Card, or Entertainment Card
- ☐ Dress shoes
- ☐ Driver's license and/or photo ID (to be kept on your person at all times when traveling through airports or on airplanes)
- ☐ Fashion accessories (leave expensive jewelry at home)
- ☐ Flip-flops or beach shoes
- ☐ Golf clubs or tennis racquet
- ☐ Hair care products (most hotels provide hair dryers)
- ☐ Hat or cap (You'll want to wear something comfortable, such as a baseball cap, to protect your head and face from sun and/or rain.)
- ☐ Jacket, lightweight or medium weight but definitely waterproof
- ☐ Jeans
- ☐ Long-sleeve shirts
- ☐ Medications/prescriptions
- ☐ Pajamas/nightgown
- ☐ Pantyhose
- ☐ Pocketbook/handbag
- ☐ Prescription eyeglasses
- ☐ Raincoat
- ☐ Shaving equipment
- ☐ Shorts
- ☐ Short-sleeve shirts
- ☐ Skirts

- ☐ Slacks
- ☐ Socks
- ☐ Sports jacket and tie
- ☐ Sunblock (Even if you're traveling in the winter or the weather is overcast, the sun can cause a serious sunburn.)
- ☐ Sunglasses
- ☐ Sweaters/sweatshirts
- ☐ Toiletries
- ☐ Traveler's checks
- ☐ T-shirts
- ☐ Underwear/bras
- ☐ Waist pack
- ☐ Wallet
- ☐ Watch
- ☐ Workout clothing

💼 TRAVEL TIP

While the use of cellular telephones and two-way radios is permitted throughout all of the major theme parks, be considerate and refrain from using these devices while you're actually experiencing an attraction or ride.

Don't Forget the Camera!

When you visit Anaheim and/or Southern California to experience the various theme parks and tourist attractions, you're in for a memorable vacation! Chances are you'll want to capture at least some of these memories on film. All of the theme park and tourist attraction operators count on the fact that people forget their cameras, film, and batteries and charge exorbitant prices for these items. You'll also find that the cost of one-hour photo processing within the theme parks is rather high.

To save money, pack plenty of film and batteries. When buying film, keep in mind that you'll probably want to take pictures both indoors and outdoors, so using general purpose film, such as Kodak's MAX 35mm film, will provide the best results in traditional cameras. Instead of purchasing one roll of film at a time, you can also save money by purchasing packages of three or more rolls.

Ultimately, when you have your film developed, you can save money by using an overnight film processing service as opposed to a one-hour photo processor. The quality of your pictures will most likely be better if you take your film to a professional camera store rather than the one-hour processing offered through your local supermarket or pharmacy; however, these services tend to be cheaper.

Another alternative is to use America Online's You've Got Pictures service. You will receive prints, and your photos will also be e-mailed directly to you, so you can easily e-mail them to friends or family, or post them on a family Web site. For more information about this service, log on to America Online and click on the You've Got Pictures icon or ask your local photo developer.

Stay in Touch

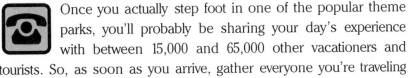

Once you actually step foot in one of the popular theme parks, you'll probably be sharing your day's experience with between 15,000 and 65,000 other vacationers and tourists. So, as soon as you arrive, gather everyone you're traveling with and select a central meeting location and determine meeting times. For example, if anyone gets separated, plan to meet at the top of the hour at your meeting place. Within Disneyland, one of the most central meeting locations is called "the Hub." It's located in front of the main castle, at the end of Main Street, U.S.A. You'll see a giant statue of Mickey Mouse and Walt Disney in the center of the Hub.

If you plan on separating, one way to stay in touch with the people you're traveling with is to have everyone carry a two-way radio. Motorola offers a complete line of two-way radios that have a two-mile range, which means that the people you're traveling with will be able to communicate from anywhere inside one of the major theme parks.

The price of the two-way radios varies between $50 and $175 per unit. You must have at least two units to communicate. The full-featured Motorola Talkabout T6320 two-way radios offer more than just the ability to communicate. They contain a built-in digital compass, altimeter, thermometer, and barometer. You can also tune into the National Oceanic and Atmospheric Administration's weather broadcasts and listen to up-to-the-minute weather reports for your current location. Thus, you can predict what the weather will be like for your day in the theme parks and dress accordingly.

Before Leaving Home

As you get ready to leave on vacation, here's a quick checklist of things you might want to do before you go. Due to increased airport security, make sure to arrive at least ninety minutes (or even two hours) before your flight's scheduled departure. With this in mind, plan your schedule accordingly.

Here are a few things to do before leaving on vacation:

- ☐ Arrange for someone to care for your pets and plants.
- ☐ Ask a friend, relative, or neighbor to check on your home or apartment while you're gone.
- ☐ Ask the post office to hold your mail (and fill out the appropriate form).
- ☐ Clean all dirty dishes.
- ☐ Close and lock all windows (and close the blinds/curtains).
- ☐ Contact your child's teacher if he/she will be missing classes.
- ☐ Empty your refrigerator of perishable items.
- ☐ Empty your trash.
- ☐ Get a haircut, manicure, and so on.
- ☐ Give a copy of your house keys to a nearby friend or relative.
- ☐ Leave your contact information (hotel name and phone number) with coworkers, friends, or relatives, or anyone who might need to reach you in case of an emergency.

☐ Pay your mortgage, rent, credit card bills, and other bills.

☐ Refill all prescription medications.

☐ Stop daily newspaper delivery or arrange for newspapers to be placed in an area that's out of sight. You don't want to make it obvious that you're on vacation.

☐ Turn down the heat or air-conditioning.

☐ Turn on your telephone answering machine, but don't announce that you're on vacation.

☐ Unplug electrical appliances.

☐ Visit a bank to get cash and traveler's checks.

CHAPTER 4

Choosing Your Hotel Accommodations

ALTHOUGH YOU PROBABLY WON'T BE spending too much time in your hotel room while on vacation, you'll definitely want accommodations that are comfortable and that offer the amenities you need and want, at a price that suits your budget. In the Anaheim area and The Disneyland Resort, there are literally hundreds of hotels, motels, and inns that cater to vacationing families.

Defining Your Needs

If you want to experience the ultimate Disney vacation and the superior service and hospitality that Disney is known for, you'll probably want to stay at one of The Disneyland Resort hotels. If, however, you're looking for a clean, fully functional hotel room or suite, or even a less expensive motel, either of which will save you a lot of money, staying at a non-Disney hotel is an excellent idea, especially if you're planning on renting a car.

You've Got the Answer

Before making any hotel reservation, consider the following:

- What type of accommodations do you need? How many beds and what size (twin, queen, or king)? How many bedrooms, bathrooms? Will you be requiring extra cots or a crib in the room? If so, how much does the hotel charge per night for extra cots or cribs?

- Since most room rates are based on double occupancy, is there an extra charge per person for children staying in your room?

- What type of amenities do you need or want?

- What type of hotel services are you looking for? Should the hotel have a swimming pool (indoor or outdoor), hot tub, exercise room/fitness center, tennis courts, or an on-site restaurant? Will you require or want self-service (coin-operated) laundry facilities?

- Is a complimentary shuttle bus offered to and from the airport? Is a shuttle bus offered to and from The Disneyland Resort?

- How close is the hotel to The Disneyland Resort and other attractions you plan on visiting?

- Does the hotel offer complimentary parking (if you're renting a car)? If not, how much will parking fees increase your overall hotel bill?

- Does the hotel charge for local phone calls or for calling toll-free numbers? If so, how much? Is the hotel equipped with phone jacks that allow you to connect a laptop computer and access the Internet, check your e-mail, or access one of the major online services?

- Does the hotel offer incoming and outgoing fax service? What about a full-service business center?

- What types of dining options are available? What about in-room dining (room service)?

- Is an in-room safe provided so you can store your valuables?

- Will the hotel be able to guarantee you a nonsmoking room (if you request one when you make your reservation)?

- What is your nightly budget for a hotel/motel room?

Shop Around for Rates

As you make your hotel reservation, shop around for the best room rates. Non-Disney hotel rates are often negotiable, plus most will honor some type of discount program (AAA, the Entertainment Book, etc.). Before mentioning that you're a member of any discount program, ask the hotel for their best rate and negotiate the best deal you can; then mention that you'd like the added discount.

If you need help finding accommodations and making a reservation, especially during peak travel times, consider contacting any of these organizations:

Anaheim Chamber of Commerce: ☏(714) 758-0222
Anaheim/Orange County Visitor & Convention Bureau:
☏(714) 765-8888, ✐ *www.anaheimoc.org*
Anaheim Visitor Center: ☏(714) 239-1340,
✐ *www.teleguideinc.com*
Los Angeles Convention & Visitors Bureau: ☏(213) 624-7300
✐ *www.lacvb.com*
Orange County Tourism Council: ☏(714) 278-7491

💼 TRAVEL TIP

To ensure that you'll get the best room selection and best rates, make your hotel reservations as far in advance as possible, and be prepared to guarantee your reservation using a major credit card. If you're having trouble locating a hotel with rooms available that offer the accommodations you're looking for, consider using the services of a travel agent.

The Disneyland Hotel

🖾 1150 Magic Way
   Anaheim, CA 92802
☏ (714) 956-MICKEY
✐ *www.Disneyland.com*

This Disneyland landmark, complete with a tropical sandy beach, fine restaurants, and a handful of its own activities and attractions, offers 990 rooms, and is located a short walk from the Disney theme parks. While this 65-acre hotel complex offers plenty of convention space, banquet rooms, and meeting facilities, it's definitely a resort hotel that caters to families traveling with kids and teens.

As a resort hotel, The Disneyland Hotel offers a wide range of amenities and activities, including three swimming pools, along with the Never Land theme pool (which features tropical landscaping, a 110-foot water slide, a pirate ship, and the "mermaid lagoon" spa). You'll also find several souvenir gift shops and clothing boutiques. There's also a fully equipped fitness center.

Dining

Throughout the hotel, you'll find a handful of fine-dining restaurants, places to grab a quick snack, plus several full-service bars and lounges. If you don't find what you're looking for on the hotel's property, Downtown Disney is a short walk away.

The hotel's popular fine-dining options, which are ideal for romantic dinners or celebrating special occasions, include **Granville's Steak House** (offering a large selection of steaks, prime rib, poultry, and fresh Maine lobsters) and the **Hook's Pointe & Wine Cellar** (serving mesquite-grilled American cuisine in an upscale atmosphere, along with more than twenty-five acclaimed California wines). These restaurants are rather fancy. While they offer kid's menus, younger people will most likely enjoy less formal dining options.

Goofy's Kitchen offers more affordable, family-oriented dining options, with a popular all-you-can-eat buffet. This restaurant is where you and your kids can have breakfast with the popular Disney characters, so be sure to bring along a camera. For a light snack or that morning cup of gourmet coffee, you'll want to drop into the **Coffee House,** which features espresso, cappuccino, specialty coffee drinks, muffins, and freshly baked cookies.

Guest Room Accommodations

The guest room accommodations are available at several different price points. The concierge-level rooms offer upgraded in-room amenities and complimentary access to a special Concierge Lounge, which serves a continental breakfast, beverages, wine, and cheese. The hotel also offers sixty-two suites, ranging in size from 740 to 3,400 square feet.

Basic room rates (subject to change based on availability, the view from the room, and the season) for The Disneyland Hotel range between $200 and $290 per night for a regular room. For a concierge room, add between $65 and $75 per night to the room rate. Suites are priced somewhat higher, between $450 and $2,500 per night, based on availability and season. All rates are based on single or double occupancy. Children under the age of seventeen can share the room (using existing beds) for no additional charge.

Although there is no additional cost for a rollaway bed, there is a $15 per night per adult charge for each adult (beyond two) staying in a room. Valet parking is also available for a $15 per night extra fee, while self-parking costs $5 per night.

Keep in mind, when making a reservation, The Disneyland Hotel has a seventy-two-hour reservation cancellation or change policy. Special promotional rates, package rates, and other discounts are available throughout the year, based on availability. To learn more about these special rates, call a travel agent or The Disneyland Hotel reservation number.

▐ TRAVEL TIP

The best way to save money when staying at any of the Disney-owned hotels is to visit during nonpeak travel periods (January 1 through April 13, April 30 through June 1st, and August 27 through December 21). You can also take advantage of the discounts offered to Disney Club members on travel packages, as well as other package deals offered by The Walt Disney Travel Company, ☎(714) 520-5050.

Guest Services and Perks

Optional guests services, which can be coordinated through the front desk or the concierge, include child-care services, self-service laundry facilities, and a fully equipped business center.

One of the perks of staying at The Disneyland Hotel is that on predetermined days, guests can enjoy early admission to the theme parks (ninety minutes before they open to the general public). This provides an awesome opportunity to experience the most popular rides, without having to wait in long lines. Another perk is that anything you purchase within the hotel, the theme parks, or at Downtown Disney can be delivered to your hotel room, free of charge. Finally, on particularly busy days, guests of The Disneyland Hotel are guaranteed admission to the theme parks (with the purchase of a ticket or travel package) even if the parks are at capacity.

The Disneyland Hotel also offers its own attraction, the Fantasy Waters show, which has been entertaining guests for decades. Combining choreographed fountains of water with colorful lights and popular Disney music, this twenty-minute show is presented nightly (after dark) and is definitely worth experiencing.

⊕ HOT SPOT

The Disneyland Hotel, along with the Paradise Pier Hotel and Grand Californian Hotel, offer nonsmoking rooms and rooms especially designed for guests with disabilities. Make sure you request these special accommodations at the time you make your reservation, not when you show up to check into the hotel.

Disney's Paradise Pier Hotel

🖃 1717 Disneyland Drive
   Anaheim, CA 92802

📞 (714) 956-MICKEY

✎ *www.Disneyland.com*

At the same time Disney's California Adventure theme park opened, the nearby resort hotel, formally known as the Disneyland Pacific Hotel, got a total makeover and reopened as the luxurious Disney's Paradise Pier. This hotel connects directly to Disney's California Adventure and now offers a California theme, both inside and out.

The two primary buildings that make up this hotel include a fifteen-story and a fourteen-story tower, which combined contain a total of 502 rooms, including twelve suites and poolside cabana rooms. In addition to the guest rooms, you'll find a lovely rooftop swimming pool, whirlpool, two fine-dining restaurants, a video arcade, a lobby and pool bar, a fitness center, and a coffeehouse among the amenities.

Like The Disneyland Hotel, this one also offers premium concierge rooms, which offer additional services and in-room amenities (such as a newspaper delivered to your room each morning, turndown service, in-room VCR and video library, extra workspace, and a lounge area located on the concierge floor).

Dining

For a midpriced dining experience (for breakfast, lunch, or dinner), the **Pacific Coast Highway (PCH)** restaurant within the hotel serves wood-fired specialty pizzas, sea bass, baby back ribs, and a selection of other entrées. The kids you're traveling with will particularly enjoy the Minnie & Friends breakfast (served daily), which features a meal with some of Disney's most popular characters that roam the dining room interacting with guests.

If you're in the mood for a somewhat fancy and utterly delicious Japanese dining experience, the hotel's **Yamabuki** restaurant serves fresh sushi, tempura, and other entrées. **The Tatami Room** offers both Japanese and Western-style seating. A less formal dining experience can be found within a traditional English tearoom, located on the hotel's second floor.

Guest Room Accommodations

As for the room accommodations, you can expect contemporary Disney and California-themed furnishings, one king-size bed (or two extra-long double beds), plus a foldout twin sofa bed in the room's sitting area. Room rates vary greatly, depending on availability, time of year, view, and room type. But expect to spend between $200 and $250 per night for a standard, double occupancy room. Add between $65 and $75 per night for a concierge room.

If more than two adults (persons over seventeen years old) will be staying in the room, there's an additional $15 per night charge for the extra adult(s). Suite prices range from $850 to $1,300 per night. Parking is an additional $5 per night, and valet parking is an additional $15 per night.

Guest Perks

As with the other Disney-owned hotels, there are several additional perks if you stay at this hotel. For starters, it's located less than a one-minute walk from Disney's California Adventure theme park. On predetermined days, guests can enjoy early admission to the theme parks (ninety minutes before they open to the general public). This provides an awesome opportunity to experience the theme parks' most popular rides, without having to wait in long lines. Another perk is that anything you purchase within the hotel, the theme parks, or at Downtown Disney can be delivered to your hotel room, free of charge. Finally, on particularly busy days, guests of the Paradise Pier Hotel are guaranteed admission to the theme parks (with the purchase of a ticket or travel package) even if the parks are at capacity.

⊕ HOT SPOT

The magic of the Disneyland theme parks can continue throughout the length of your stay in the Anaheim area if you choose to lodge at one of the hotels on the resort's property. These top-quality family-oriented hotels include The Disneyland Hotel, Disney's Grand Californian Hotel, and Disney's Paradise Pier Hotel.

Disney's Grand Californian Hotel

▣ 1600 South Disneyland Drive
   Anaheim, CA 92802
✆ (714) 300-7170 or ✆ (714) 956-MICKEY
✍ *www.Disneyland.com*

Located next to Disney's California Adventure theme park and a short hop, skip, and a jump from Downtown Disney, Disney's Grand Californian Hotel is the most upscale of the Disney-owned hotels that make up The Disneyland Resort. This 750-room low-rise hotel is surrounded by trees and was designed to re-create an early-1900s style, which features lovely wood paneling inside and out. Inside, the furnishings and even the hotel staff's wardrobe reflect this hotel's theme which is layered in the memories of the arroyo craftsmen, the mission pioneers, and the Plein Air school of painters and architecture.

Amenities

Some of the upscale amenities you'll find in the standard rooms include two phone lines (with data jacks), an in-room safe and refrigerator, a 27-inch television, iron and ironing board, coffeemaker, triple-sheeted beds, robes, and an Italian marble vanity in the bathroom. Additional amenities are included in the slightly more expensive concierge rooms, as well as in the significantly more expensive suites.

In the hotel itself, you'll find a beautiful (and always lit) fireplace in the lobby, an outdoor pool, two spas, a children's pool, a dry and steam sauna, a business center, and a fully equipped workout facility.

Room Rates

Standard room rates vary based on the season, availability, view, and room type; however, you can expect to spend between $250 and $300 per night. As with the other Disney-owned hotels, there is no charge for children (under the age of seventeen) to stay in a room with at least one adult. If more than two adults are in a room, there's an additional per night charge of $15 per adult. For a concierge room, add between $65 and $75 per night to the standard room rate. Suites range in price from $350 to $2,500 per night. Self-service parking is an additional $5 per night, and valet parking is an additional $15 per night. This hotel does not offer rollaway beds. Cribs are, however, available.

Child-Care Services

Located in Disney's Grand Californian Hotel is **Pinocchio's Workshop**, a child activity center that's available every evening, so that parents can enjoy a quiet dinner alone or explore Downtown Disney's nightlife without the kids. This child-care center is open from 5:00 P.M. to midnight every night. Space is limited, especially during the peak season, so be sure to make reservations in advance by calling ✆ (714) 956-6755.

Open to kids, between the ages of five and twelve only, the cost of this child-care service is $9 per hour per child. Snacks are provided, but for an additional $5 charge, dinner can be served. Private babysitters are also available. Contact the hotel's front desk or concierge for details.

⊕ HOT SPOT

When you get hungry, you can take a very short walk to Downtown Disney or enjoy the dining options within the hotel, which include the **Napa Rose** (a fine-dining restaurant serving California wine country cuisine), **Storytellers Café** (family dining), the **Hearthstone Lounge** (serving gourmet coffees and homemade baked goods), and **White Water Snacks** (a poolside snack area).

Anaheim-Area Accommodations

 Located just outside of the Disney property are dozens of hotels, motels, and restaurants that give you a vast choice about where you can sleep and eat. The prices vary greatly, but most are extremely affordable for families traveling on a budget. The hotel/motel business in Anaheim is highly competitive. So, no matter what rates a hotel/motel advertises, be sure to negotiate in order to get the best deals possible.

≡FAST FACT

There are now over 20,000 hotel rooms available in Anaheim at over 150 different hotels and motels. Throughout the year (not just during peak seasons), average occupancy is around 86.5 percent.

Close and Convenient

Just about all of the hotels/motels listed here are located just outside The Disneyland Resort. Although you can walk to and from the park, most of these hotels offer a complimentary shuttle bus. Using a shuttle bus as opposed to driving your own car to the park will save you that daily parking fee.

As you select a hotel/motel, don't be fooled by advertised rates that seem too good to be true. Most of the time, they are. Many advertise extremely low rates, but when you actually try to make a reservation, all of the rooms at the advertised price are already taken. If you do manage to find a room that's dirt cheap, keep in mind that you always get exactly what you pay for. A hotel that charges $30 to $50 per night is going to be no-frills, to say the least.

Most vacationers find it extremely convenient to stay at a hotel that's a short walk from The Disneyland Resort, so during the day, it's easy to leave the park and return to your room to change clothing or take a nap. To experience the best possible Disney vacation, you'll definitely want to stay at one of the three Disney-owned resort hotels, but you'll pay a premium.

To save money, your best bet is to find a comfortable non-Disney-owned hotel/motel that's located near the theme parks. You can always visit The Disneyland Hotel, for example, dine at any of the excellent restaurants that are located in the Disney-owned hotel, and see the Fantasy Waters show at night.

As soon as you know you'll be visiting the Disney theme parks, make your hotel reservations as far in advance as possible, and be prepared to secure your reservation by supplying your credit card number. As you do this, ask about the hotel's policy for canceling reservations. Often (but not always), you can cancel a reservation up until 6:00 P.M. on the evening your hotel stay is scheduled to begin. Many hotels offer additional discounts for reservations made more then seven days in advance.

≡ FAST FACT

If you're staying along the 1400 or 1500 block of Harbor Boulevard, you'll find it extremely convenient to walk to and from your hotel or motel to the Disneyland theme parks. This will save you the cost of parking and the time required to wait for a shuttle bus to and from where you're staying.

Nearby Hotel/Motel One Room, Double Occupancy Rates

The following key will help you to determine the cost of a room per night for the hotels/motels listed in the table.

In many cases, to describe the distance between The Disneyland Resort and each hotel/motel, the number of blocks is used. When walking, each block represents a five-minute or so walk. Virtually all of the hotels/motels listed offer a free shuttle bus to and from the Disney theme parks.

KEY:

🛏 = Hotel/Motel Name

📞 = Phone Number

$ = Price Range per Night
   $: $0–$50 per night
   $$: $51–$75 per night
   $$$: $76–$99 per night
   $$$$: $100–$150 per night
   $$$$$: $151–$200 per night
   $$$$$$: $201+ per night

🚗 = Distance from The Disneyland Resort by Car

🛏 **Abby's Anaheim Inn,** 📞(714) 774-0211, **$$**, 🚗 1 block

🛏 **Adam's Mark of Orlando,** 📞(407) 859-1500 or 📞(800) 231-7883, 🚗 20 minutes, **$$$/$$$$**

🛏 **Akua Motor Inn,** 📞(714) 871-2830, **$**, 🚗 3 miles

🛏 **Alamo Inn & Suites,** 📞(800) 378-9696 or 📞(714) 635-8070, **$$/$$$**, 🚗 2 blocks

🛏 **Alpine Motel,** 📞(800) 772-4422, **$$/$$$**, 🚗 1 block

🛏 **Anaheim Angel Inn,** 📞(800) 358-4400, **$**, 🚗 1 mile

🛏 **Anaheim Best Inn,** 📞(714) 635-3630, **$$$/$$$$**, 🚗 1½ blocks

🛏 **Anaheim Coachman Inn,** 📞(714) 971-5556, **$**, 🚗 2½ blocks

🛏 **Anaheim Comfort Inn Maingate,** 📞(800) 228-5150 or 📞(714) 750-5211, **$/$$/$$$**, 🚗 1 mile

🛏 **Anaheim Courtesy Lodge,** 📞(714) 533-2570, **$**, 🚗 ½ mile

🛏 **Anaheim Desert Inn & Suites,** 📞(714) 772-5050, **$$/$$$**, 🚗 block

🛏 **Anaheim Desert Palm Inn & Suites,** ☎ (714) 535-1133, **$$/$$$**, 🚗 ½ mile

🛏 **Anaheim Fairfield Inn,** ☎ (714) 772-6777, **$$$/$$$$**, 🚗 1 mile

🛏 **Anaheim Hilton & Towers,** ☎ (800) 445-8667 or ☎ (714) 750-4321, **$$$$$/$$$$$$$**, 🚗 2 blocks

🛏 **Anaheim Maingate Inn,** ☎ (714) 533-2500, **$/$$**, 🚗 ½ mile

🛏 **Anaheim Marriott Hotel,** ☎ (800) 228-9290 or ☎ (714) 750-8000, **$$$$/$$$$$**, 🚗 2 blocks

🛏 **Anaheim Plaza Hotel,** ☎ (714) 772-5900, **$$$**, 🚗 1 block

🛏 **Anaheim Ramada Inn,** ☎ (800) 272-6232 or ☎ (714) 978-8088, **$/$$**, 🚗 1 mile

🛏 **Anaheim Sportstown Travelodge,** ☎ (800) 634-1920 or ☎ (714) 634-1920, **$/$$**, 🚗 1.5 Miles

🛏 **Best Western Courtesy Inn,** ☎ (800) 233-8062 or ☎ (714) 772-2470, **$/$$**, 🚗 1 block

🛏 **Best Western Park Place Inn,** ☎ (800) 528-1234 or ☎ (714) 776-4800, **$$$/$$$$**, 🚗 1 block

🛏 **Best Western Raffles Inn & Suites,** ☎ (800) 528-1234 or ☎ (714) 750-6100, **$$$/$$$$**, 🚗 2 blocks

🛏 **Best Western Stovall's Inn,** ☎ (800) 528-1234 or ☎ (714) 778-1880, **$$**, 🚗 1 block

🛏 **Brea's Hyland Motel,** ☎ (714) 990-6867, **$/$$**, 🚗 7 miles

🛏 **Brookhurst Plaza Inn,** ☎ (800) 909-1220, **$$/$$$**, 🚗 1½ miles

🛏 **Candy Cane Inn,** ☎ (800) 345-7057 or ☎ (714) 774-5284, **$$/$$$**, 🚗 1 block

🛏 **Carousel Inn & Suites,** ☎ (714) 758-0444, **$$/$$$**, 🚗 1 block

🛏 **Castle Inn & Suites,** ☎ (800) 227-8530 or ☎ (714) 774-8111, **$$/$$$**, 🚗 1 block

🛏 **Courtesy Lodge,** ☎(800) 999-1367, **$**, 🚗 2 blocks

🛏 **Crystal Inn,** ☎(800) 999-3545 or ☎(714) 535-8444, **$/$$**, 🚗 3 miles

🛏 **Crystal Suites Hotel,** ☎(800) 237-8811 or ☎(714) 535-7773, **$$$/$$$$**, 🚗 2 blocks

🛏 **Days Inn–Disneyland,** ☎(800) 331-0055 or ☎(714) 520-0101, **$/$$**, 🚗 1½ blocks

🛏 **Days Inn Park South,** ☎(800) 654-7503 or ☎(714) 703-1220, **$/$$/$$$**, 🚗 2 blocks

🛏 **Days Inn Suites,** ☎(800) 654-7503 or ☎(714) 533-8830, **$$/$$$/$$$$**, 🚗 2 blocks

🛏 **DoubleTree Hotel–Anaheim,** ☎(800) 222-TREE or ☎(714) 634-4500, **$$$/$$$$**, 🚗 2½ miles

🛏 **Econo Lodge East Main Gate,** ☎(800) 553-2666 or ☎(714) 772-5721, **$/$$**, 🚗 1 mile

🛏 **Economy Inn,** ☎(714) 220-2882, **$**, 🚗 4 miles

🛏 **Embassy Suites–Disneyland Park Area,** ☎(800) 362-2779 or ☎(714) 632-1221, **$$$$/$$$$$**, 🚗 6 miles

🛏 **Frontier Lodge,** ☎(714) 774-1818, **$**, 🚗 1 block

🛏 **Hacienda Inn & Suites,** ☎(800) 858-7006, **$$/$$$**, 🚗 1 mile

🛏 **Hilton Suites,** ☎(800) 916-2221 or ☎(714) 938-1111, **$$/$$$/$$$$**, 🚗 2 miles

🛏 **Holiday Inn Anaheim at the Park,** ☎(800) 545-7275 or ☎(714) 758-0900, **$$$/$$$$**, 🚗 1½ blocks

🛏 **Holiday Inn Conestoga,** ☎(714) 535-0300, **$$$/$$$$**, 🚗 1 mile

🛏 **Holiday Inn Express,** ☎(800) 833-7888 or ☎(714) 772-7755, **$$$**, 🚗 1 block

🛏 **Howard Johnson Hotel,** ☎(800) 446-4656 or ☎(714) 776-6120,

$$/$$$, 🚗 1 block

🛏 **Hyatt Regency Alicante,** 📞 (800) 233-1234 or 📞 (714) 750-1234, **$$$$/$$$$$**, 🚗 1 mile

🛏 **Islander Motel,** 📞 (800) 882-8819 or 📞 (714) 778-6565, **$/$$**, 🚗 2 blocks

🛏 **Jolly Roger Inn Hotel,** 📞 (800) 446-1555 or 📞 (714) 772-7621, **$$/$$$/$$$$**, 🚗 1 block

🛏 **Legacy Suites,** 📞 (800) 669-5617, **$**, 🚗 1 mile

🛏 **Marriott Hotel,** 📞 (800) 624-8213, **$$/$$$**, 🚗 ½ mile

🛏 **Park Inn International,** 📞 (800) 828-4898 or 📞 (714) 635-7275, **$$$$/$$$$$**, 🚗 1 block

🛏 **Parkside Inn & Suites,** 📞 (800) 200-4539 or 📞 (714) 971-5511, **$/$$**, 🚗 1 block

🛏 **Parkside Regency Inn & Suites,** 📞 (800) 582-4270 or 📞 (714) 776-2600, **$/$$**, 🚗 2 miles

🛏 **Park View Inn,** 📞 (800) 334-7021, **$$**, 🚗 1 block

🛏 **Peacock Suite Resort,** 📞 (800) 522-6401 or 📞 (714) 535-8255, **$$$/$$$$**, 🚗 2 blocks

🛏 **Polynesian Motel,** 📞 (800) 362-6433, **$**, 🚗 3 miles

🛏 **Portofino Inn & Suites,** 📞 (888) 297-8761, **$$/$$$**, 🚗 1 block

🛏 **Quality Hotel Maingate,** 📞 (800) 228-5151 or 📞 (714) 750-3131, **$$/$$$/$$$$**, 🚗 1 mile

🛏 **Radisson Hotel Main Gate–Anaheim,** 📞 (800) 333-3333 or 📞 (714) 750-2801, **$$$/$$$$**, 🚗 1 block

🛏 **Radisson Resort Knott's Berry Farm,** 📞 (800) 422-4444 or 📞 (714) 995-1111, **$$$/$$$$**, 🚗 7 miles

🛏 **Ramada Inn Anaheim,** 📞 (800) 854-6097 or 📞 (714) 772-0440, **$$/$$$**, 🚗 1 block

📠 **Ramada Suites,** ☎ (800) 526-9444 or ☎ (714) 971-3553, **$$$/$$$$**, 🚗 2½ blocks

📠 **Red Roof Inn,** ☎ (800) THE-ROOF or ☎ (714) 635-6461, **$$/$$$**, 🚗 3 Miles

📠 **Residence Inn by Marriott,** ☎ (800) 331-3131 or ☎ (714) 533-3555, **$$$$$/$$$$$$**, 🚗 0.2 miles

📠 **Riviera Motel,** ☎ (714) 776-9100, **$**, 🚗 3 blocks

📠 **Sheraton-Anaheim Hotel,** ☎ (800) 325-3535 or ☎ (714) 778-1700, **$$$$$**, 🚗 1 block

📠 **Super 8 Motel Anaheim Park,** ☎ (800) 248-4400 or ☎ (714) 778-0350, **$/$$**, 🚗 3 blocks

📠 **Super 8 Motel Disneyland Park,** ☎ (800) 248-4400 or ☎ (714) 778-6900, **$/$$**, 🚗 2 blocks

📠 **Travelodge,** ☎ (714) 761-4200, **$/$$**, 🚗 2 miles

📠 **Travelodge,** ☎ (800) 578-7878 or ☎ (714) 774-7817, **$$/$$$**, 🚗 ½ mile

📠 **Travelodge International Inn & Suites,** ☎ (714) 971-9393, **$/$$**, 🚗 2½ blocks

📠 **Tropicana Inn,** ☎ (800) 828-4898 or ☎ (714) 635-4082, **$$$/$$$$**, 🚗 1 block

📠 **Vagabond Inn,** ☎ (800) 532-4358 or ☎ (714) 772-5900, **$$**, 🚗 1 block

📠 **West Coast Anaheim Hotel,** ☎ (714) 750-1811, **$$$**, 🚗 1 block

For additional information about any of these hotels, contact the hotel directly. AAA members can also request a free copy of the *AAA California/Nevada TourBook*, which rates many of the hotels/motels located near The Disneyland Resort and provides sample rates and what amenities each offers. Any of AAA's

TourBooks can be obtained by visiting an **AAA** office or by calling ☎ (800) 222-4357 or ☎ (800) AAA-HELP. On the Internet, visit ☞ *www.aaa.com*, or on America Online use keyword: AAA.

 TRAVEL TIP

> During peak travel times, finding a vacancy at one of the hotels or motels in Anaheim can be a challenge. If you're having trouble finding adequate accommodations, try calling the Anaheim/Orange County Visitor & Convention Bureau at ☎ (714) 765-8888, or visit the organization's Web site at ☞ *www.anaheimoc.org*.

To discover other special discounts and deals, check out the **Traveler Coupon Guide** on the Internet at ☞ *www.exitinfo.com* or ☞ *www.hotelcoupons.com*. This publication is also given out free of charge at many California-area hotels, tourist locations, and restaurants. Other useful services for finding discounted hotel accommodations in Anaheim include **Anaheim Hotels Online,** ☎ (800) 826-0533 or ☞ *www.anaheimhotelsonline.com*, **Anaheim Reservations,** ☎ (619) 578-7820 or ☞ *www.anaheimreservations.com*, and the **Hotel Reservations Network,** ☎ (800) 964-6835 or ☞ *www.hoteldiscount.com*.

 TRAVEL TIP

> Aside from theme parks, there are countless other activities in the Anaheim area. Be sure to obtain a copy of the quarterly *Anaheim/Orange County Calendar of Quarterly Events* published by the Anaheim/Orange County Visitor & Convention Bureau. The newsletter lists hundreds of theater, dance, music, arts, cultural, sports, recreation, and kid-oriented activities taking place in Anaheim.

If you'd prefer to stay at a cozy bed and breakfast as opposed to a hotel or motel, call **Bed & Breakfast International of California,**

☎ (800) 872-4500, ✑ *www.bbintl.com*, for information about bed and breakfasts in the Anaheim, Los Angeles, or San Diego areas.

The Hilton Anaheim

▢ 777 Convention Way
   Anaheim, CA 92802-3497
☎ (714) 750-4321 or ☎ (800) HILTONS
✑ *www.anaheim.hilton.com*

During peak travel times, you could easily find the Disney-owned hotels booked at capacity. Thus, if you want to stay in the Anaheim area, you'll need to stay off-property. The Walt Disney Company started a program, called The Disneyland Resort Good Neighbor Hotel Program, which is a selection of nearby hotels that meet Disney's tough requirements and quality standards. One of the premier hotels in this program and one of the very best family- and business-oriented hotels in the Anaheim area (located just blocks from The Disneyland Resort) is the four-star Hilton Anaheim.

Not only is the Hilton Anaheim the largest hotel in Southern California, it's also one of the best equipped. Originally opened in 1984, the hotel underwent a massive $18.5 million renovation in 1997. It now offers 1,572 guest rooms, including ninety-five suites.

The Hilton Anaheim actually overlooks Disneyland and Disney's California Adventure and provides free shuttle service. The hotel is also a mere 50 feet away from the Anaheim Convention Center.

TRAVEL TIP

If you're traveling with a family, be sure to request a room on a high floor that overlooks Disneyland and Disney's California Adventure. This will ensure you have a view of the nightly fireworks display at the nearby theme parks. Many of the rooms have a spacious outdoor balcony, so you can watch the fireworks and even hear the accompanying music.

Amenities

In addition to offering clean and comfortable rooms at an affordable price, this hotel offers a ton of family-oriented amenities including a lovely pool, a fully equipped health club, several restaurants, shops, a business center, three rooftop recreation decks, and a game center. You'll also receive top-notch service from a friendly staff.

Standard in-room amenities include:

- Air-conditioning
- Alarm clock
- Cable T.V. with CNN, HBO, and Disney Channel
- Clock radio
- Coffeemaker
- Data port hookup
- Dual-line phones (2)
- Fire sprinklers
- Hair dryer
- Iron and ironing board
- Neutrogena toiletries
- On-demand videos
- Smoke detectors
- Stationery and postcards
- Voice mail

The hotel's Executive Floor guest rooms also offer the following amenities:

- Bottled water
- Plush bathrobes
- Complimentary coffee, tea, soft drinks, and snacks all day long
- Complimentary continental breakfast
- Complimentary daily newspaper on weekdays
- Evening turndown service
- Fax machine in every room
- Ice service

- Private lounge with bar
- Private registration

Guest Services

From late May to the Labor Day weekend, the Hilton Anaheim participates in the Hilton Family Vacation Station program, offering families added services, such as special children's programs and free gifts. There's also the Vacation Station Lending Desk, which allows guests with children to check out an array of games, toys, books, and other kid-oriented items for use during their stay. A special children's menu is offered at Café Oasis, one of the midpriced restaurants in the hotel that serves breakfast, lunch, and dinner.

Throughout the year, children are invited to stay at the hotel free of charge, providing they're in a room with a parent or grandparent. The Hilton Anaheim is a midpriced hotel and worth every penny. The accommodations are clean, comfortable, spacious, and conveniently located near the Disney theme parks as well as near several affordable restaurants (McDonald's, Tony Roma's, IHOP, Denny's, etc.).

If your vacation needs take you beyond Disneyland, you'll find a tour and sightseeing desk and car rental desk on-site, a florist, post office, one-hour photo processing, and multiple gift shops, along with the ability to purchase Disneyland Resort Park Hopper tickets.

Room Rates

Room rates vary, based on the time of year, type of room, and availability; however, an average guest room is typically priced between $100 and $150 per night. Special package deals and discount programs (such as the Hilton HHonors program and AAA) are honored. This hotel typically fills up when major conventions are in town, as well as during the peak holiday season, so make your reservations early.

TRAVEL TIP

No matter what type of food you're looking for, chances are you'll find it at one of the more than 5,000 restaurants located in the Orange County area. Wherever you're staying, make sure to check with the hotel's concierge or front desk for dining recommendations.

Los Angeles–Area Hotels

In the Los Angeles (Southern California) area, there are literally thousands of hotels, motels, inns, and other types of accommodations. You'll find that all of the major hotel/motel chains have locations in Los Angeles (often close to the popular tourist attractions).

For assistance in finding Los Angeles–area accommodations, consider using one of the following services, contacting a travel agent, or accessing one of the popular online-based travel services (Priceline.com, Travelocity.com, etc.).

All Los Angeles hotels: ☏(800) 663-4680,
✉ www.all-los-angeles-hotels.com
Los Angeles Famous Hotels Directory: ☏(800) 984-4878,
✉ http://hotel.inlosangeles.com
Traveler.com: ☏(800) 610-5749, ✉ www.traveler.com

 TRAVEL TIP

For a directory of Los Angeles–area campgrounds and RV parks, visit ✉ www.gocampingamerica.com/california/inlandempire.html.

CHAPTER 5

Planning Your Travel Itinerary

PREPLANNING YOUR ITINERARY will help ensure you have the easiest time possible traveling to and from your destination as you start your vacation. Once you actually reach Southern California, however, there are many ways you can spend your time.

Consider This

This book focuses on some of the major tourist destinations, especially the various theme parks, including Disneyland and Disney's California Adventure. Assuming that you'll be spending the greatest amount of time at The Disney Resort, exploring what these two fun-filled theme parks have to offer, this chapter will help you create a day-to-day itinerary as you develop a plan for how your time will be spent.

Keep in mind, when planning your daily itinerary, to leave plenty of flexibility in your schedule. Then, you'll be able to enjoy unexpected events that take place or experience a ride, show, or attraction that looks exciting.

While this book provides an overview of the various rides, shows, attractions, shops, and dining options you'll encounter in the Anaheim area (and beyond), only you can determine what you will enjoy the most once you actually arrive at The Disneyland

Resort or one of the other tourist destinations.

How you ultimately spend your time will vary, based on the type of people you're traveling with. If you're traveling with fellow adults, for example, your schedule will most likely be very different than if you're traveling with young children, teenagers, or senior citizens. The same holds true if you're traveling with family members as opposed to friends.

 TRAVEL TIP

> These theme parks and resorts are always evolving. New rides, attractions, shows, parades, and activities are added, updated, or somehow changed, and outdated attractions are taken out of the various parks. Thus, when you actually visit California, don't be surprised if you encounter something new or different, that's not described in this book.

You'll find that this book is loaded with telephone numbers and Internet addresses to help you gather more information about specific theme parks and attractions, make reservations, and ultimately plan your dream vacation. If you have access to the Web, visit any Internet search engine, such as **Yahoo!** (☞ *www.yahoo.com*) or **AltaVista** (☞ *www.altavista.com*), and type in Disneyland Vacation, Disney Theme Parks, Knott's Berry Farm, or Universal Studios California as a keyword or search phrase. You'll find literally hundreds of official and unofficial Web sites dedicated to the various theme parks and attractions in the Southern California area.

TRAVEL TIP

> Although this chapter provides some general guidelines for planning your stay in the Anaheim and Southern California area, consider it a series of suggestions. You'll want to spend your time doing things you know you'll enjoy.

Itinerary Planning Strategies

 Visiting the various theme parks and tourist attractions is somewhat expensive. When you add up the cost of theme park admission, hotel/motel accommodations, food, rental car, souvenirs, snacks, and other expenses, you're about to make a rather significant investment in your vacation. While visiting the theme parks is fun and exciting, most families can also have fun enjoying a day at the beach or an afternoon at the hotel's swimming pool.

As you plan your itinerary, investigate some of the free or low-cost activities that are available. This strategy will help you save money. Likewise, choose restaurants with your budget and personal tastes in mind. You might want to enjoy a fast-food lunch to save money so you can enjoy a more expensive fine-dining experience in the evening.

If you'll be traveling with several people, including kids and teenagers, gather everyone before you leave on your vacation and ask them for ideas on the activities they'd like to do. Decide the types of things you'll do as a group and when you might want to break apart so people can explore their own interests. By providing everyone with a say, you're more apt to ensure that everyone will better enjoy the vacation. This strategy will also help avoid arguments later, when the people you're traveling with all want to go in different directions.

While you might want to see as much as possible during your time exploring the theme parks, chances are young children will want to spend a considerable amount of time in Mickey's Toontown and Fantasyland, which are both kid-oriented. (See Chapter 9 for details on enjoying The Disney Resort with children under the age of twelve.) Be sure to plan your time accordingly.

As a general rule, if you're traveling with kids or teens, you'll probably want to begin your days bright and early. If possible, take advantage of early admission days to the theme parks (if you're staying at one of the Disney-owned hotels). Thus, if your day is going to begin between 7:00 A.M. and 9:00 A.M. with breakfast, plan your time based on how long it'll take everyone to wake up, get dressed, and eat before going to the park.

Divide Your Days

Divide your days at the theme park(s) into several three- or four-hour blocks, especially if you're traveling with kids or senior citizens. Thus, your day at a theme park could be divided into a morning excursion, afternoon excursion, an evening excursion, and during the peak season, a nighttime excursion. Since visiting a theme park will require a tremendous amount of walking, you'll want to schedule several breaks throughout the day.

For example, if you're traveling with children, arrive at the park early in the morning, break for lunch (around noon), and then take a few hours to relax at the hotel. (You might want to take a dip in the pool). Once everyone is rested, you can then visit the theme park again for a few hours, say between 2:00 P.M. and 6:00 P.M., before breaking for dinner. After dinner, you might experience the nighttime shows and attractions at the various parks, such as Fantasmic! (Disneyland) or Disney's Electrical Parade (Disney's California Adventure). Especially if you're traveling with kids (under age twelve), it's critical that you plan on taking at least one or two long breaks during the day and evening to avoid exhaustion.

🧳 TRAVEL TIP

If you're visiting The Disneyland Resort for one day, there's absolutely no way to see and do everything. Thus, your best bet is to choose one theme park and choose a handful of the rides, shows, and attractions that sound the most appealing.

An alternative is to plan your itinerary to go against the crowds. Thus, you might want to sleep late in the morning, arrive at the theme park around 10:00 A.M. or noon, and then plan on staying late into the night (before experiencing the nightlife at Downtown Disney until midnight or even 2:00 A.M.).

As a general rule, you can complete one theme park in one day if you pursue a hectic, nonstop schedule and spend between ten and twelve hours within the park. (This means you'll see the majority of what the park has to offer.) Ideally, you'll want to spread out your schedule, so you can set a more casual pace and include leisurely breaks throughout the day and evening.

Pace Yourself

Although strollers are available to rent, if your child is old enough to walk, consider holding off on pushing your five- to eight-year-old child around. If your child doesn't have to walk, as the adult, you'll tire yourself out while your child will remain full of energy late into the evening. It's important to pace yourself. Remember that irritability goes hand in hand with exhaustion. In a single day, it's impossible to see and do everything, so don't even try.

TRAVEL TIP

If you're taking advantage of the early-admission perk, consider visiting the park's popular attractions first thing in the morning when the crowds are at a minimum. Otherwise, wait until lunchtime, dinnertime, or late in the evening to experience the most popular rides and attractions.

When Time Is on Your Side

 If you'll be spending multiple days at the theme park, use the first day at the park to experience the rides, shows, parades, and attractions you're most excited to see. Use subsequent days to experience everything else the theme park has to offer and do your souvenir shopping. Keep in mind, some of the stores (including all of those along Main Street, U.S.A. in Disneyland) open about thirty minutes earlier and stay open about one hour later than the rides and attractions. Also, the stores in Downtown Disney are open late.

If you have two days at The Disneyland Resort, you can either spend one day at Disneyland and the second day at Disney's California Adventure (or vice versa). Or you can focus on one theme park, spend a few hours exploring Downtown Disney, and maybe check out one of the Disney-owned hotels or spend some time at your hotel (at the pool, for example).

Three days is ideal for The Disneyland Resort. Spend the first day exploring either Disneyland or Disney's California Adventure and the second day exploring the other park. Use the third day to return to both parks (a half day in each) and experience whatever you missed. You can then spend evenings or afternoons visiting Downtown Disney.

If you have more time in the Anaheim area, you could adopt a much more casual schedule as you explore the parks, or spend a fourth or fifth day exploring other nearby parks, such as Universal Studios Hollywood, Knott's Berry Farm, or Six Flags Magic Mountain. If you want to experience some of the San Diego–based theme parks and attractions, consider taking at least two full days for this (and spending at least one or two nights in the San Diego area).

Plan on spending at least a half day in a theme park as opposed to running back and forth between the two Disney parks to experience the various rides/attractions (if you have a Park Hopper pass). Random park-hopping will waste a lot of valuable time. If you're going to visit two parks in a single day, spend the morning at one and the afternoon at the other.

💼 TRAVEL TIP

Many of the shows and parades are extremely popular. Thus, you'll want to arrive at the viewing area (or theater) anywhere from twenty minutes to an hour early to secure the best seating or viewing location.

Disneyland's Must-See Attractions

 Use the following lists of rides and attractions to help plan your itinerary. More details about these attractions, including descriptions and the age group they cater to, can be found in Chapters 9 and 10.

Attractions That Appeal to Families with Teens

- Big Thunder Mountain Railroad (thrill ride)
- Haunted Mansion (a Disney classic)
- Indiana Jones Adventure (thrill ride)
- "It's a Small World" (a Disney classic)
- Matterhorn Bobsleds (thrill ride)
- Space Mountain (thrill ride)
- Splash Mountain (thrill ride)
- Star Tours (thrill ride)

Kid-Oriented Rides and Attractions

- All rides and attractions in Fantasyland
- All rides and attractions in Mickey's Toontown
- Astro Orbitor
- Autopia (a Disney classic)
- Honey, I Shrunk the Audience
- Tarzan's Treehouse

Adult-Oriented Rides and Attractions

- Enchanted Tiki Room (a Disney classic)
- Haunted Mansion (a Disney classic)
- Indiana Jones Adventure (thrill ride)
- Innoventions
- "It's a Small World" (a Disney classic)
- Matterhorn Bobsleds (thrill ride)
- Pirates of the Caribbean (a Disney classic)
- Space Mountain (thrill ride)
- Star Tours (thrill ride)

Attractions That Appeal to Senior Citizens

- The Disney Gallery
- Enchanted Tiki Room (a Disney classic)
- Haunted Mansion (a Disney classic)
- Innoventions
- "It's a Small World" (a Disney classic)
- Main Street Cinema
- Pirates of the Caribbean (a Disney classic)
- Sailing Ship *Columbia*
- The Walt Disney Story, featuring "Great Moments with Mr. Lincoln"

 TRAVEL TIP

If the weather is extremely hot, you might want to alternate between indoor and outdoor shows and attractions. After all, for many outdoor attractions, you could wind up spending at least an hour standing in line outdoors (in the direct sunlight). When you break for lunch, find an indoor dining option, so you can sit down and relax in an air-conditioned environment.

Disney's Most Popular Rides and Attractions

The most popular rides and attractions are going to have the longest lines. According to the Walt Disney Company, in general, some of Disneyland's current most popular rides and attractions include:

- Big Thunder Mountain Railroad (thrill ride)
- Haunted Mansion (a Disney classic)
- Honey, I Shrunk the Audience
- Indiana Jones Adventure (thrill ride)
- Matterhorn Bobsleds (thrill ride)
- Peter Pan's Flight (a Disney classic)
- Pirates of the Caribbean (a Disney classic)
- Roger Rabbit's Car Toon Spin (thrill ride)

- Space Mountain (thrill ride)
- Splash Mountain (thrill ride)
- Star Tours (thrill ride)

The Disneyland Classics

Some of the rides and attractions were created by Walt Disney himself (and/or the Imagineers) and have been enjoyed for generations. If you're an adult who hasn't been to Disneyland since childhood, chances are you'll find the following rides and attractions to be nostalgic. During the midafternoons, when the park is the most crowded, the classic rides tend to have the shortest lines. Thus, this is the best time to experience these rides and attractions.

- Alice in Wonderland
- Autopia
- Big Thunder Mountain Railroad
- Casey Jr. Circus Train
- Davy Crockett's Explorer Canoes
- The Disney Gallery
- Disneyland Monorail
- The Disneyland Railroad
- Dumbo the Flying Elephant
- Enchanted Tiki Room
- Haunted Mansion
- "It's a Small World"
- Jungle Cruise
- King Arthur Carrousel
- Mad Tea Party
- Main Street Cinema
- Mark Twain Riverboat
- Matterhorn Bobsleds
- Mr. Toad's Wild Ride
- Peter Pan's Flight
- Pinocchio's Daring Journey
- Pirates of the Caribbean

- Rafts to Tom Sawyer Island
- Sailing Ship *Columbia*
- Sleeping Beauty Castle
- Snow White's Scary Adventure
- Space Mountain
- Storybook Land Canal Boats

⊕ HOT SPOT

If you're interested in some of the classic Disney theme park experiences, consider taking A Walk in Walt's Footsteps tour of the Disneyland theme park (see Chapter 1 for details).

Disney's California Adventure's Must-See Attractions

 Although this new theme park features mostly new and original rides and attractions (mixed with a few borrowed from The Walt Disney Resort in Florida), it doesn't yet have any classics. But it does feature several that are destined to be enjoyed for generations. More details about these attractions, including descriptions and the age groups they cater to, can be found in Chapter 11.

Attractions That Appeal to Families with Teens

- California Screamin' (thrill ride)
- Grizzly River Run (thrill ride)
- It's Tough to Be a Bug!
- *Jim Henson's Muppet*Vision 3D*
- King Triton's Carousel
- Maliboomer (thrill ride)
- Mulholland Madness (thrill ride)
- Orange Stinger (thrill ride)
- Soarin' over California

- Sun Wheel
- Who Wants to Be a Millionaire—Play It!

Kid-Oriented Rides and Attractions
- Disney Animation
- Golden Zephyr
- It's Tough to Be a Bug!
- *Jim Henson's Muppet*Vision 3D*
- Redwood Creek Challenge Trail
- S.S. *Rustworthy*
- Sun Wheel

Adult-Oriented Rides and Attractions
- Disney Animation
- Golden Dreams
- Golden Vine Winery
- Soarin' over California
- Sun Wheel
- Who Wants to Be a Millionaire—Play It!

Attractions That Appeal to Senior Citizens
These rides and attractions are not considered thrill rides. Many are self-paced or involve sitting down for a presentation or ride experience.

- The Boudin Bakery
- Bountiful Valley Farm
- Disney Animation
- Golden Dreams
- Golden Vine Winery
- Mission Tortilla Factory
- Sun Wheel
- Who Wants to Be a Millionaire—Play It!

⊕ HOT SPOT

Disney's Electrical Parade now has its home in Disney's California Adventure, but this nighttime parade made its original debut in Disneyland and was presented in this park for decades before being retired and then brought back in Disney's newest theme park.

Beating the Crowds

 During the peak season, when the parks are the most crowded, you'll typically find shorter lines (and smaller crowds) on Tuesdays, Wednesdays, and Thursdays. Unfortunately, Fridays and Saturdays are the busiest days in the theme parks. The good news is, during the peak season, the parks are open late (often until midnight) and typically families traveling with young kids tend to leave the park before or right after the peak dinner hours. That leaves the late evening and nighttime to experience the parks with fewer crowds. The late-night fireworks show in Disneyland, however, tends to draw large crowds nightly. During this presentation (which happens over the castle), the ride and attraction lines will typically be the shortest of the day. Here are the best times to experience busy rides or attractions:

- Anytime on Tuesdays, Wednesdays, or Thursdays when the parks tend to be less crowded
- During early-admission hours (if you're staying at a Disney-owned hotel)
- During parade time(s)
- During peak lunchtime (11:30 A.M. to 1:00 P.M.)
- During peak dinnertime (5:00 P.M. to 7:00 P.M.)
- One hour (or so) before the park closes

💼 TRAVEL TIP

If this is your first visit to Disneyland or Disney's California Adventure, spend time familiarizing yourself with the layout of each park as well as the rides, shows, and attractions you most want to experience before you get there. This planning will keep you from getting lost and help you best use your time.

Avoiding the Lines

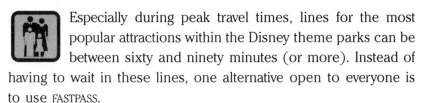 Especially during peak travel times, lines for the most popular attractions within the Disney theme parks can be between sixty and ninety minutes (or more). Instead of having to wait in these lines, one alternative open to everyone is to use FASTPASS.

FASTPASS

Using FASTPASS is easy. At the entrance of the participating ride or attraction, you'll see the FASTPASS machine. Insert your theme park ticket into the machine. In addition to receiving your park ticket back, you'll receive a special FASTPASS ticket that will display a specific time you should return to the ride or attraction. (You have a one-hour window.) When you return, go directly to the special FASTPASS entrance of the ride/attraction. You'll have little or no wait.

It's important to plan your use of the FASTPASS and use it initially for the attractions you most want to experience. You can only use FASTPASS for one attraction at a time. Thus, once you insert your park ticket into a FASTPASS machine for one attraction, you can't use it again until after you've experienced that attraction. In some cases, this could be a two- or three-hour window, so you'll only be able to use this line-eliminating perk a few times during a typical day.

Use FASTPASS at these Disneyland rides and attractions:

- Autopia
- Big Thunder Mountain Railroad
- Haunted Mansion
- Indiana Jones Adventure
- Pirates of the Caribbean
- Roger Rabbit's Car Toon Spin
- Space Mountain
- Splash Mountain
- Star Tours

And also at these Disney's California Adventure rides and attractions:

- California Screamin'
- Grizzly River Run
- It's Tough to Be a Bug!
- *Jim Henson's Muppet*Vision 3D*
- Mulholland Madness
- Soarin' over California
- Who Wants to Be a Millionaire–Play It!

💼 TRAVEL TIP

Be sure to drink plenty of fluids to avoid dehydration. Spending too much time in the sun if you're not used to it could result in heat stroke as well as serious sunburn, so plan accordingly.

Child Pass

If you're traveling with several adults as well as young kids, one adult, or sometimes two, in the group can avoid long ride lines by taking advantage of Disneyland's Child Pass perk. Basically, some rides are not suitable for young kids. For the adult(s) who hangs out with the young child while the rest of the group waits in a long ride line and experiences the ride, the Child Pass allows the baby-sitting adult to visit the adult-oriented ride (without the child) and not have to wait in the line.

With the Child Pass, the adult goes directly to the front of the line at several popular attractions. You can obtain a Child Pass from a cast member near the entrance to many of the rides that aren't suitable for young kids (i.e., the thrill rides, like Space Mountain, Star Tours, and Indiana Jones Adventure). The Child Passes are ride-specific, so you must obtain one for each ride. These passes are only good on the day they're obtained and other restrictions apply. For more information, visit City Hall or speak with a cast member at the entrance to any of Disneyland's thrill rides.

The Right Path

Virtually all of the popular rides at Disneyland and Disney's California Adventure require you to wait in long lines. Sometimes, the lines are divided and guests are asked to follow one of two paths. Most people, by habit, choose the path or line that goes right. Thus, the left line is often somewhat shorter.

The Singles Line

Some of the popular rides also have separate Singles lines. No, this has nothing to do with your marital status. If you don't mind experiencing a ride with a group of strangers, instead of the people you're traveling with, get into the Singles line. The line is always much shorter and moves faster. This is not a good idea if you're traveling with kids, because you will be separated from them when you experience the actual ride.

Travel Tips

As you read this book and start thinking about how you want to spend your time, take notes and keep track of which rides, shows, attractions, parades, and activities are of interest to you and the people you'll be traveling with. Once you think you know what you want to experience, start planning out the actual days of your trip. Keep in mind that each of the various theme parks is massive, so plan on doing a lot of walking.

To save yourself a considerable amount of time traveling between theme parks and activities, plan out your itinerary in half-day chunks. Also, when making up your schedule, don't forget to leave time to eat, rest, experience the popular rides and attractions, and wait in line.

Make sure everyone you're traveling with gets to experience activities that he or she is most excited about. This may mean making compromises or separating at various times. There's no reason for every family member to be dragged to activities that others aren't interested in. Although you'll definitely want to plan some "quality family time," that time will be more enjoyable if everyone is happy and excited about the activities.

 TRAVEL TIP

Depending on what time of year you visit the various theme parks and attractions, the wait for each of the popular rides, for example, could be from thirty to sixty minutes (or more!).

With all there is to see and do while visiting Los Angeles County, Anaheim, and San Diego, focus on those activities that are most suited for the people you're traveling with and keep the following travel tips in mind.

Tips for Single Travelers

Unfortunately, many of the theme parks in California were designed to be family vacation destinations, so there aren't too many opportunities for singles to meet other singles (after all, this isn't the Love Boat). If you're single, you might consider inviting a friend or relative along with you on vacation. Otherwise, your best chances for meeting other singles is to take in the nighttime activities at Downtown Disney or Universal Studios CityWalk, where you'll find bars, restaurants, and dance clubs that are frequented by tourists as well as California residents, especially on weekends.

 **TRAVEL TIP**

Los Angeles County has countless nightclubs, comedy clubs, and bars that cater to the singles crowd. Ask the concierge at your hotel for recommendations as to the hottest nightspots in the area you're visiting.

Tips for Senior Citizens

One of the nicest things about vacationing at The Disneyland Resort and visiting the other California tourist attractions is that there's so much to do, yet you can set your own pace. Senior citizens should consider staying at one of the resort hotels that attract primarily adults (as opposed to families). In Anaheim, Los Angeles, and San Diego, you'll find golf courses, museums, galleries, guided tours, theaters, and many other activities that don't involve long lines, crowds, and thrill rides.

If you're interested in exploring the various theme parks, don't get too overwhelmed by their size. Instead of visiting one park per day, consider a more casual approach. If you tire easily or don't enjoy a lot of walking, seriously consider renting a wheelchair or Electronic Convenience Vehicle. Also, spend more time enjoying the various fine-dining experiences available throughout The Disneyland Resort, Los Angeles County, and San Diego. Take time in the middle of the day to relax and enjoy a two-hour lunch, for example. You might also consider arriving at a park early in the morning, exploring for three or four hours, taking several hours to relax in the afternoon, and then venturing back out in the late afternoon or evening for several more hours.

In addition to a lot of walking, one of the biggest concerns when visiting tourist attractions in California is dealing with the heat and sun. Overexposure to the sun can cause health problems. Be sure to wear plenty of sunblock, a hat, sunglasses, and light clothing that covers your entire body. Also, drink plenty of fluids and take rests often. During the afternoon hours (when the weather is the hottest), plan to visit the indoor air-conditioned attractions.

To help pace your travels during each day, consider participating in the various organized tours and sightseeing expeditions both inside and outside the theme parks. Also, consider planning your vacation during the off-peak season, so that you won't have to deal with large crowds and long lines for the theme park attractions.

Tips for Traveling with Young Kids

Traveling with young children (preschoolers) can be a bit of a burden when visiting the various theme parks because they will tire easily, while older people will have the energy to spend hour after hour exploring the rides, shows, and attractions. When visiting the park, make sure to pace yourself and plan your schedule based on your children's schedule. If they typically nap in the afternoon, schedule a midday nap into your daily vacation itinerary.

Also, keep in mind that you can rent a stroller at the parks. Although you'll want to leave your own stroller at home, in the hotel, or in your car, make sure to bring with you anything else your young child will need throughout the day, such as diapers, snacks, baby food, formula, a change of clothes, toys. You can carry these items with you or store them in a locker (at the park) until they're needed. As you explore the theme parks, there are various places (such as all of the rides) where strollers cannot be taken. Instead, you'll need to leave the stroller in designated areas. If you leave your own stroller in one of these areas, chances are, it could disappear.

Many of the hotels and resorts in Anaheim, Los Angeles

County, and San Diego can help you arrange for professional baby-sitting services or day care, if you choose to leave your child for a few hours during the day or evening. If you plan on keeping your kids with you, the decisions you make about how you'll spend your time in the theme parks and where you eat, for example, should all be made with the kids' wants and needs in mind. Even in the kid-oriented areas of the various theme parks, such as Mickey's Toontown in Disneyland, *never* leave your child unattended or unsupervised.

 **TRAVEL TIP**

Whenever you leave your rented stroller at a designated "stroller parking" area near a ride, show, or attraction, always take your belongings with you. Don't leave purchases, wallets, or other items in the storage compartment of the unattended stroller.

CHAPTER 6

Ticket Prices and Admission Policies

TO HELP YOU PREPLAN your travel budget and create your itinerary, this chapter outlines the 2001–2002 ticket prices and admission policies for the theme parks and attractions highlighted in this book. The prices and special offers listed here are subject to change, as are blackout dates for annual passes.

The Disneyland Resort

 The following table reflects the current tickets/passes and prices available for The Disneyland Resort, which includes both Disneyland and Disney's California Adventure.

One-day/one-park Disneyland Admission Tickets can be used for either Disneyland or Disney's California Adventure and are valid for a single day. Guests can re-enter the park as often as they wish during the day of use. A special one-day ticket is available to senior citizens (ages sixty and up) for $41.

The three- and four-day Disneyland Resort Passports include unlimited same day re-entry to Disneyland or Disney's California Adventure up to the total number of days the passport is valid for. Disneyland Resort Passports may not be used for admittance to more than one park per day, and they expire thirteen days after their first day of use. Thus, if you choose to visit Disneyland on the first day of your three-day pass, you can come and go from the park as often as you wish on that first day, but you cannot enter Disney's California Adventure during the first day.

Ticket Type	Adult	Child*
1-Day/1-Park Admission Ticket	$43	$33
3-Day Disneyland Resort Passport	$111	$87
4-Day Disneyland Resort Passport	$137	$107
Online 4-Day Park Hopper Ticket	$111	$87
Online 5-Day Park Hopper Ticket	$137	$107
Premium Annual Passport—1 Park	$199	N/A
Premium Annual Passport—2 Parks	$299	N/A
Deluxe Annual Passport—1 Park	$139	N/A
Deluxe Annual Passport—2 Parks	$199	N/A
Southern California Annual Passport—1 Park	$89	N/A
Southern California Annual Passport—2 Parks	$149	N/A
* (Ages 3 to 9)		

When purchased online from the official **Disneyland Web site** (✎ *www.disneyland.com*), a Multi-Day Park Hopper Ticket entitles guests admittance to both the Disneyland Park and Disney's California Adventure over a specified number of days, including visits to both parks on the same day (which is referred to as "park hopping").

💼 TRAVEL TIP

When purchasing multiday passes for Disneyland and/or Disney's California Adventure, pay attention to expiration dates. Some multiday passes expire; others don't. In some cases, expired but unused passes can be exchanged for current passes; however, guests are responsible for paying any price differences between a current pass and the expired pass.

The Premium Annual Passport is good for unlimited admission to one or both theme parks on all 365 days of a given year, starting from the first day of use. The passport also entitles you to various discounts on food, beverages, Disney merchandise purchased within the theme parks or at Downtown Disney, and at Disney-owned hotels. This premium passport also includes parking in the theme park's main Mickey & Friends parking lot.

The Deluxe Annual Passport is valid for unlimited admission to either one or both theme parks on 320 preselected days of the year. This passport excludes forty-five "blackout" dates, which include Saturdays throughout the year as well as most major holidays. Although discounts are offered on food, beverages, merchandise, and Disney-owned hotel accommodations, parking is not included.

The Southern California Annual Passport is available only to Southern California residents living in zip code areas 90000 to 93599. This pass has a larger number of blackout dates, including all Saturdays throughout the year, some Fridays, and virtually all major holidays. Although discounts are offered on food, beverages, merchandise, and Disney-owned hotel accommodations, parking is not included.

TRAVEL TIP

> To save time and not have to wait in line to purchase your Disneyland admission tickets, you can purchase them in advance (using a major credit card) by calling ☎(714) 781-4043. They're also available online at the Disneyland Web site (✎ www.disneyland.com) or from any Disney Store.

Special discounted admission tickets are available to members of the Disney Club, AAA, AARP, or the United States military. Inquire about these special offers at any Disneyland ticket counter or call ☎(714) 781-4043. The ticket booths at the theme parks do not honor the Disney Club discount. To obtain this discount, you must buy tickets online or from a Disney Store.

Universal Studios Hollywood

 The following table reflects the current tickets/passes and prices available for Universal Studios Hollywood. See Chapter 18 for more information about this park.

Type of Pass	Adult	Child*	Senior**
1-Day Pass	$43	$33	$37
CityWalk Nighttime Party Pass with Single Day Ticket	$58	N/A	N/A
Front of the Line Pass	$79	N/A	N/A
Director's Pass	$69	N/A	N/A
Southern California Value Pass	$75	N/A	N/A
Celebrity Annual Pass	$49	$39	$44
Deluxe Celebrity Annual Pass	$72	$62	$67
* (Ages 3 to 11), **(Ages 60 and up)			

Here is what the passes include:

One-Day Pass: Admission to the theme park for one day (all rides and attractions).

CityWalk Nighttime Party Pass with Single Day Ticket: Enjoy the theme park during the day and the CityWalk nightclubs at night, all for one price.

Front of the Line Pass: Don't wait in ride lines—go right to the front, plus get the best seats for the shows. This is a one-day pass.

Director's Pass: Participate in aftershow demonstrations and special character meet-and-greet events. This is a one-day pass.

Southern California Value Pass: This is a fourteen-day pass (good on consecutive days only) that offers admission to Universal Studios Hollywood and the clubs within CityWalk.

Celebrity Annual Pass: This is an annual pass good for 333 days of the year. In addition to park admission, special discounts are offered on food and merchandise.

Deluxe Celebrity Annual Pass: This annual pass is good every day of the year.

To save nearly 50 percent on admission tickets to Universal Studios Hollywood, along with six other Hollywood-area attractions, including the Starline Tours of Hollywood, American Cinematheque at the Egyptian Theatre, Petersen Automotive Museum, the Museum of Television & Radio, the Hollywood Entertainment Museum, and the Autry Museum of Western Heritage, consider purchasing the Hollywood CityPass (available from **Welcome Magazine**, *www.welcomemagazine.com*) for only $59 per adult and $39 per child. The seven tickets offered with this pass are valid for thirty days from the day of first use.

≡FAST FACT

Welcome Magazine (*www.welcomemagazine.com*) offers discounted admission tickets to virtually all Southern California theme parks and tourist attractions. These tickets must be purchased online.

Six Flags Magic Mountain

The following table reflects the current tickets/passes and prices available for Six Flags Magic Mountain. See Chapter 15 for more information about this park.

Type of Pass	Adult	Child *	Senior **
1-Day/1-Park Pass (Magic Mountain Only)	$42.99	$21.50	$21.50
Magic Mountain & Hurricane Harbor Combo Pass	$52.99	N/A	N/A
Season Pass (Individual)	$85	N/A	N/A
Family Annual Pass	$280	N/A	N/A
Annual Combo Magic Mountain and Hurricane Harbor Pass	$115	N/A	N/A
* (Under 48" tall), ** (Ages 55 and up)			

The Individual Season Pass is good at all Six Flags theme parks across America. The Family Annual pass is good for up to four people and costs $70 for each additional person beyond four.

Six Flags Hurricane Harbor

The following table reflects the current tickets/passes and prices available for Six Flags Hurricane Harbor. This water park is open seasonally, from mid-May through September. See Chapter 15 for more information about this park.

Type of Pass	Adult	Child *	Senior **
1-Day Pass	$21	$14.99	$14.99
Magic Mountain/Hurricane Harbor Combo Pass	$52.99	N/A	N/A
Individual Season Pass	$70	N/A	N/A
Family Season Pass	$220	N/A	N/A
* (Under 48" tall), ** (Ages 55 and up)			

The Magic Mountain/Hurricane Harbor Combo Pass includes two tickets that can be used on the same day, on two separate days, or for a return visit. The Family Season Pass is good for up to four people and costs $55 for each additional person beyond four.

Knott's Berry Farm

The following table reflects the current tickets/passes and prices available for Knott's Berry Farm. See Chapter 16 for more information about this park.

Type of Pass	Adult	Child *	Senior **
1-Day Pass	$40	$30	$30
1-Day–After 4:00 P.M. Admission	$20	$15	N/A
Annual Passport	$109.95	$49.95	$65.95
Annual Passport for Knott's Theme Park and Soak City U.S.A.	$159.90	$99.90	$115.90
* (Ages 3 to 11), ** (Ages 60 and up)			

 **TRAVEL TIP**

Special money-saving tickets are available directly from the Knott's Berry Farm ticket booths. There's a Non-A.M. ticket, which offers admission from noon until closing for $30 (adults) and an Entry after 4:00 P.M. ticket for $16.95 (all ages).

Knott's Soak City

 The following table reflects the current tickets/passes and prices available for Knott's Soak City. This park is open seasonally. Hours and months of operation vary. See Chapter 16 for more information about this park.

Type of Pass	Adult	Child *	Senior **
1-Day Pass	$21.95	$14.95	N/A
Seasonal Passport	$59.95	$49.95	$59.95
Annual Passport for Knott's Theme Park and Soak City U.S.A.	$159.90	$99.90	$115.90
* (Under 48" tall), ** (Ages 55 and up)			

Bring a Pepsi can or any other Pepsi product to Soak City and receive admission (adults and kids) for only $12.95 per person. (A family of four saves up to $36.) Knott's Soak City also offers a special to all U.S. military personnel. A one-day admission ticket is priced at $10 with a valid active military I.D.

SeaWorld San Diego

 The following table reflects the current tickets/passes and prices available for SeaWorld in San Diego. See Chapter 20 for more information about this park.

Type of Pass	Adult	Child *	Senior **
1-Day Pass	$41.95	$31.95	N/A
Southern California Value Pass	$65	$45	N/A

Type of Pass	Adult	Child *	Senior **
Annual Pass	$94.95	$74.95	$79.95
Two-Year Annual Pass	$199.95	$94.95	$99.95
* (Under 48" tall), ** (Ages 55 and up)			

During the off-season, SeaWorld runs special promotions, such as a two-day ticket for the price of a one-day ticket. The Southern California Value Pass ($65 for adults, $45 for children) is also offered. This promotion allows unlimited access to SeaWorld San Diego and Universal Studios Hollywood for fourteen consecutive days, starting from the first day of use.

TRAVEL TIP

Priced at $79 (adults) and $56 (kids), SeaWorld offers a five-day ticket that's valid at SeaWorld San Diego, the San Diego Zoo, and the San Diego Wild Animal Park. This special ticket is available at the ticket counters of these attractions.

LegoLand California

 The following table reflects the current tickets/passes and prices available for LegoLand in Carlsbad, California, about 30 miles north of San Diego. See Chapter 20 for more information about this park.

Type of Pass	Adult	Child *	Senior **
1-Day Pass	$39.00	$33.00	$33.00
Primo Annual Pass	$109.00	$89.00	$89.00
Block Party Pass	$79.00	$59.00	$59.00
* (Under 48" tall), ** (Ages 55 and up)			

The Primo Annual Pass is good all year with no blackout dates, and parking is included. The Block Party Pass has blackout dates, including weekends and holidays, and parking is not included with this pass.

The San Diego Zoo

 The following table reflects the current tickets/passes and prices available for the San Diego Zoo. See Chapter 20 for more information about the zoo.

Type of Pass	Adult	Child *	Senior **
1-Day Pass	$24	$13	N/A
Annual Membership	$66	$19	N/A
Annual Membership (2 People)	$84	N/A	N/A
* (Under 48" tall), ** (Ages 55 and up)			

Annual membership includes unlimited admission to the San Diego Zoo and Wild Animal Park.

The San Diego Wild Animal Park

 The following table reflects the current tickets/passes and prices available for the Wild Animal Park in San Diego. See Chapter 20 for more information about this park.

Type of Pass	Adult	Child *	Senior **
1-Day Pass	$19.95	$12.95	N/A
Annual Membership	$66	$19	N/A
Annual Membership (2 People)	$84	N/A	N/A
* (Under 48" tall), ** (Ages 55 and up)			

Annual membership includes unlimited admission to the San Diego Zoo and Wild Animal Park.

≡FAST FACT

The **Zoological Society of San Diego**, a nonprofit organization that operates the San Diego Zoo and the Wild Animal Park, accepts donations from individuals as well as corporations. For more information about the various programs sponsored by the zoo, visit ✍ *www.sandiegozoo.org/society/donors.html*.

CHAPTER 7

An Overview of The Disneyland Resort

OUT OF ALL THE MAN-MADE TOURIST attractions in the world, The Disneyland Resort in Anaheim, California (along with Walt Disney World in Orlando, Florida), is definitely among the most well known. This chapter scratches the surface of what makes this resort so unique and incredible.

What The Disneyland Resort Offers

 Originally when it opened, Disneyland was a single theme park. It contained a mere eighteen major attractions and had The Disneyland Hotel located adjacent to it. Today, The Disneyland Resort encompasses two large and evergrowing theme parks, three large resort hotels, a separate shopping and dining area, and plenty of other activities.

Vacationers can easily lose themselves in The Disneyland Resort for five days to a full week, exploring the theme parks, spending time enjoying what the hotels have to offer, and shopping. With the opening of Downtown Disney, the excitement extends late into the night, with the handful of restaurants, bars, and clubs that remain open during the peak travel seasons until 2:00 A.M.

Throughout this book, you'll find Web site links that will provide you with even more detailed information about The Disneyland

Resort. In some cases, these sites provide photos and full-motion videos of various activities at the resort. For a sneak preview before leaving home, the official **Disneyland Web site** (⌨ *www.disney land.com*), operated by The Walt Disney Company, is certainly an excellent resource. Simply type the search phrase Disneyland into any Internet search engine, such as **Yahoo!** (⌨ *www.yahoo.com*), and you'll find countless other Web sites created by fans and travel-related businesses alike, all of which pay tribute to The Disneyland Resort or can help you plan your vacation.

One excellent, albeit unofficial, Disneyland Web site is **the Disneyland Source** (⌨ *www.disneylandsource.com*), which allows you to see and hear video clips of many Disneyland attractions, parades, and shows, right on your computer screen. Another great unofficial Web site is **Intercot West: Disneyland Inside Out** (⌨ *www.intercotwest.com*). This site offers great detail about the history of many attractions and excellent vacation-planning strategies and information about the resort.

The Theme Parks

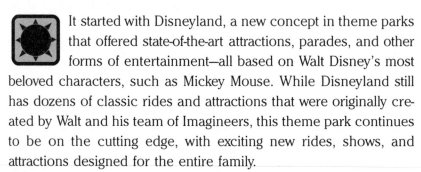 It started with Disneyland, a new concept in theme parks that offered state-of-the-art attractions, parades, and other forms of entertainment—all based on Walt Disney's most beloved characters, such as Mickey Mouse. While Disneyland still has dozens of classic rides and attractions that were originally created by Walt and his team of Imagineers, this theme park continues to be on the cutting edge, with exciting new rides, shows, and attractions designed for the entire family.

Today's Disneyland theme park offers over sixty rides, shows, and attractions. As you'll discover in Chapters 8 and 9, the park is divided into areas, known as lands. Each land has a different theme and offers totally different experiences. If you're traveling with kids, plan on spending extra time in Fantasyland and Mickey's Toontown, which are both designed primarily for young people (ages twelve and under).

Most rides within Disneyland aren't considered thrill rides, like a traditional roller coaster. On most Disney rides, you won't be dropped, swung, spun, tossed, or forced into a state of nausea or dizziness (with a few exceptions). What you will experience are classic moments in Disney history presented in innovative ways, often using special effects, audio animatronics (robots), and beautifully designed sets or architecture.

≡ FAST FACT

The Disneyland theme park combines the "classic" Disney experience created by Walt with exciting new rides, shows, and attractions. Many of the new activities are based on Disney characters, T.V. shows, and movies that were created after Walt's death and yet remain faithful to his overall vision.

All of the rides are designed to tell (or retell) a story featuring popular Disney characters. These rides tap all of your five senses to create a fantasy-like experience. Of course, there are a few exceptions, like Space Mountain and Indiana Jones Adventure, for example, that tell stories, yet offer the thrill-ride element that kids, teens, and young adults crave.

The second theme park within The Disneyland Resort is much less focused on Disney characters and finds inspiration in its home state. As the name suggests, Disney's California Adventure (which opened in February 2001) is an exciting theme park that salutes the culture, history, and lifestyle of America's West Coast.

Many of the experiences offered at Disney's California Adventure are unique to this theme park. Yet, this park offers a touch of Disney magic mixed into the theme-park formula for entertaining people of all ages. In Chapter 11, you'll discover exactly what makes Disney's California Adventure such a special place to visit.

Downtown Disney

 What happens when you take the beauty and décor of a Disney theme park; add a growing selection of upscale stores, boutiques, and one-of-a-kind shops; throw in several themed restaurants, clubs, bars, and a twelve-screen movie theater (with state-of-the-art sound and projection systems, plus stadium seating in each theater)? The answer is, Downtown Disney.

 TRAVEL TIP

Based on the time of year, each park's operating hours vary. To determine either park's operating hours during the time you'll be visiting, call ✆ (714) 781-4565 or visit the **Disneyland Web site** at ✑ *www.Disneyland.com*.

Whether you're looking for something to do after a fun-filled day at the Disney theme parks, you want to spend an entire afternoon shopping, or you're looking to relax for a few hours and see a current blockbuster movie, Downtown Disney is the place to be. During the day and evening, Downtown Disney is a great place for the entire family to eat and shop. At night, however, the majority of the bars and clubs are open to adults only, allowing the older crowd to experience Disney's nightlife until around 2:00 A.M. (during peak seasons).

As you'd expect, not only does Downtown Disney offer stunning landscaping and architecture, you can expect to be treated like royalty by the Disney cast members, just as you're treated in the Disney theme parks and hotels.

The Disney-Owned Resort Hotels

 The Disneyland Resort now contains three resort-quality hotels, including the classic Disneyland Hotel (which has recently been totally renovated and updated), Disney's

Paradise Pier (formally the Disney Pacific Hotel), and Disney's Grand Californian Hotel. While you can expect to receive top-notch service when visiting any of these hotels, each has a different theme.

In addition to offering room accommodations (like what you'd find at any upscale Hilton or Sheraton, for example), all of the Disney hotels offer resort accommodations, beautiful décor, and world-class service. Great efforts have also been made to ensure that the magical experience families have within the theme parks is extended to their hotel stay, so a typical Disney vacation is enjoyed twenty-four hours a day, even when the guests are sleeping.

The Disney-owned hotels keep the magic going, for example, by having Disney characters meeting and greeting guests. Many of the swimming pools and other amenities also carry on the Disney theme.

Unlike ordinary hotels, Disney hotels offer their own shows and attractions. For example, at The Disneyland Hotel, the classic Fantasy Waters fountain show has captivated the hearts and imaginations of guests for decades.

⊕ HOT SPOT

The Disney Monorail stops adjacent to the hotel, offering a direct route to Disneyland. When you ride the monorail system, even getting to and from the theme parks is a fun and memorable experience.

Though quite the Disney experience, the Disney hotels can be very expensive. In addition to the hotel room's nightly charge, determine in advance any extra charges you'll incur, such as phone surcharges, parking charges, shuttle bus charges, an extra fee for a rollaway bed, and so on. All of these charges can easily add up. When ordering room service, pay attention to the fine print on the menu to determine what the surcharges and delivery charges are. Often, the price of the room service will almost double once these additional charges are added to the bill. When you sign for your room service (when it's delivered), determine if a tip has already been added to the bill. Typically, the hotel will automatically add a 15 to 20 percent tip but not list it prominently, so many guests give an additional tip.

The Disneyland Monorail System

While it's technically not part of the Disney theme parks, one of the all-time favorite attractions among people of all ages is the Disneyland Monorail system, which runs between The Disneyland Hotel/Downtown Disney and Disneyland. This monorail system made its debut back in 1959 and was the first system of its kind to operate on a daily basis. Since then, the system has undergone multiple upgrades, yet it still offers a unique 2.5-mile journey (nine-minute round-trip) in and around The Disneyland Resort, along what's commonly referred to as Disney's "highway in the sky."

The monorail system operates nonstop throughout the day and evening. To ride the monorail, you must have a valid admission ticket to Disneyland. For an added thrill, ask the cast member at the monorail station's loading area if you and your group can ride in the front car (inside the pilot cabin). This area holds up to five people and offers an incredible view as the monorail travels around the resort. Kids, in particular, will really enjoy this special treat.

If you're visiting Disneyland, a ride in the monorail is enjoyable, memorable, and relaxing. It's definitely part of the whole Disney experience, so don't miss it!

Perks for Staying On-Property

You will pay a bit more if you choose to stay at one of the Disney-owned hotels, located within The Disneyland Resort, but there are a great number of perks that other off-property hotels can't offer. For example, guests have the ability to ride the Disney Monorail from The Disneyland Hotel/Downtown Disney to the theme parks.

Guests of the Disney hotels are also granted early admission on predetermined days to either Disneyland or Disney's California Adventure. This means that for a full ninety minutes, guests of the hotels can enjoy the theme parks before the general public is admitted (virtually guaranteeing shorter lines and fewer crowds). In addition to the world-class service and upscale accommodations, there are other benefits of staying in one of the Disney-owned hotels (see Chapter 4).

⊕ HOT SPOT

Located across the street from the main entrance of the theme parks, the Anaheim Resort Center offers a pizza parlor, Subway, doughnut shop, Chinese food, a chicken/taco place, and a liquor store. Located across the street from this strip mall is a 7-Eleven and ABC Market convenience store. If you travel about a block down to the Harbor, you'll also find a McDonald's, Denny's, Tony Roma's, and IHOP.

Special Shows, Parades, and Attractions

 For decades, people of all ages from around the world have enjoyed many of the rides at Disneyland, such as "It's a Small World" and the Haunted Mansion. In addition to the rides that have made the Disney theme parks famous around the world, the parks offer incredible parades and live shows, which add immensely to the overall Disney vacation experience.

During the day, there are character-based parades, featuring popular Disney music, singing, dancing, colorful floats, and hundreds of performers. At night, the theme parks offer parades and shows that will truly capture your imagination. Fantasmic! is a not-to-be-missed combination of lights, motion pictures, live action, dancing waters, lasers, fireworks, and incredible special effects. Disney's Electrical Parade is a Disney classic that lights up the parade route with millions of colorful lights, Disney characters, and music. And the legendary Believe: There's Magic in the Stars fireworks spectacular is presented nightly over Sleeping Beauty Castle.

Throughout the days and evenings, you'll also find a wide range of other live shows, many featuring popular Disney characters and performers. Information about Disneyland's parades and shows can be found in Chapter 10, whereas detailed descriptions of the parades and shows offered at Disney's California Adventure can be found in Chapter 12.

TRAVEL TIP

As soon as you arrive at either theme park, be sure to pick up a free copy of *Disneyland Today* or the *Souvenir Map and Guide to Disney's California Adventure*. These colorful brochures list exact show and parade times for the day(s) you'll be visiting the respective theme parks.

Parking

 If you choose to arrive at The Disney Resort by car, you'll have no trouble finding a place to park. Separate parking lots are available for guests of each Disney hotel, the theme parks, and for Downtown Disney. Once you're on resort property, however, it's often best to leave your car parked and use Disney transportation to get around the resort. In addition to the Disneyland Monorail, trams, trains, and other types of vehicles are available to get you exactly where you need to go.

For those who will be parking in one of the theme park's large parking lots, be prepared for crowds early in the morning (starting one hour before the park opens). It could take up to thirty minutes just to get into the parking lot and into a space. Because the theme park parking lots are tremendous, plan on taking a free tram from your car to the theme park entrance.

Parking at one of the theme park lots costs $7 per day for cars and $8 for RVs. As long as you keep your ticket stub, you're allowed to enter and exit the lot during the day as often as you wish. No overnight parking is permitted. Don't worry about the park running out of available spots. The main parking structure holds over 10,250 cars. An additional nearby lot holds 4,300 more cars.

If you're traveling with young children, senior citizens, or someone who is disabled, you may want to use the passenger drop-off/pickup areas in front of the theme parks' main entrance before parking your car. There are designated passenger drop-off/pickup areas in front of the theme parks, the Disney hotels, and near Downtown Disney.

At the Disney hotels, self-parking costs $5 per night (a twenty-four-hour period) and valet parking costs $15 per night (twenty-four-hour period). The parking rates for Downtown Disney vary based on which lot you choose. See Chapter 14 for details.

Unless you're planning to visit some of the other attractions, theme parks, and tourist destinations in Southern California, there's really no need to have a car when you're visiting The Disneyland Resort. If you do have a car and choose to explore Anaheim (and beyond), you'll find dozens of additional restaurants, shopping opportunities, and activities to experience.

TRAVEL TIP

When you park your car anywhere in The Disneyland Resort, make sure you write down exactly where you leave your car. If you're driving a rental, also write down the make and model of the car, along with its color and license plate number. Once a parking lot gets filled up, finding your car can be like looking for a needle in a haystack.

As you drive up to The Disneyland Resort, you'll notice hundreds of hotels, motels, and restaurants surrounding the Disney property. Many of these outside locations have their own parking lots (and don't charge for parking). These lots, however, are reserved for hotel/motel guests or customers of the restaurants. The majority of these parking lots are patrolled twenty-four hours per day, and nonguests/customers are not welcome! If you're not staying at one of these hotels/motels or eating at one of the restaurants, don't park in their parking lot and walk to the Disney theme parks. You will be towed!

Something Special for Everyone

 If there's a special occasion or holiday to be celebrated, The Disneyland Resort will help you do it in style. Whether you choose to plan your own special event or take advantage of the organized events set up by the resort, you won't be disappointed in the celebration style of Disney!

Holidays

Throughout the year, in conjunction with holidays, such as Christmas, New Year's Eve, Thanksgiving, the Fourth of July, Easter, and Valentine's Day, Disneyland and Disney's California Adventure offer special events and/or attractions to celebrate the holidays . . . Disney style.

Around Christmas, for example, Main Street, U.S.A. (in Disneyland) is decorated for the holidays with thousands of lights and poinsettias, along with a 60-foot-tall Christmas tree decorated with over 6,000 twinkling lights. Carolers can be found throughout the park and the classic Christmas Fantasy Parade is presented daily.

To learn more about the **special holiday-oriented events**, see Chapters 10 and 12, or call ☎ (714) 781-4565.

TRAVEL TIP

When it comes to dining, you have literally dozens of options without having to leave Disney property. Whether you're looking for a quick bite to eat or a formal (multicourse) breakfast, lunch, or dinner that's prepared by a world-class chef, you'll find what you're looking for.

Wedding Bells

Everyone dreams of a fairytale wedding in a beautiful setting. Well, at Disneyland, weddings are a specialty. Whether you're planning a small, intimate ceremony and honeymoon or an all-out extravaganza with hundreds of invited guests, Disneyland's Fairy

Tale Wedding program will help you plan the ultimate wedding and honeymoon experience.

Choose to hold the ceremony and reception indoors or outdoors, within the Disneyland theme park or one of the Disney hotels. Oh, and if you want to add Mickey and Minnie Mouse to your guest list, appearances are possible.

When you plan your wedding through the **Disney Fairy Tale Wedding program**, a special events coordinator will help you plan every aspect, from choosing Disney-themed invitations to what will be on the menu during the reception. For more information about planning a wedding at The Disneyland Resort, call ✆ (714) 956-6527.

The Disneyana Convention

Every year, thousands of true Disney fans flock to The Disneyland Resort for the annual Disneyana Convention. This is a fun-filled convention/gathering where Disney merchandise collectors and historians gather. **The Disneyana Convention** is held each year, either at The Disneyland Resort (Anaheim) or Walt Disney World (Orlando). For details, visit ✑ *www.officialdisneyana.com* or call ✆ (407) 827-7600.

Throughout the year on **eBay** (✑ *www.ebay.com*), Disneyana collectors participate in auctions of highly collectible Disney-related art and merchandise from the past and present. For details, visit ✑ *http://members.ebay.go.com/aboutme/disneyauctionears*.

Gay Day 2

Although not officially sponsored or sanctioned by the Walt Disney Company, every October, Gay Day 2 is held at Disneyland. According to the organization that sponsors this unofficial event, "Years ago, Disneyland used to have a private party one night of the year for gays and lesbians. When the event was canceled in 1998, we created Gay Day 2. We derived our name from our big sister event in Orlando, Gay Day (1), which attracts over 100,000 gays and lesbians from around the world each June. Like the Orlando event, Gay Day 2 is a 'mix in,' meaning gay people and straight people mingle together; the park is open to the general public. Also, like Gay Day, we wear red shirts to identify one another and show our numbers."

Held in 1998, the first **Gay Day 2** at Disneyland attracted about 2,500 people. In 1999, over 5,000 people attended. By 2000, the crowd grew to nearly 10,000. There are separate gay days held at Disneyland and at Disney's California Adventure. For more information, visit *www.gayday2.com.*

TRAVEL TIP

While you're waiting in line for each ride or attraction, strike up conversations with the people around you. Find out what they've enjoyed thus far on their vacation, seek out recommendations for things to see and do, or places to eat, and most important, don't be afraid to make new friends!

CHAPTER 8

The Disneyland Theme Park

THE DISNEYLAND THEME PARK is divided into a series of separate and distinct areas, known as lands. Each land has its own theme, and each has its own unique sets of rides, attractions, and shows. This chapter gives detailed information about the family-oriented lands of Disneyland.

Main Street, U.S.A.

 Once you purchase your Disneyland Passport(s) and pass through the ticket gate, you're officially inside Disneyland, and will be standing in what Walt Disney called the Lobby. Facing you will be the Disneyland Train Station and a giant floral Mickey Mouse. (This is a great photo spot.) Walt Disney considered Disneyland to be a 3-D interactive show, which is why people visiting Disneyland are called guests and the people who work at Disneyland are called cast members.

If you look down at your feet in the lobby area, you'll notice that the pavement is painted red, to symbolize a red carpet. Walk to the left or right of the floral Mickey Mouse to pass under the train tracks and enter Disneyland's Main Street, U.S.A. area. On a typical summer day, more than 65,000 guests will pass under these tracks to begin their day exploring Disneyland.

As you pass under the train tracks, look up. You'll see a sign that reads, "Here you leave today and enter the world of yesterday, tomorrow, and fantasy." Just ahead is Main Street, U.S.A. At the far end of this street is Sleeping Beauty Castle, and along the two sides of Main Street, U.S.A. are souvenir shops, arcades, and places to eat. You'll also find City Hall, the main Disneyland Railroad Station, the Opera House, and what looks like the Disneyland fire station.

Located in between the Opera House and City Hall is a circular park area, which offers a nice place to sit (benches are provided) and an excellent place to watch the daily character parade. (You'll need to be on one of the sidewalks of Main Street, U.S.A. to see several of the parades.) This park area is also an excellent meeting spot if you get separated from the people you're traveling with.

While Main Street, U.S.A. is primarily an area offering shops, places to eat, and various guest services, there are a few attractions here that will be of particular interest to true Disney fans and Disney historians.

⊕ HOT SPOT

At the center of the park is the Hub on which stands a life-size statue of Walt Disney and Mickey Mouse. The Hub is the center of Disneyland, from which you can easily travel to any of the lands. The Hub is also one of the most photographed areas in Disneyland.

The Disneyland Opera House

Ages 2–4:	N.S.
Ages 5–10:	★
Ages 11–15:	★
Ages 16–Adult:	★★
Senior Citizens:	★★★

Located in The Disneyland Opera House (which was a lumber mill when Disneyland was first being constructed, and later a television studio where scenes for the original *Mickey Mouse Club* were filmed) is a salute to two American icons: Walt Disney and President Abraham Lincoln.

First, guests are free to roam around the lobby of this building and look at various pieces of Disney memorabilia, plus see a reconstruction of Walt Disney's office, which was located at Disney's Burbank Studios. You can also see the actual car Walt used to travel around Disneyland in every morning before the park opened. Finally, there's a fifteen-minute movie that summarizes Walt's incredible life. This entire salute to Walt Disney was created after his death.

The second attraction is a salute to President Lincoln. Guests will see an Audio-Animatronics version of America's sixteenth President giving a speech, after watching a brief slide presentation.

The Disneyland Railroad

Ages 2–4:	★★
Ages 5–10:	★★
Ages 11–15:	★★
Ages 16–Adult:	★★
Senior Citizens:	★★★

All aboard! This is one of Disneyland's true landmarks. This train begins its circular path around the park at the main entrance of Disneyland, and makes stops in Frontierland, Tomorrowland, and Mickey's Toontown, providing a transportation alternative to using your feet.

If you want to ride the Disneyland Railroad and not have to wait too long, your best bet is to climb aboard at the Main Street, U.S.A. station. Be sure, however, to ride the train between Tomorrowland and Main Street, U.S.A., because that's the only way you'll get to see a few hidden attractions at Disneyland, including Primeval World, which features huge Audio-Animatronics (robotic) dinosaurs that kids will love. Taking an entire loop around the park by train takes about twenty minutes, but you can get off and later reboard at any stop, providing seats are available.

Riding the train offers a great overview of virtually the entire theme park. It also provides for some excellent photo opportunities.

The Main Street Cinema

Ages 2–4:	N.S.
Ages 5–10:	★
Ages 11–15:	★
Ages 16–Adult:	★★
Senior Citizens:	★★★

When you're standing on Main Street, U.S.A. and facing Sleeping Beauty Castle, on the right side of the street is a movie theater. There's no charge to enter this theater, and what you'll see inside is rather special. Shown on a rotation basis are some of Mickey Mouse's original animated films, including Mickey's motion picture debut in *Steam Boat Willie*, along with *Plane Crazy*, *Mickey's Polo Team*, *The Moose Hunt*, *Traffic Trouble*, and *Dog Napper*.

All of these films are in black and white. Each features Walt Disney providing Mickey's voice. This attraction runs constantly, so you're free to enter and exit the theater whenever you wish. This theater is almost never crowded, so you can enjoy a short movie in a nice air-conditioned theater. (Sorry, adults have to remain standing, but there's a place for kids to sit down.) True Disney fans and historians shouldn't miss this attraction. Kids, however, might find it somewhat dull.

TRAVEL TIP

Many of the services offered, such as the Lost & Found and Baby Care Center, are located along Main Street, U.S.A. This is also the primary parade route for several of this park's most popular daytime and evening parades.

Main Street Vehicles

Old-fashioned nineteenth-century horse-drawn street cars, horseless carriages, an old motorized fire engine, and even a double-decker Omnibus are among the vehicles that travel up and down Main Street, U.S.A., providing free transportation from a stop near the Main Street Train Station to Sleeping Beauty Castle. These vehicles certainly add to Disneyland's overall atmosphere. If you want to experience a short ride, hop aboard the vehicle of your choice.

The Penny Arcade

Ages 2–4:	N.S.
Ages 5–10:	★
Ages 11–15:	★
Ages 16–Adult:	★
Senior Citizens:	★

Forget about the hottest video games that contain violence, awesome 3-D graphics, and surround sound. This arcade, located along Main Street, U.S.A., will take you back to the days before Pac-Man, Space Invaders, and Mortal Kombat. Here, you'll see arcade machines from the early 1900s. The arcade machines that still work cost money to try. If you want to check out the latest and greatest arcade machines, trek on over to Tomorrowland.

TRAVEL TIP

In addition to souvenirs of all kids, several of the shops on Main Street sell necessities, such as sunglasses, aspirin, diapers, rain ponchos, and other items. These items aren't always on display, so if you're looking for something in particular, be sure to ask a cast member.

Shop and Explore

In addition to buying film, camera supplies, and other necessities for taking pictures (and having your film developed) during your stay at Disneyland, a free service offered at the Main Street Photo Supply Co. is that you can drop off your camcorder battery and have it recharged. Ask the cashier about this service, and be sure to get a pickup ticket for your battery.

Kodak film (the official film of Disneyland) and same-day film developing is available at this store and at gift shops and souvenir stands throughout the park. The prices for film and batteries at Disneyland are rather high. To save money, buy your film, batteries, and other photo supplies at a convenience store or camera shop before you arrive at Disneyland, and wait until you get home to have your film developed.

Whether you're looking to make some purchases or you just

want to see some beautiful Disney-related artwork and products, be sure to spend some time browsing in the various shops located along Main Street, U.S.A. Much of the merchandise sold in these shops can't be purchased from the Disney Stores, the Disney Catalog, or anywhere else.

If you're staying at one of the Disneyland hotels, your purchases can be delivered to your hotel room, free of charge, so you won't have to carry them. The shops along Main Street, U.S.A. include:

- 20th Century Music Company
- Candy Palace and Candy Kitchen
- China Closet
- Crystal Arts
- Disneyana Emporium
- Disney Clothiers, Ltd.
- Disney Showcase
- The Mad Hatter
- Main Street Magic Shop
- Market House
- New Century Jewelry
- New Century Timepieces
- Newsstand
- Silhouette Studio

⊕ HOT SPOT

If you're looking to purchase a pair of monogrammed Mickey (or Minnie) Mouse ears, one of the few places in the Walt Disney Resort to get this classic souvenir is The Mad Hatter shop, located on Main Street, U.S.A., near Town Square. Adult ears are priced at $6.25, while kid-size ears cost $5.25 (includes monogramming).

If you're staying at a Disney hotel, to avoid overspending, which is extremely easy to do, you may want to refrain from using your room key as your Disney credit card. When using your room key, all purchases you make are added to your hotel bill, and it's very easy to lose track of how much you're spending. There will, no doubt, be a long list of things you want to purchase. Set a strict budget for yourself and stick to it. You might want to save your souvenir shopping until the last day of your trip.

Adventureland

 Your true adventure within Disneyland can begin in any of the lands. This one, however, takes you to exotic locales and recreates Africa, Asia, and the South Pacific. Here, you'll find exciting attractions and rides suitable for the entire family.

Enchanted Tiki Room

Ages 2–4:	★
Ages 5–10:	★★
Ages 11–15:	★★
Ages 16–Adult:	★★
Senior Citizens:	★★★

Walt Disney created a technology called Audio-Animatronics, which allowed him to make models (robots) of people and animals appear to come alive within the attractions at Disneyland and later Disney World. The Enchanted Tiki Room was the very first Disneyland attraction to feature this roboticlike technology, as dozens of Audio-Animatronics birds appear to come to life in a seventeen-minute, fun-filled musical performance that's suitable for the entire family. Sit down, relax, and sing along with 225 Audio-Animatronics performers.

The Enchanted Tiki Room has been a popular attraction at Disneyland since 1963, and while it certainly doesn't offer state-of-the-art entertainment, it does offer a taste of what Walt Disney helped to create. This attraction is presented on an ongoing basis throughout the day. The lines typically aren't too bad, and once you're inside, you'll find the room is air-conditioned.

While you're waiting to enter this attraction, there's a small park area, complete with benches and a kiosk that sells tropical treats, such as pineapple. The Enchanted Tiki Room is truly one of Disneyland's classic attractions. If you visit the Walt Disney World Resort in Orlando and visit this attraction in The Magic Kingdom there, you'll find the show has been totally revamped. This version at Disneyland, however, is faithful to Walt's original vision.

 TRAVEL TIP

In addition to walking through this theme park, there are several other modes of transportation. Most notable is The Disneyland Railroad, which has stops in several of the lands. There are also various vehicles that run up and down Main Street, U.S.A.

Indiana Jones Adventure

Ages 2–4:	N.S.
Ages 5–10:	★★★
Ages 11–15:	★★★
Ages 16–Adult:	★★★
Senior Citizens:	★★

One of the most popular attractions at Disneyland is the Indiana Jones Adventure. It's based on the live-action movies. As you board a twelve-passenger off-road vehicle, you'll embark on a fast-paced and extremely turbulent ride that explores the simulated jungles of India and the Temple of the Forbidden Eye.

Although not a roller coaster in the traditional sense of the word, Indiana Jones Adventure isn't for elderly people, young children (under 46 inches), or people who don't enjoy exciting and turbulent thrill rides.

Since it is one of the most popular attractions at Disneyland, you can expect to wait in extremely long lines. The best times to experience this ride are early in the morning, late at night, or during a parade. Indiana Jones Adventure is an awesome ride, but probably not worth waiting more than ninety minutes for. After all, the ride itself only lasts about 3½ minutes. This will probably be the longest line you'll have to wait in at Disneyland, but if you go at a nonbusy time of day, the wait will be reasonable. If you're going to use FASTPASS to avoid a long line, this is the attraction you'll definitely want to use it on!

Be sure to stop at the Information Desk/Wait Board located near the Hub or in Tomorrowland, and ask about wait times before joining the line. When you actually do get on this ride, take off your hat and make sure your purse, camera bag, and other belongings are secure.

👍 This is a must-see attraction.

💼 TRAVEL TIP

> If you're in a hurry to begin exploring this theme park, keep in mind that the shops along Main Street, U.S.A. stay open about one hour later than the rides and attractions, so you might want to save some of your shopping for later in the day.

The Jungle Cruise

Ages 2–4:	N.S.
Ages 5–10:	★★
Ages 11–15:	★★
Ages 16–Adult:	★★
Senior Citizens:	★★

Prepare to embark on an eight-minute boat ride that's hosted by a Disney cast member who has been trained to entertain you with really dumb jokes as you pass Animatronic animals and animated exhibits along a man-made river. The Jungle Cruise is cute, somewhat entertaining, and suitable for people of all ages. (Don't worry; you won't get seasick or wet on this ride.) To keep you entertained, you'll probably see a live steel drum band performing throughout the day near the Jungle Cruise.

Tarzan's Treehouse

Ages 2–4:	N.S.
Ages 5–10:	★★★
Ages 11–15:	★★
Ages 16–Adult:	★★
Senior Citizens:	★

Designed for children, this artificial tree was formally the Swiss Family Treehouse, modeled after Disney's 1960 movie *The Swiss Family Robinson,* but was recently refurbished and redesigned to offer a Tarzan jungle theme. This 70-foot tree might look real, but it's all man-made and perfectly safe for climbing and exploration. Think of this attraction as a giant jungle gym for your kids (although it's suitable for adults, too). There's almost never a long line for this attraction, and it's something that kids really enjoy.

Frontierland

 Take a look back at the adventure of the pioneers of the Old West as you experience what this area of Disneyland has to offer.

Big Thunder Mountain Railroad

Ages 2–4:	N.S.
Ages 5–10:	N.S.
Ages 11–15:	★★★
Ages 16–Adult:	★★★
Senior Citizens:	★

The most action-packed ride in this land is a runaway railroad (roller coaster) that takes sharp turns at pretty fast speeds, but offers no really big drops, making it pretty tame as far as thrill rides go. At the time Disneyland was built, this ride represented the park's most expensive and massive construction effort, but in terms of cost, it has since been surpassed many times by more recent attractions.

Add Big Thunder Mountain Railroad to the list of thrill rides that'll appeal to guests over 40 inches tall who don't suffer from any physical limitations that prevent them from experiencing high-speed, turbulent rides. Lots of attention was paid in putting great detail and realism into this ride, but Big Thunder Mountain Railroad, like all of the other structures within Disneyland, was man-made.

Frontierland Shootin' Exposition

Ages 2–4:	N.S.
Ages 5–10:	★
Ages 11–15:	★
Ages 16–Adult:	★★
Senior Citizens:	★

How's your aim? You can find out at this arcade-style shooting range that features replicas of rifles from the 1800s. These rifles use infrared beams instead of bullets as you aim and shoot at targets. Just like all of the arcades in Disneyland, the cost of shooting is extra—fifty cents for twenty shots.

Golden Horseshoe Variety Show (and Other Western Shows)

Ages 2–4:	N.S.
Ages 5–10:	★★
Ages 11–15:	★★
Ages 16–Adult:	★★
Senior Citizens:	★★

You'll need to make a reservation early in the day if you want to catch one of the comedy/musical performances with a Western flair that are presented several times per day at the Golden Horseshoe Stage. If you want to check out one of these shows, go to the reservation desk at the theater first thing in the morning after you arrive at Disneyland. All reservations are on a first-come basis. The show is free, but food or drinks cost extra.

Mark Twain Riverboat

Ages 2–4:	N.S.
Ages 5–10:	★★
Ages 11–15:	★★
Ages 16–Adult:	★★
Senior Citizens:	★

Not only was this one of Disneyland's original attractions, it was one that Walt Disney paid for partially out of his own pocket. Located in the heart of Disneyland is Tom Sawyer Island, and surrounding this island is a man-made body of water (the Rivers of America) that the Mark Train Riverboat travels around.

This paddle-wheel steamboat offers a fourteen-minute cruise and provides a look at parts of Frontierland, New Orleans Square, Critter Country, and Tom Sawyer Island. If you climb to the upper decks, your view of Disneyland is even better.

On nonbusy days, if you participate in the A Walk in Walt's Footsteps tour, you might be lucky enough to ride on the bridge of this ship, meet the captain, and actually get to steer this large vessel (that is, with a bit of help from Disney's Imagineers who ensured that this boat will never travel off course). This boat operates constantly during the day; however, cruises end in the early evening so preparations can be made for the Fantasmic! show.

Mike Fink Keel Boats

Ages 2–4:	N.S.
Ages 5–10:	★★
Ages 11–15:	★★
Ages 16–Adult:	★★
Senior Citizens:	★

These boats provide yet another opportunity to take a ride around the Rivers of America.

Sailing Ship *Columbia*

Ages 2–4:	★★
Ages 5–10:	★★
Ages 11–15:	★★
Ages 16–Adult:	★★
Senior Citizens:	★★★

In addition to the Mark Twain Riverboat, the sailing ship *Columbia* is Disneyland's other large ship that travels in the waters around Tom Sawyer Island. When not sailing, *Columbia* remains moored at Fowler's Harbor, located near the Haunted Mansion. If you have the opportunity to take a short cruise in this vessel, be sure to visit the maritime museum that's located below deck.

Tom Sawyer Island

Ages 2–4:	N.S.
Ages 5–10:	★★
Ages 11–15:	★★
Ages 16–Adult:	★★
Senior Citizens:	★

In the center of Rivers of America (the water that surrounds this island) is a man-made landmass that's filled with dozens of places to explore and climb, just as Tom Sawyer would have done. Be sure to drop by Injun Joe's cave. This island is open only during daylight hours and can only be reached by taking a raft. (Don't worry, a Disneyland cast member will do all the work, you just have to board the raft and be a passenger for the short journey.)

New Orleans Square

 This special land offers two classic Disneyland attractions that have been loved for generations: the Haunted Mansion and Pirates of the Caribbean. Both are suitable for people of all ages, but might be a bit scary for very young kids.

 TRAVEL TIP

The Disneyland Railroad stops at New Orleans Square and will bring you to one of the other stations located throughout Disneyland, such as the Main Entrance, Mickey's Toontown, or Tomorrowland.

The Disney Gallery

This area, located above the Pirates of the Caribbean ride, was originally designed to be a private apartment for Walt Disney and his family; however, Walt died before its completion. This area is now an art gallery that showcases original concept drawings, paintings, and design blueprints for many of Disneyland's past, present, and future attractions.

You'll also see animation cells from Disney's animated movies and have a chance to buy limited editions or prints of many of the works on display. The Disney Gallery also invites special guests, such as Disney Imagineers or animators, to make appearances, conduct demonstrations, and answer guests' questions. If you're a Disney fan, you'll want to spend at least a few minutes walking through this gallery, where Disneyland's past, present, and future all come together as works of art. Since this is an art gallery, what's on display will appeal mainly to older guests.

⊕ HOT SPOT

> Every evening, Fantasmic! combines dancing waters, Disney characters, fireworks, motion picture technology, countless special effects, and classic Disney music. It's a breathtaking live presentation that's memorable, exciting, and highly entertaining. In other words, don't miss it!

The Haunted Mansion

Ages 2–4:	N.S.
Ages 5–10:	★★★
Ages 11–15:	★★★
Ages 16–Adult:	★★★
Senior Citizens:	★★★

Before this attraction opened at Disneyland, Walt Disney participated in interviews with the media during which he invited all homeless ghosts to come live at Disneyland's Haunted Mansion. Construction for this attraction began in 1963, but it wasn't completed and opened to Disneyland guests until 1969.

Since then, millions of guests have dropped in on the many ghosts that live within this mansion. Perhaps one of the most elaborate haunted houses anywhere, this one uses all sorts of special effects to entertain and scare visitors. Guests ride in moving love seats, as they receive the seven-minute grand tour of this haunted mansion. This is one of Disneyland's classic attractions that shouldn't be missed.

👍 This is a must-see attraction.

The Pirates of the Caribbean

Ages 2–4:	★
Ages 5–10:	★★★
Ages 11–15:	★★★
Ages 16–Adult:	★★★
Senior Citizens:	★★★

Pirates always fascinated Walt Disney, which is the main reason he insisted that Disneyland guests have the opportunity to embark on a musical boat ride through a Caribbean village that's populated by pirates. Although not a thrill ride, this thirteen-minute boat ride is one of Disneyland's most popular attractions and shouldn't be missed. During your voyage, you'll see over sixty-four Audio-Animatronics pirates and fifty-five Audio-Animatronics animals. Throughout the cruise, the song, "Yo-Ho, Yo-Ho, A Pirate's Life for Me" is played, so by the end of the cruise, you'll probably be singing along.

Just after your cruise begins, expect the boat to take two very short (three-second drops); otherwise your cruise will be smooth, slow, and extremely enjoyable. This entire attraction is air-conditioned, so it's an ideal way to cool off and relax in the middle of a hot day. Located inside the same building as this attraction is the Blue Bayou restaurant, which offers a fine-dining experience for lunch or dinner. Reservations for this restaurant are required.

 This is a must-see attraction.

 TRAVEL TIP

No matter which ride you're experiencing, your safety and well-being are Disneyland's primary concerns. As a result, you are under almost constant video surveillance at Disneyland. Failure to follow the basic rules of conduct at Disneyland could result in your being evicted from the park.

Tomorrowland

 Step into the future for an exciting and positive look at what's yet to come. Here, you can check out cutting-edge technology and experience a handful of space-age attractions, including Space Mountain, Disneyland's famous roller coaster. This land was entirely redesigned back in 1998. As part of the redesign, classic rides from the past, such as the Astro Orbitor, were brought back, but others were retired.

In the Magic Eye Theater, which used to be the home of the 3-D *Captain EO* movie starring Michael Jackson, is a new attraction called Honey, I Shrunk the Audience. This attraction is extremely popular with people of all ages. It combines 3-D film techniques with all sorts of special effects, picking up where the popular Disney movies left off.

The Carousel Theater, which over the years has presented two shows, *The Carousel of Progress* and *America Sings*, is now the home of Innoventions, a two-level interactive pavilion that showcases near-future technology and consumer electronics we'll soon find in our homes and workplaces. This is a hands-on exhibit.

Located near Innovations is a state-of-the-art interactive fountain called Cosmic Waves. On hot days, guests can cool off as they are sprayed by water shooting and flowing in synchronized patterns. In addition to all of these new rides and attractions, plans to revamp the Circle-Vision Theater and the former Mission to Mars attractions are under way.

Since Disneyland first opened, the rides and attractions in Tomorrowland have evolved and changed with the times. As a child, you might recall visiting Disneyland and experiencing rides and attractions like: Space Station X-1 (1955–1960), TWA Moonliner (1955–1962), Douglas Moonliner (1962–1966), Circarama (1955–1964), Circle Vision 360 (1964–1997), Astro Jets (1956–1964), Tomorrowland Jets (1964-1967), Rocket Jets (19671997), Clock of the World (1955–1966), House of the Future (1957–1967), Flying Saucers (1961–1966), Flight to the Moon (1967–1975), Adventure Through Inner Space (1967–1985),

Carousel of Progress (1967–1973), PeopleMover (1967–1996), *America Sings* (1974–1988), Mission to Mars (1975–1992), Magic Journeys (1984–1986), and *Captain EO* (1986–1996).

All of these rides and attractions have now been replaced to provide a peek into the future, which is what Tomorrowland is all about. Currently, the only attraction in Tomorrowland that has remained opened since Disneyland's grand opening in 1955 is Autopia, which was originally called the Freeway of the Future.

 TRAVEL TIP

Unfortunately, Astro Orbitor is a popular ride among kids, which means the wait can be long. Although the experience is fun, if there's a long wait, you might want to think twice about experiencing this rocket ship flying experience.

Autopia

Ages 2–4:	N.S.
Ages 5–10:	★★★
Ages 11–15:	★★★
Ages 16–Adult:	★
Senior Citizens:	★

Autopia allows guests to ride in model sports cars (sort of like go-carts) along a predefined track. These cars, which are about 10 feet long, weigh 1,100 pounds and have real motors. They travel at a fast-paced 7 miles per hour but can't leave their track. Kids (over 52 inches tall) will find Autopia provides a lifelike, fun driving experience. Kids over the age of seven can ride Autopia alone. Adults who already have a driver's license will probably want to skip this ride, unless they're traveling to Disneyland with kids.

Disneyland Monorail Station

Hop the Disneyland Monorail for a ride through Disneyland to The Disneyland Hotel/Downtown Disney. Once you reach your destination, be prepared to leave the Monorail and then reboard for a return trip to Disneyland. Round trips are not permitted.

Disneyland Railroad Station

Walt Disney had a fascination with trains. The Disneyland Railroad circles Disneyland and allows guests to travel between Disneyland's different areas. Riding the Disneyland Railroad is an excellent opportunity to get off your feet and receive a grand, narrated tour of Disneyland.

Space Mountain

Ages 2–4:	N.S.
Ages 5–10:	★★
Ages 11–15:	★★★
Ages 16–Adult:	★★★
Senior Citizens:	★

Perhaps one of Disneyland's most famous and popular attractions, this roller coaster takes you for a fast-paced ride through space. You'll find yourself traveling in the dark at speeds up to 30 miles per hour as you whiz around sharp turns. Hollywood-style special effects surround you with stars and galaxies as you rocket through space. Twelve people at a time ride each vehicle.

There's always a wait to ride this attraction, but if you're excited by high-speed thrill rides, Space Mountain is well worth it. What sets this ride apart from most roller coasters is that this one travels fast, but offers no steep drops. Instead, you'll experience countless sharp turns. Thus, even if you tend to get scared riding a traditional roller coaster, since you're in virtual darkness and won't experience any massive drops, the whole experience is rather enjoyable.

Make sure you secure all loose articles of clothing. Space Mountain should not be experienced by young children (under the age of seven or less than 40 inches tall), pregnant women, anyone with a heart condition, weak back, or any type of physical problems. Avoid eating right before this ride. To save time, take advantage of FASTPASS.

👍 This is a must-see attraction.

Starcade

Ages 2–4:	N.S.
Ages 5–10:	★
Ages 11–15:	★
Ages 16–Adult:	★
Senior Citizens:	★

Check out some of the hottest new arcade games, plus some of your old favorites. All of the arcades located at Disneyland accept tokens (which are not included in the cost of admission to the park).

Star Tours

Ages 2–4:	N.S.
Ages 5–10:	★★
Ages 11–15:	★★★
Ages 16–Adult:	★★★
Senior Citizens:	★★

What happens when you combine the creative talent of Disney's Imagineers with the imagination of George Lucas? The result in this case is Star Tours, a ride that's based on the *Star Wars* movies and features characters like R2-D2 and C3-PO. As an intergalactic tourist, you and thirty-nine other guests will board a StarSpeeder and experience a whirlwind tour of the galaxy.

Using flight simulator technology, the StarSpeeder is on hydraulics and is perfectly synchronized with the movie you'll be watching on the ship's main view screen. The overall effect is that you'll actually feel as if you're traveling at ultra fast speed through space, when in reality, your StarSpeeder is only a few feet off the ground. Star Tours is a fast-paced, turbulent roller-coasterlike ride with a *Star Wars* twist.

Be prepared for long lines, but while you're waiting to board the StarSpeeder, you'll be entertained by an elaborate preshow that includes Audio-Animatronics characters from the *Star Wars* movies and video monitors that feature Star Tours travel information.

This ride is suitable for people of all ages, except very young children (under the age of three) and people who suffer from back problems, heart conditions, motion sickness, and so on. Once you board the StarSpeeder, stow all of your loose articles and fasten your seat belt. This ride is bumpy but not scary.

This is a must-see attraction.

⊕ HOT SPOT

The best time to ride the Star Tours attraction is late in the evening. If the line for this ride doesn't go outside of the building, the wait will be less than twenty minutes.

Tomorrowland Terrace Stage

As you chow down on snacks from the nearby Tomorrowland Terrace Refreshment Stand (where hamburgers, hot dogs, french fries, drinks, and other goodies are available), you can often enjoy live musical performances or hang out with Disney characters. This is also a great place to sit down (at tables covered with large umbrellas to block the sun) and rest for a few minutes. The little birds that fly around this area aren't afraid of people and they love eating leftover french fries.

TRAVEL TIP

In the Tomorrowland Terrace area are some of the radio studios for Radio Disney, Disney's own national radio network for kids. From here, you might be able to check out a live broadcast of "Just Plain Mark & Zippy," presented every weekday, between 1:00 P.M. and 5:00 P.M.

Meeting Your Disney Pals

 During your visit to Disneyland, if you want to meet and greet Disney characters, and maybe even snap a few pictures with them, the best places to find the characters are the following:

Adventureland, at Aladdin's Oasis, near the exit to the Jungle Cruise, meet Aladdin and Princess Jasmine

Critter Country, at the Thotful Spot, meet Winnie the Pooh and his pals (Check the *Disneyland Today* booklet for exact times.)

Fantasyland, near Pinocchio's Daring Journey, in conjunction with the Classic Princess Storytelling presentations (See the *Disneyland Today* booklet for exact times.)

Main Street, U.S.A., in front of the Walt Disney Story, featuring "Great Moments with Mr. Lincoln" (periodically throughout the day)

Mickey's Toontown (throughout the day)

Throughout the park (Stop by the Information Desk/Wait Board near the Hub or in Tomorrowland to discover where some of these characters can be found during your visit.)

Tomorrowland Terrace Stage (periodically throughout the day)

⊕ HOT SPOT

Be sure to make a lunch or dinner reservation, as early in the day as possible, at the following fine-dining restaurants: Blue Bayou restaurant, Golden Horseshoe Stage, and Disney Gallery Fantasmic! Dessert.

Club 33 Membership

 Just behind the Disney Gallery, around the corner from the Pirates of the Caribbean attraction entrance, and above the Blue Bayou restaurant (on 33 Royal Street) is a private, members-only club, known as Club 33. Years ago, Walt Disney entertained dignitaries, celebrities, and other special guests at Disneyland, and he wanted a quiet, fancy, and secure place where he could offer them a fine-dining experience. Walt and his wife traveled to New Orleans and handpicked all of the art that continues to be displayed in Club 33.

Club 33 was completed and opened in May 1967, just a few months after Walt's death. Today, some of the best chefs from around the world are invited to showcase their talents for Club 33 members. Membership in this club is rather exclusive.

Corporate memberships to Disneyland's Club 33 cost $20,000, plus annual dues of $1,800 per member. Individual memberships are available for a onetime fee of $7,500, plus $1,500 per year. Members and up to nine of their guests are given free, unlimited admission to Disneyland, as long as the member and/or guests plan to dine at Club 33. Membership rates do not include dining charges. All membership fees are subject to change, and a Club 33 representative reported that there is a several year waiting list to become a member.

≡FAST FACT

As a regular Disneyland guest, unfortunately you can't see the inside of Club 33 firsthand, but if you happen to be in the New Orleans Square area when a dignitary or celebrity enters or exits the club, you might catch a glimpse of them. It's been reported that at any given time, Club 33 has about 400 members.

Disneyland's Lost & Found

During your visit to Disneyland, if you happen to lose something, you're not alone. Disneyland's main Lost & Found office is located just off the east side of Main Street, U.S.A., around the corner from the Market House. Each day, literally hundreds of eyeglasses, sunglasses, hats, wallets, purses, cameras, and other items are found and returned to guests. If your lost item turns up and is returned to the Lost & Found office after you leave Disneyland, it will be mailed to your home, at Disneyland's expense, if the item is reported lost and identified to be yours.

If you're visiting Disneyland and someone in your party happens to get lost, you can leave a written message for that person at City Hall, located on the left near the entrance to Disneyland once you pass under the Disneyland Train Station. It's also an excellent idea to choose a meeting location, such as the Hub, before you enter the park. For example, you can agree to meet on the half-hour or at the top of the hour at the Hub if someone in your party gets lost.

Lost children are taken to a special area located near Disneyland's First Aid center. If a young child (under the age of twelve) gets lost in Disneyland, report the missing child immediately to any Disneyland cast member and follow their instructions. Of course, keep a close eye on your children at all times. **Disneyland's Lost Children** department's phone number is ✆ (714) 781-4210. Disney security is highly trained in dealing with lost child situations; so before you panic, seek help from Disney security.

CHAPTER 9

Disneyland's Kid-Oriented Lands

WHILE THE ENTIRE DISNEYLAND theme park was created to entertain and inspire people of all ages, there are certain lands specifically for children under the age of twelve. So, if you're traveling with kids, plan on spending extra time within these areas.

Critter Country

 As you'll soon discover, this is one of Disneyland's smaller lands. Although it offers cute kid-oriented attractions and shops, it's also the land of Splash Mountain, one of Disneyland's most popular thrill rides.

Country Bear Playhouse

Ages 2–4:	★★
Ages 5–10:	★★★
Ages 11–15:	★★★
Ages 16–Adult:	★
Senior Citizens:	★

Get ready for an old-fashioned country hoedown, starring a cast of over twenty lifelike Audio-Animatronics animals that sing, dance, and entertain audiences of all ages. This sixteen-minute show, however, is designed primarily for Disneyland's younger guests. Be prepared to tap your feet and clap along. The Country Bear Playhouse is an indoor theater.

TRAVEL TIP

Near the entrance of the Country Bear Playhouse, you and your kids can meet Pooh, Eeyore, and Tigger at their favorite Thotful Spot. This is a great photo and autograph opportunity for kids. Check the *Disneyland Today* brochure for exact appearance times during the day(s) you're visiting the park.

Davy Crockett's Explorer Canoes

Ages 2–4:	N.S.
Ages 5–10:	★★
Ages 11–15:	★★
Ages 16–Adult:	★★
Senior Citizens:	★

In the heart of Disneyland is the Rivers of America, a man-made circular river where Fantasmic! is presented nightly. In the center of this river is Tom Sawyer Island. One of the ways you can ride along Rivers of America is in a 35-foot fiberglass canoe.

If you're up to the challenge, you can even help with the rowing. If not, you can kick back and enjoy the scenic ride. Davy Crockett's Explorer Canoes operate only during certain times of the year and only during daylight hours. Check with the Information Desk/Wait Board at the Hub or in Tomorrowland, or visit the canoe dock for details.

Splash Mountain

Ages 2–4:	N.S.
Ages 5–10:	★★★
Ages 11–15:	★★★
Ages 16–Adult:	★★★
Senior Citizens:	N.S.

Based on Disney's 1946 movie *Song of the South*, Splash Mountain gives you a chance to once again experience the adventures of Brer Rabbit, Brer Fox, and Brer Bear, along with a colorful cast of more than 100 other Audio-Animatronics creatures.

This nine-minute ride starts off as a slow-paced, calm, and relaxing boat ride. Your heart and imagination will be captivated by the classic Disney music and exciting visuals. The adventure concludes with a rather scary 52½-foot drop (at a 47-degree angle) that culminates in a big splash. (Yes, you'll probably get wet, especially if you're sitting in front.)

If you're wondering what your face looks like when you let out a scream as you plummet downward during the ride's final drop, you can purchase an 8" × 10" color photo of yourself as you leave the ride. With or without the picture, Splash Mountain is not something you'll soon forget. Guests must be over 40 inches tall and older than three to experience this thrill ride.

Splash Mountain is not recommended for anyone who can't handle roller-coasterlike drops, and don't go on it right after a meal. After riding Splash Mountain, you'll probably be singing "Zip-A-Dee-Doo-Dah" for the rest of the day. This ride nicely combines Disney's unique storytelling abilities with Audio-Animatronics technology and the excitement of a thrill ride.

☞ This is a must-see attraction.

Teddi Barra's Swinging Arcade

Ages 2–4:	N.S.
Ages 5–10:	★
Ages 11–15:	★
Ages 16–Adult:	★
Senior Citizens:	★

This attraction combines old-fashioned arcade machines with some of the newest arcade hits. You'll need to purchase tokens to play these games because they're not included in the Disneyland admission price.

Sleeping Beauty Castle

Ages 2–4:	★★★
Ages 5–10:	★★★
Ages 11–15:	★★★
Ages 16–Adult:	★★★
Senior Citizens:	★★★

The best-known landmark in Disneyland is Sleeping Beauty Castle, which can be found at the end of Main Street, U.S.A. Inspired by various medieval European castles, this colorful 77-foot-tall castle was created specifically for Disneyland.

The water-filled moat is home to many fish and is visited often by ducks and swans. The same white swans in the moat have been guests of Disneyland for over fifteen years. Each year, one or two baby swans are born in this moat.

You won't want to leave Disneyland without walking through the enchanted castle. Having your picture taken while standing in front of the castle will also make the perfect addition to your family photo album.

Does the castle look a bit backward to you? When the blueprints and plans for Disneyland were first created, the castle was supposed to face the opposite direction, but Walt Disney turned things around just before construction actually began in order to make the castle look more inviting to guests.

 This is a must-see attraction.

═FAST FACT

> The drawbridge at the castle's front entrance (which marks the entrance into Fantasyland) can go up and down. However, the drawbridge was lowered at Disneyland's opening in 1955 and hasn't been raised since.

Fantasyland

 Located behind Sleeping Beauty Castle is Fantasyland, a magical place designed for children and the young-at-heart. Each of the rides and attractions in Fantasyland features some of Disney's most famous and beloved characters.

To meet Mickey, Minnie, Goofy, and the rest of the classic Disney gang, however, you'll probably need to trek over to Mickey's Toontown, located just a hop, skip, and a jump from Fantasyland.

Families traveling with children, between the ages of four and twelve, should plan on spending plenty of time in Fantasyland. Virtually all of the rides are kid-oriented and based on classic Disney characters, movies, and stories that young people know and love.

Alice in Wonderland

Ages 2–4:	★★★
Ages 5–10:	★★★
Ages 11–15:	★
Ages 16–Adult:	★
Senior Citizens:	★

Generations have grown up hearing the *Alice in Wonderland* story, but only at Disneyland can you take a leap down the rabbit hole and meet up with Tweedledee, Tweedledum, the Cheshire Cat, the Queen of Hearts, and other characters from this classic story.

Guests ride in caterpillar-shaped vehicles as they experience this colorful, enchanting ride. Like all of the attractions in Fantasyland, Alice in Wonderland is designed for kids but is suitable for guests of all ages. The ride itself lasts for about four minutes and ends with a very sweet surprise—an exploding "unbirthday" cake.

TRAVEL TIP

Sometimes, you'll see the Disney characters wandering around the park meeting guests. They also appear at preset locations, which are listed in the *Disneyland Today* brochure. Throughout the day and evening, however, you're guaranteed to meet the classic Disney characters in Mickey's Toontown.

Casey Jr. Circus Train

Ages 2–4:	★★★
Ages 5–10:	★★★
Ages 11–15:	★
Ages 16–Adult:	★
Senior Citizens:	★

Scenes from Disney's *Dumbo* animated classic are the basis for this ride. A train engine, named Casey Jr., pulls guests along in a train-shaped vehicle that takes a 3.5-minute journey around Disneyland's Storybook land. Young children will enjoy this ride, while older guests may find it nostalgic.

Dumbo the Flying Elephant

Ages 2–4:	★★★
Ages 5–10:	★★★
Ages 11–15:	★
Ages 16–Adult:	★
Senior Citizens:	★

Young children (who should definitely be accompanied by parents) can hop on Dumbo's back and take a two-minute journey into the air as they fly in circles at a speed that'll thrill most young people, without scaring them.

Of all the rides at Disneyland, Dumbo the Flying Elephant is one of the true classics. It's been experienced by guests since Disneyland's earliest days.

Fantasyland Theatre

Ages 2–4:	★★★
Ages 5–10:	★★★
Ages 11–15:	★★★
Ages 16–Adult:	★
Senior Citizens:	★★★

Located near the entrance of Mickey's Toontown and one of the Disneyland Train Stations, Fantasyland Theatre is the home of a musical stage show that has changed many times over the years. As this book was being written, *Disneyland Presents Animazement—The Musical* was the featured presentation. (See Chapter 10 for more information on this charming live show.)

 TRAVEL TIP

Some of the rides and attractions in the lands described in this chapter will certainly appeal to adults as well as kids. There's Splash Mountain (in Critter Country), for example. While this is certainly a very cute and lighthearted ride, it ends with a rather thrilling drop and splash!

The show is presented primarily during the park's peak season(s) only on Monday through Thursday, with a few shows per day. The Fantasyland Theatre is large and holds several hundred people; however, for the best seats, arrive at least thirty minutes early. This is an outdoor theater, so on hot and sunny days, be prepared to sit outside (exposed to the sun). Wear plenty of sunscreen and a hat, and drink plenty of fluids. Check the *Disneyland Today* booklet for show times and details.

"It's a Small World"

Ages 2–4:	★★★
Ages 5–10:	★★★
Ages 11–15:	★★★
Ages 16–Adult:	★★★
Senior Citizens:	★★★

Prepare yourself for a twelve-minute boat ride through a series of colorful and magical sets filled with Audio-Animatronics children, representing countries from around the world, all singing "It's a Small World" in multiple languages.

Walt Disney's team of Imagineers created this attraction, which originally opened in New York on April 22, 1964, at the World's Fair. The theme is world peace, understanding, and friendship, and it's been dubbed "the happiest cruise that ever sailed." During the Christmas holiday season, this ride receives an annual makeover, giving it a festive look.

As you wait to board this ride, you'll witness the charm of the pastel-colored building, life-size animal topiaries, and the giant clock. No matter how old you and your traveling companions are, this is one of the truly timeless attractions at Disneyland that you won't want to miss!

 This is a must-see attraction.

King Arthur Carrousel

Ages 2–4:	★★★
Ages 5–10:	★★★
Ages 11–15:	★★★
Ages 16–Adult:	★
Senior Citizens:	★★★

Located in the heart of Fantasyland, this musical carousel ride will capture the imagination of all who climb aboard. King Arthur Carrousel is a classic carousel featuring seventy-two handmade horses. Each horse was created in Germany more than 100 years ago and is considered a priceless work of art. Every aspect of this ride is visually stunning and great care goes into keeping this classic carousel in perfect condition.

Mad Tea Party

Ages 2–4:	N.S.
Ages 5–10:	★★★
Ages 11–15:	★★★
Ages 16–Adult:	★★
Senior Citizens:	N.S.

Here's a classic ride for anyone who wants to take a spin in a giant teacup. Inspired by a scene in Disney's *Alice in Wonderland* animated movie, this was the first thrill ride that opened in Disneyland back in 1955. (It's been spinning ever since.)

Guests climb into a giant teacup-shaped vehicle that automatically spins around in circles around other teacups. At the same time, riders can cause their own teacup to spin quickly or slowly around its own axis, adding to the dizzying thrill. It's probably better to ride Mad Tea Party (a.k.a. the Teacups) before lunch, since once this ride begins you're in for about ninety seconds of rather high-speed spinning. Extremely young children and anyone who tends to suffer from motion sickness should skip this ride.

Matterhorn Bobsleds

Ages 2–4:	N.S.
Ages 5–10:	N.S.
Ages 11–15:	★★★
Ages 16–Adult:	★★★
Senior Citizens:	★

This 2½-minute roller coaster was state-of-the-art when it first opened in Disneyland. It's since been upgraded, so it continues to make you feel as if you're riding in an actual bobsled down, through, and around a giant mountain. This is more of a teen- and adult-oriented thrill ride that is not suitable for very young children.

In reality, this attraction soars about 147 feet into the sky, but the Disney Imagineers use forced perspective to make this artificial snow-covered mountain look a lot taller than it actually is. Like Space Mountain and Big Thunder Mountain Railroad, Matterhorn Bobsleds is a high-speed ride that should not be experienced by guests who suffer from a weak back, heart condition, motion sickness, or any other ailment that would keep them from enjoying this attraction.

Matterhorn Bobsleds can be seen from miles around Disneyland

and is the tallest structure in the theme park. You can expect this attraction to have one of the longest waits on a busy day, but if you enjoy roller coasters, it's worth it.

 This is a must-see attraction.

TRAVEL TIP

Most families visit the park early. As the day progresses, however, kids get hungry and tired. So, by evening, most families with kids tend to leave the park. Thus, late afternoons, evenings, or nights are the best times for adults to experience the areas of Disneyland described in this chapter.

Mr. Toad's Wild Ride

Ages 2–4:	★★★
Ages 5–10:	★★★
Ages 11–15:	★★
Ages 16–Adult:	★
Senior Citizens:	★

As one of the classic rides at Disneyland, Mr. Toad's Wild Ride is based on the 1949 Disney movie *The Adventures of Ichabod and Mr. Toad.* Guests ride in high-speed carlike vehicles driven by Mr. Toad.

In addition to the kid-oriented thrill element of this ride, there's a lot to see along the two-minute journey, so keep your eyes open. This ride is suitable for guests of all ages, because it's much tamer than Disneyland's other thrill rides—Space Mountain, Big Thunder Mountain, Splash Mountain, or Matterhorn Bobsleds.

This classic ride has been closed at The Magic Kingdom at The Walt Disney World Resort in Orlando, so Disneyland is now the only place in America to experience it.

Peter Pan's Flight

Ages 2–4:	★★★
Ages 5–10:	★★★
Ages 11–15:	★★
Ages 16–Adult:	★
Senior Citizens:	★

Special effects (including many that use fiber optics) throughout this colorful attraction allow guests to feel just like Peter Pan as they soar through the air in Never Land and see many familiar sights from Disney's popular animated movie *Peter Pan*.

This ride is suitable for guests of all ages. Although guests ride in a moving vehicle that simulates flight, the movement isn't too fast-paced or scary. Families with children shouldn't miss this attraction. As you wait in line, listen carefully and you may actually hear Peter Pan and Wendy laughing.

Pinocchio's Daring Journey

Ages 2–4:	★★★
Ages 5–10:	★★★
Ages 11–15:	★★
Ages 16–Adult:	★
Senior Citizens:	★

Inspired by Disney's *Pinocchio* movie, which premiered in 1940, guests ride in slow-moving vehicles as the story of Pinocchio unfolds before their eyes. Audio-Animatronics, holograms, fiber optics, and other effects add a touch of Disney-style magic that kids in particular will enjoy.

Snow White's Scary Adventure

Ages 2–4:	★★
Ages 5–10:	★★★
Ages 11–15:	★★
Ages 16–Adult:	★
Senior Citizens:	★

Riding in specially designed vehicles, guests see scenes from Disney's classic animated film *Snow White and the Seven Dwarfs* come to life before their eyes. Expect to see Bashful, Happy, Dopey, and the rest of the dwarfs, and hear music from the movie's original soundtrack.

Snow White's Scary Adventure is far more enchanting than scary, since it's designed primarily for Disneyland's young guests. Like many of the rides in Fantasyland, this one lasts about two minutes.

Storybook Land Canal Boats

Ages 2–4:	★★
Ages 5–10:	★★
Ages 11–15:	★
Ages 16–Adult:	★
Senior Citizens:	★★

Here's a chance to take a seven-minute cruise along a manmade canal. Along the slow-moving boat route are expertly crafted miniatures that re-create scenes from many Disney movies and other classic stories. Adults will truly appreciate the incredible detail of the miniatures, while kids will enjoy the actual boat ride.

Story Time with a Princess

Ages 2–4:	★★★
Ages 5–10:	★★★
Ages 11–15:	★★
Ages 16–Adult:	★
Senior Citizens:	★

Located near Pinocchio's Daring Journey, young guests have a chance to meet and greet Snow White, Cinderella, Princess Aurora, or Belle in person, and hear her tell a story.

Personalized photos of children who participate in the story time are taken with the featured princess. Photos can be purchased for $10 (for a 6" × 8" color photo) or $15 (for an 8" × 10" color photo). Be sure to check the *Disneyland Today* booklet for the exact time(s) each princess will be appearing. Space is definitely limited, so show up early and be prepared to hang out and wait.

═FAST FACT

This chapter offers detailed information about Fantasyland, Critter Country, and Mickey's Toontown. Information about all of the parades, shows, and special events held in this park can be found in the next chapter. For descriptions of the special services offered to guests, such as the park's Baby Care Centers, be sure to read Chapter 13.

Mickey's Toontown

 Hollywood may be where human celebrities hang out, but the stomping ground for Disney's animated stars is Mickey's Toontown. This is Disneyland's newest land designed specifically for kids. Throughout the day and evening, guests can meet and greet Mickey, Minnie, and other classic Disney characters. In fact, the entire area has the look and feel of a three-dimensional cartoon.

If you're traveling with children (between the ages of two and twelve), plan on spending at least two or three hours in Mickey's Toontown. Adults traveling without the company of young people can head directly to the Roger Rabbit's Car Toon Spin ride, which will appeal to anyone who loved Disney's *Who Framed Roger Rabbit?* animated/live-action movie. The other areas of Toontown are kid-oriented.

In addition to the major rides and attractions, even the buildings, mailboxes, fire hydrants, and manholes are interactive and make cartoonlike sounds. This land is a great place to bring the kids for a snack or lunch. The food court area of Mickey's Toontown specializes in foods that kids love, such as pizza, chicken fingers, burgers, ice cream, and hot dogs.

▐▊ TRAVEL TIP

Mickey's Toontown often closes earlier than the rest of Disneyland, because preparations need to be made for the Believe: There's Magic in the Stars fireworks spectacular, which is presented nightly. Check with Guest Services or the Information Desk/Wait Board Kiosk (located on Main Street, U.S.A. and in Tomorrowland) for exact operating hours.

Chip 'n Dale Treehouse and Acorn Crawl

Ages 2–4:	★★★
Ages 5–10:	★★★
Ages 11–15:	★★
Ages 16–Adult:	N.S.
Senior Citizens:	N.S.

The home of Chip and Dale is really a "ball crawl," where kids can jump around and play in piles of tiny multi-colored plastic balls shaped like acorns. Sorry, adults and kids under the age of three will have to stay out of this area, but a special viewing area for parents is provided. Remember, never leave your children unsupervised anywhere in Disneyland.

Donald's Boat

Ages 2–4:	★★★
Ages 5–10:	★★★
Ages 11–15:	★★
Ages 16–Adult:	N.S.
Senior Citizens:	N.S.

Everyone knows Donald Duck, but did you know he has a passion for sailing? Donald keeps his colorful, cartoonlike boat docked (on land) in Toontown. Young guests can explore this boat, climb rope ladders, turn the steering wheel, and pretend they're sailing the high seas with Donald.

Gadget's Go Coaster

Ages 2–4:	★★★
Ages 5–10:	★★★
Ages 11–15:	★★★
Ages 16–Adult:	N.S.
Senior Citizens:	N.S.

This brightly colored roller coaster was created just for Disneyland's young guests. You might have to wait awhile for this mini-thrill ride, but it's an experience your kids won't want to miss, especially if they're too young for Space Mountain.

Goofy's Bounce House

Ages 2–4:	★★★
Ages 5–10:	★★★
Ages 11–15:	N.S.
Ages 16–Adult:	N.S.
Senior Citizens:	N.S.

This giant inflatable house allows kids to kick off their shoes and bounce around . . . literally. Kids can climb all over the furniture and peek out the rope-covered windows to see their parents and other onlookers. Kids must be at least three years old and 52 inches tall to experience this attraction.

Jolly Trolley

Ages 2–4:	★★★
Ages 5–10:	★★★
Ages 11–15:	★★
Ages 16–Adult:	★
Senior Citizens:	★

For a quick tour of Toontown, hop aboard the Jolly Trolley. This fun (and somewhat bouncy) ride will take you from one end of this cartoonlike town to the other. It's a short ride, but exciting for kids.

Roger Rabbit's Car Toon Spin

Ages 2–4:	★★★
Ages 5–10:	★★★
Ages 11–15:	★★★
Ages 16–Adult:	★★
Senior Citizens:	★★

Although not a roller coaster, this fast and turbulent ride offers a lot of quick turns as guests ride in taxilike vehicles and explore scenes from Disney's *Who Framed Roger Rabbit?* This is one ride in Mickey's Toontown that will appeal to most adults as well as to kids. It's a fast-moving ride, but it's not at all scary.

⊕ HOT SPOT

The Gag Factory/Toontown Dive & Dime offers a large selection of kid-oriented Disney merchandise, including plush toys, costumes, and other products featuring Mickey Mouse and the famous Disney characters.

Meet Mickey and Minnie

 Both Mickey Mouse and Minnie Mouse make appearances throughout the day and evening in the parades and live shows. In addition, these popular characters can often be found roaming the park and meeting guests. However, you'll definitely find Mickey and Minnie all day (and evening) in Mickey's Toontown.

If you don't have time to wait so your kids can meet these characters, consider taking them to one of the character breakfasts, held every morning in Disneyland and at all three of the Disney hotels. For more information about these character breakfasts, contact Guest Services or the front desk of any Disney hotel.

Mickey's House

Ages 2–4:	★★★
Ages 5–10:	★★★
Ages 11–15:	★★
Ages 16–Adult:	★
Senior Citizens:	★

If you want to meet Mickey Mouse during your visit to Disneyland, head directly to this attraction found in Mickey's Toontown. Kids (and their parents) can be personal guests of Mickey Mouse as they explore his house and ultimately meet him. A visit to Mickey's house gives you the perfect opportunity to snap a photo of Mickey with your kids.

Because you're guaranteed to meet Mickey, this attraction tends to have a long line during peak times of the day. Be patient! For kids, meeting Mickey is typically a highlight of their trip to Disneyland, and the picture you take of your kids with Mickey will probably be worth the wait.

Minnie's House

Ages 2–4:	★★★
Ages 5–10:	★★★
Ages 11–15:	★★
Ages 16–Adult:	★
Senior Citizens:	★

Being the ultimate host, Minnie Mouse loves to meet and greet her guests as they roam around her house. Here's a chance for your kids to meet Minnie and get a photo taken with this popular Disney character.

Last-Minute Advice

 Wear comfortable shoes and plan on doing a lot of walking! If the weather looks bad, bring along a raincoat or plan on purchasing a Mickey Mouse rain poncho. Umbrellas are permitted, but you'll find it difficult to navigate through the crowds if you're carrying an open umbrella. Plan on getting wet, but having a lot of fun on days when it's raining. The good news is that when it rains, the park is usually less crowded. A few of the outdoor attractions, however, will be closed.

On sunny days, wear light-colored, lightweight clothing, and apply plenty of sunblock to all areas of skin that are exposed. Also, wear a hat and sunglasses.

Throughout the day, drink plenty of liquids. You can purchase soda, juice, or bottled water throughout Disneyland, or you can take advantage of the free water fountains that are also located throughout the park. Avoid becoming dehydrated by drinking liquids even if you're not thirsty.

Plan your day in advance. Choose which attractions you absolutely don't want to miss, and then determine the best time of the day or night to see each of them, based on the waits reported at either of Disneyland's two Information Desks/Wait Boards.

If your day (or night) at Disneyland includes dining at a restaurant that requires a reservation or seeing a show that requires a reservation, make that reservation first thing in the morning.

Plan on having lunch before 11:00 A.M. or after 2:00 P.M. During this midday period, the lines for the popular attractions are the shortest, while the lines at Disneyland's various eating establishments are the longest. Whenever possible, go against the crowds to avoid extra waiting. As for dinner, the peak dinner hours are between 5:00 P.M. and 8:00 P.M. Once again, it's best to experience the popular attractions during these times. Right after a meal, avoid the more turbulent rides or you might feel queasy.

Disneyland reports that the wait times posted at the Information desk are usually overstated by about ten minutes. So, if you're told an attraction has a sixty-minute wait, chances are you'll only wait about fifty minutes.

Let's face it, before you leave Disneyland, you'll probably want to buy some souvenirs. The best time to do your shopping is midday. The busiest time for the shops is at the end of the day (the hour or so before Disneyland closes).

If you're planning on staying at Disneyland into the night (until the park closes), be sure to take a break at midday to avoid overexerting yourself. If you're staying at a nearby hotel, consider taking a midday nap.

Keep in mind, chewing gum is not sold anywhere on Disney property. While you're allowed to bring your own chewing gum into the park, Disneyland's cleanup crew asks that you dispose of it properly, and not spit it out onto the ground or place it under the seat of an attraction. Be courteous!

═FAST FACT

Each year, Disneyland serves over 4 million hamburgers, 3.4 million orders of french fries, 3.2 million boxes of popcorn, 3.2 million servings of ice cream, 1.2 million gallons of soft drinks, and 1.6 million hot dogs, but there are plenty of other dining choices available.

CHAPTER 10

Disneyland's Parades, Live Shows, and Fireworks

THIS CHAPTER DESCRIBES the majority of the parades, shows, and live entertainment offered throughout Disneyland. Whether you're traveling with kids, you're a kid at heart, or you have a soft spot for anything Disney, be sure to check out at least some of this entertainment during your visit.

Disneyland's Parades

Most Disney vacationers take time out of their busy theme park schedules to catch a parade. While the parades may not seem as enticing as the exciting rides and fireworks displays, to truly capture the essence of Disneyland, you should try to make it to at least one of the parades offered.

A Christmas Fantasy Parade

Ages 2–4:	★★★
Ages 5–10:	★★★
Ages 11–15:	★★★
Ages 16–Adult:	★★★
Senior Citizens:	★★★

LOCATION: **Main Street, U.S.A.**

Starting in early November, Disneyland (a.k.a. "The Happiest Place on Earth") is transformed into "The Merriest Place on Earth." Throughout the holiday season (late November through early January), a Christmas Fantasy Parade has become a classic at Disneyland. All of your favorite Disney characters, dressed in holiday attire, participate in this festive parade along Main Street, U.S.A. Suitable for the entire family, it's definitely a parade worth seeing. As with all of the parades, stake out your spot about one hour early.

Disneyland's Parade of Stars

Ages 2–4:	★★
Ages 5–10:	★★★
Ages 11–15:	★★★
Ages 16–Adult:	★★
Senior Citizens:	★★★

LOCATION: **Main Street, U.S.A.**

Once or twice per day (depending on the season), Main Street, U.S.A. is transformed into a lavish parade route, compete with colorful floats, upbeat music, dancing performers in colorful costumes, and, of course, all of the popular Disney characters. You're guaranteed to see Mickey, Minnie, Donald Duck, and many other Disney favorites as part of this parade, so have your camera handy.

Although the theme of the parade changes at least once each year, the daytime character parade has been a staple since the early days. This parade represents the fun and excitement this park offers—especially to young people. Disneyland's Parade of Stars is a salute to Disney Animation's classic characters. It lasts approximately twenty minutes.

⊕ HOT SPOT

As you're waiting for the parade to begin, check out the Blue Ribbon Bakery for fruit, muffins, sandwiches, cookies, and gourmet coffee. Or how about some delicious chocolate, chocolate-chip muffins and Mickey Krispie Treats? They all make great snacks.

When the park is busy, you'll want to stake out your viewing spot about one hour early. Kids will enjoy sitting on the curb (along Main Street, U.S.A.) for the best up close view as the characters go by and often wave to onlookers. The first parade of day begins at the end of Main Street, U.S.A. (in the Town Square area), proceeds along the entire length of Main Street, U.S.A., around the Hub (to the right of the castle), continues toward the Matterhorn Bobsleds (in Fantasyland), and concludes near "It's a Small World." For the second parade of the day, the route is reversed. For exact show times on the day(s) of your visit to Disneyland, see the *Disneyland Today* brochure or stop by the Information Desk/Wait Time Board on Main Street, U.S.A. or in Tomorrowland.

If you've only got time to see one parade during the day at Disneyland and you're visiting with kids and plan to leave before nightfall, this is the parade to see. If there are two showings on the day of your visit, the second parade (which is identical) will always be less crowded. If you'll be visiting Disneyland over several days, the best time to experience the park's most popular rides and attractions is during the parade, because the lines will be shorter.

 ## TRAVEL TIP

The best viewing locations include on the platform of the Disneyland Railroad or in and around Town Square (in front of the train station, near the flagpole). From anywhere along Main Street, U.S.A., however, you'll be able to see and hear everything.

Entertainment for One and All

 There are several live shows taking place on any given day in Disneyland. Whether you're in the mood to laugh, sing, or just relax and enjoy a show, the live entertainment may just be exactly what you are looking for.

Aladdin and Jasmine's Story Tale Adventures

Ages 2–4:	★★★
Ages 5–10:	★★★
Ages 11–15:	★★
Ages 16–Adult:	★
Senior Citizens:	★★

LOCATION: Aladdin's Oasis, Adventureland

The main characters from Disney's *Aladdin* gather amongst Disneyland's guests to retell the exciting story of their adventure. This is a kid-oriented show that involves audience participation in a relatively intimate setting. The show is presented on weekends, holidays, and throughout the summer season. After the show, Aladdin and Jasmine will meet and interact with guests, sign autographs, and take pictures.

Billy Hill & the Hillbillies

Ages 2–4:	N.S.
Ages 5–10:	★
Ages 11–15:	★★
Ages 16–Adult:	★★
Senior Citizens:	★★★

LOCATION: The Golden Horseshoe Stage, Frontierland

In keeping with the theme of Frontierland, Billy Hill & the Hillbillies offers a mix of foot-stomping bluegrass and slapstick comedy. The show stars four brothers, all named Billy, who are rather funny and extremely entertaining. This upbeat musical show is presented several times throughout the day. Check the *Disneyland Today* booklet for show times. Billy Hill & the Hillbillies will appeal primarily to adults.

TRAVEL TIP

While you'll, no doubt, find many rides and attractions that you'll thoroughly enjoy, your Disneyland experience isn't complete unless you experience at least some of the incredible live shows, parades, and entertainment offered throughout the day, evening, and night.

Calling All Space Scouts . . .
A Buzz Lightyear Adventure

Ages 2–4:	★★★
Ages 5–10:	★★★
Ages 11–15:	★★
Ages 16–Adult:	★
Senior Citizens:	★

LOCATION: Club Buzz Stage, Tomorrowland

All of the rides, shows, and attractions in Tomorrowland have a futuristic or sci-fi theme, so it makes perfect sense that a live musical show starring Buzz Lightyear from *Disney's Toy Story* movies would have its home in this area of the park.

This is a totally original musical show that's kid-oriented (like the movies). Nearby, you'll find an assortment of dining options in the Club Buzz–Lightyear's Above the Rest food pavilion. The menu here is primarily food that kids will enjoy (pizza, burgers, hot dogs, etc.). Check the *Disneyland Today* brochure for daily show times.

Disneyland Presents Animazement—The Musical

Ages 2–4:	★★★
Ages 5–10:	★★★
Ages 11–15:	★★★
Ages 16–Adult:	★★★
Senior Citizens:	★★★

LOCATION: Fantasyland Theatre, Fantasyland

Characters from *The Lion King, The Little Mermaid, Beauty and the Beast, Pocahontas, The Hunchback of Notre Dame,* and *Hercules* are among the stars of this twenty-five-minute original musical stage show that features lavish sets and costumes. This is definitely a kid-oriented show; however, it'll appeal to people of all ages. While you'll want to arrive about thirty minutes early to get a good seat, The Fantasyland Theatre holds 1,200 people in a covered, out-door-style theater. During peak seasons, the show is presented five times per day. If you're traveling with kids (or you're young at heart) it's definitely worth seeing as scenes from Disney's more recent animated features come to life on stage.

Laughing Stock Co.

Ages 2–4:	N.S.
Ages 5–10:	N.S.
Ages 11–15:	★★
Ages 16–Adult:	★★
Senior Citizens:	★★★

LOCATION: The Golden Horseshoe Stage, Frontierland

Presented four days per week, this comedy troupe offers a performance that's in keeping with the theme of Frontierland, but that's also somewhat ridiculous. The storyline that unfolds will ultimately involve audience members. It seems that in the old Western town where this comedy takes place, the mayor's daughter wants to marry the sheriff, who simply isn't interested. The mayor's daughter, however, won't take no for an answer, because she desperately wants to be married to someone.

This show will appeal mainly to adults. Check the *Disneyland Today* booklet for the days and times the show is presented.

Sword in the Stone Ceremony

Ages 2–4:	★★
Ages 5–10:	★★
Ages 11–15:	★★
Ages 16–Adult:	★
Senior Citizens:	★★

LOCATION: King Arthur Carrousel, Fantasyland

Merlin the magician hosts this daily presentation in which a young king or queen (a Disneyland guest) is invited to pull the legendary Excalibur sword from the stone that's located in front of the King Arthur Carrousel. If you and your kids happen to be in the Fantasyland area at the time this show is presented, it's worth checking out. If you're short on time, however, there are plenty of other rides, shows, and attractions that you can spend your valuable time experiencing.

═FAST FACT

> One reason the public areas of the park always look spotless is because the streets are swept and steam-cleaned every night after the park closes. During a typical day, 30 tons of trash is removed from the park; however, each year, the park recycles 3.1 million pounds of cardboard, 500,000 pounds of office paper, and over 9,400 pounds of aluminum cans.

Fireworks Spectacular

 Anyone who enjoys a spectacular fireworks show will thoroughly enjoy Believe: There's Magic in the Stars fireworks spectacular. It features over 200 pyrotechnics synchronized to classic Disney music (plus a special appearance by Tinker Bell) and is presented directly over Sleeping Beauty Castle, which makes for an awesome sight. And of course we cannot forget the ever-popular Fantasmic! During this show, you will relive classic moments from Disney's animated masterpieces as Mickey Mouse battles against the forces of evil.

Believe: There's Magic in the Stars Fireworks Spectacular

Ages 2–4:	★★★
Ages 5–10:	★★★
Ages 11–15:	★★★
Ages 16–Adult:	★★★
Senior Citizens:	★★★

LOCATION: **Above Sleeping Beauty Castle**
At Disneyland, July 4th can be celebrated every night of the summer and during holiday seasons, as a spectacular fireworks presentation is offered high above Sleeping Beauty Castle. More than 200 pyrotechnics are accompanied by synchronized Disney classics, along with some patriotic favorites. As part of the show, Tinker Bell even flies through the air between the top of the Matterhorn Bobsleds and Sleeping Beauty Castle, where this fantasy in the sky takes place.

Believe: There's Magic in the Stars fireworks spectacular is definitely a must-see show, however, the loud bangs and bright flashes may frighten young children. This fireworks show is typically presented late in the evening but is coordinated with Fantasmic! so guests can experience both shows in a single evening. You can take some stunning souvenir photos of your family in front of the castle with the fireworks exploding overhead during the Believe: There's Magic in the Stars show.

 TRAVEL TIP

Toward the end of Main Street, U.S.A. (near the Main Street Photo Supply Company) or anywhere in or around the Hub are excellent viewing locations for this fireworks presentation. Basically, if you have an unobstructed view of the castle, look up and you'll see the entire fireworks show without a problem.

Fantasmic!

Ages 2–4:	★★★
Ages 5–10:	★★★
Ages 11–15:	★★★
Ages 16–Adult:	★★★
Senior Citizens:	★★★

LOCATION: New Orleans Square

Prepare yourself for twenty-two minutes of spectacular special effects and breathtaking entertainment as the Rivers of America area of Disneyland literally lights up the night with stunning fireworks, lasers, fog, fiber optics, lighting effects, shooting waters, motion picture effects, and dozens of the popular Disney characters.

This show combines live action with 70mm motion picture footage displayed on giant (30 feet by 50 feet) screens made of water. It's unlike anything else you'll see at any theme park; so don't miss it! This musical show is impressive and suitable for the entire family; however, the loud noise created by the fireworks and pyrotechnics that are an intricate part of the show may frighten very young children.

Fantasmic! is typically presented twice each night during peak seasons and on weekends. For the best seats, stake out your viewing location at least an hour early. The "stage" is the entire Rivers of America area in front of Tom Sawyer Island, so you can see the show from almost anywhere in New Orleans Square. The very best seats are directly in front of Pirates of the Caribbean and The Disney Gallery.

If you want to enjoy a wonderful dessert buffet and the very best seats in Disneyland for Fantasmic!, reserve a spot away from the crowds on the balcony of the Disney Gallery. Space is extremely limited, and the cost is $41 per person. Reservations can be made through Guest Relations. The Fantasmic! Dessert Buffet is an excellent (and romantic) way for adults to commemorate a special occasion, such as an anniversary or birthday.

⊕ HOT SPOT

During peak seasons, Fantasmic! is presented twice each night. The second show is typically less crowded. If the crowds are overwhelming, start searching for a viewing spot near Pirates of the Caribbean, but walk toward the Haunted Mansion. As you get closer to the Haunted Mansion, you should find a good viewing location, even on very crowded nights.

Other Live Entertainment

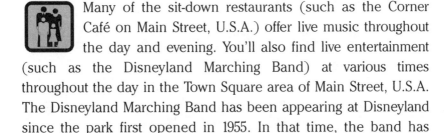 Many of the sit-down restaurants (such as the Corner Café on Main Street, U.S.A.) offer live music throughout the day and evening. You'll also find live entertainment (such as the Disneyland Marching Band) at various times throughout the day in the Town Square area of Main Street, U.S.A. The Disneyland Marching Band has been appearing at Disneyland since the park first opened in 1955. In that time, the band has marched over 3,500 miles up and down Main Street, U.S.A.

In addition to musicians, "Streetmosphere" performers and Disney characters roam the park adding to the ambiance of the various lands. This is live music on weekends and holidays at the Tomorrowland Terrace (the central stage in Tomorrowland) and various street performers show off their skills in New Orleans Square.

Meeting the Disney Characters

Mickey, Minnie, and any number of other Disney characters can often be found roaming the park greeting guests, signing autographs, and taking pictures. While you can always find Mickey and Minnie within Mickey's Toontown and in the daily character parade, Disney characters all make appearances throughout the day in the Town Square area of Main Street, U.S.A.

You'll typically find characters from *The Little Mermaid* at Ariel's Grotto, near Triton Garden in Fantasyland. Pooh, Tigger, and Piglet seem to prefer greeting guests in Critter Country.

In front of the Tinker Bell Toy Shop in Fantasyland, you might encounter Snow White, Cinderella, Belle (from *Beauty and the Beast*), or another popular Disney character. Near Tarzan's Treehouse in Adventureland, it's not uncommon to spot Tarzan and/or Terk.

≡FAST FACT

Throughout the year, Disneyland celebrates many popular holidays by hosting special events. Christmas and New Year's Eve are two of the most extravagant annual celebrations within the park. For details about the holiday happenings at Disneyland, contact **Guest Relations** at ✆(714) 781-4560 or check out the **Disneyland Web site** (✉ *www.Disneyland.com*).

For details on where to find the various Disney characters, check the *Disneyland Today* brochure or ask any cast member at the Information Kiosks/Wait Time Boards on Main Street, U.S.A. or Tomorrowland.

For about $5, many of the gift shops sell character autograph books for kids. So, when children meet the Disney characters, they'll love collecting their autographs as well as having a photo taken with them.

Future Disneyland Expansion

Most people agree that the rides and attractions at Disneyland are unique and amazing. This is one reason that tens of thousands of people return to Disneyland year after year for an annual vacation. With rides, shows, and attractions always being added, the park continually has new things to see and do, along with timeless favorites. It's typically the live shows and parades that change the most often.

Disneyland is an ever-changing theme park. New rides, shows, and attractions are added, while some are retired, destined to become part of Disneyland's rich history. Don't be surprised if a ride, show, attraction, shop, or restaurant described in this book has changed by the time you actually visit the park.

≡FAST FACT

To keep Disneyland looking its best, over 5,000 gallons of paint are used each year. In addition, the park uses over 100,000 lightbulbs, including 11,000 rim lights to outline the buildings along Main Street, U.S.A.

You might visit the park during nonpeak times and find one or more popular attractions closed for refurbishment. At least once each year, many of the popular attractions are shut down for a week or two at a time to be refurbished. This is typically done, however, during the least busy times at the park, and the closings of the rides are usually staggered, so only one or two will be closed at any given time.

As for what's in development by Disney's Imagineers—well, the company is pretty tight-lipped about new rides and attractions. Now that Disney's California Adventure is open, rumors are flying about

Disney's plans to build a third theme park at The Disneyland Resort, slated to open around 2010. Building of the new 78-acre theme park could begin as early as 2003.

Although space within Disneyland is pretty much maxed out, Disney's California Adventure has about 28 acres still available for expansion. You can bet new rides and attractions are being developed to fill this space.

CHAPTER 11

Disney's California Adventure

THIS CHAPTER OFFERS an up close look at Disney's California Adventure and provides details about all of its rides and attractions. Also highlighted are some tips for choosing the best dining options and pointers for souvenir shopping.

Park Information

Located directly across from Disneyland, Disney's California Adventure (DCA) is an entirely new, 55-acre theme park that pays tribute to the state of California through its unique rides, shows, and attractions. Everything you'll see and do within this park somehow tells a story about the state's culture, diversity, history, present, or future. According to Barry Braverman, Walt Disney Imagineering Executive Producer for DCA, "California represents fun, celebration, diversity and freedom."

Like all of the Disney theme parks, DCA is divided into separate areas. "You can navigate easily in this park, and in that way, it feels intimate and understandable. Then as you wander into an area, Hollywood Pictures Backlot, for example, you become immersed in that experience," added Braverman. "DCA was planned to enhance, not compete with, the Disneyland resort experience. Disneyland is a classic, it's the original and it's had over forty-five years to evolve into what it is today. We wanted Disneyland's sister park to be a really different kind of place telling a different kind of story."

DCA is divided into three main areas of rides and attractions but also contains the Sunshine Plaza area (featuring shops and a few dining options). As you'd probably guess, the Hollywood Backlot area pays tribute to show business and California's T.V. and motion picture industries. The Golden State area of DCA salute's California's diversity and heritage, while the Paradise Pier area focuses on the "fun in the sun" theme.

≡ FAST FACT

Since the Walt Disney Company is the owner of several motion picture studios, as well as several cable T.V. networks and the ABC Television Network, you'll find rides, shows, attractions, and even restaurants that promote these businesses.

A Combination of New and Borrowed

DCA opened to the public in February 2001 and immediately became one of California's top tourist attractions. Like Disneyland, this park is always evolving. Since its opening, new parades, shows, and attractions have been added, including what is probably the most popular attraction in the park, Who Wants to Be a Millionaire—Play It!, based faithfully on the television game show.

Much of what DCA offers is totally new—never before seen in any theme park. This park did, however, borrow a few attractions from other Disney parks. For example, the *It's Tough to Be a Bug!* 3-D movie can also be seen at Disney's Animal Kingdom theme park in Orlando. DCA is also the new home of what used to be Disneyland's Main Street Electrical Parade (now called Disney's Electrical Parade), a staple at Disneyland since 1972. *Jim Henson's Muppet*Vision 3D* was also copied from the Disney/MGM Studios theme park in Orlando.

What Is Offered

Much of what Disneyland has to offer somehow revolves around the Disney characters (as well as the company's T.V. and movie franchises). DCA, on the other hand, has the look and feel of a Disney theme park, but many of its rides, shows, and attractions have no direct commercial tie-in. In other words, the key rides aren't based on Disney movies, T.V. shows, or characters. Some of what's offered might even be considered somewhat educational or culturally enlightening.

DCA is much more teen- and adult-oriented than Disneyland. The majority of the rides here could easily be classified as thrill rides, while many of the attractions will appeal to adults. As you'll see, however, there are some exceptions, which make this theme park suitable for the entire family.

Like Disneyland, DCA will provide a family with at least one full day's worth of entertainment. The park offers all of the basic guest services you'd expect from a theme park (such as pay phones, ATM machines, first aid, lockers, stroller rental, and wheelchair rental—all of which are described in Chapter 13), plus a wide assortment of dining options and shops. Combine all this with the park's rides, shows, parades, and attractions, and what's in store is an exciting adventure for the entire family.

 TRAVEL TIP

DCA offers a few kid-oriented attractions. Teens and adults will certainly appreciate the park's multiple thrill rides, while older guests will thoroughly enjoy the educational attractions. You might want to split up for part of the day so everyone can enjoy the type of attractions or rides that are most appealing.

Admission Tickets

Depending on how long you'll be spending at The Disneyland Resort, you can choose to purchase admission tickets good for either Disneyland or DCA, or you can purchase passes that offer admission into both parks. If you plan on visiting both theme parks, you can choose from two types of passes.

When you purchase a multiday pass, typically "park-hopping" is not permitted. Park-hopping is when you have free access to both parks in a single day and can travel between both parks using a single ticket (passport). There are, however, certain types of Disney resort passports that allow park-hopping.

If you're just planning to visit DCA, you can choose to purchase a one-day ticket, three-day ticket, four-day ticket, or an annual pass. For information on the various types of tickets and pricing, see Chapter 6 or call **Guest Relations** at ✆ (714) 781-4565.

TRAVEL TIP

If you plan on park-hopping, be sure to keep your admission ticket handy *and* get your hand stamped as you leave each park. If you leave DCA and try to return later that day without a stamp, you will be stopped by security even if you're holding a valid ticket.

Hours of Operation

Throughout the year, DCA's hours of operation are typically from 8:00 A.M. to 10:00 P.M. Monday through Thursday, and from 8:00 A.M. to midnight on Friday, Saturday, and Sunday. During certain times of the year, however, hours of operation will vary. For example, you may find the park opens at 10:00 A.M. and closes at 10:00 P.M. For details, call Guest Relations or visit the **Disneyland Web site** at ✑ *www.Disneyland.com.*

Whatever time the park officially opens, the main gate opens about one hour earlier. As you explore the shops and sights in the Sunshine Plaza area, you'll hear announcements and music counting down the minutes until the opening of the park. Don't be surprised if a photographer approaches you and takes your photo. You can purchase copies of this photo in the Everything under the Sun gift shop located near the entrance to DCA (next to Guest Relations and the Lost & Found).

≡FAST FACT

If you're staying at any of the three Disney hotels, one of the perks is that you can get into DCA one hour before the general public (starting at 7:00 A.M.) on predetermined days of the week. This pretty much guarantees you'll be able to experience some of the park's most popular rides and attractions with minimal wait during the first hour of your visit.

Sunshine Plaza

 As you enter DCA from the main entrance, you'll pass under a model of the Golden Gate Bridge (a San Francisco landmark) and face a giant 50-foot golden sun perched atop a fountain. This is the Sunshine Plaza area of the park. From here, you can access each of the park's other areas. Many of the park's guest services are located here because of its centralized location. Sunshine Plaza is also an ideal place to arrange to meet the people you're traveling with if you get separated during your visit.

Here you'll find a few shops, including **Engine-Ears Toys** (a well-stocked toy store that's shaped like a train) and **Greetings from California** (offering a wide range of DCA-, California-, and Disney-themed merchandise). If you're in the mood for a quick snack, try **Baker's Field Bakery** (offering baked goods and gourmet coffees) or **Bur-r-r Bank Ice Cream**. The shops open an hour before the park and close about thirty minutes after the park.

At various times throughout the day, you'll be able to meet and greet popular Disney characters, get autographs, and take pictures. You'll also find one of the park's Information Kiosks/Wait Boards, where you can determine how long ride and attraction wait lines are and see listings of show times for the live entertainment (shows and parades).

Hollywood Pictures Backlot

 Lights, cameras, action! This fun-filled area salutes Hollywood's past and present. Here you'll get a behind-the-scenes look at Disney animation, see a hysterical 3-D movie starring the Muppets, and even be a contestant on America's most popular T.V. game show, *Who Wants to Be a Millionaire?*

For soap opera fans, you'll definitely want to dine at the ABC Soap Opera Bistro, which re-creates sets from ABC's popular soaps and displays props from shows like General Hospital. This is the ultimate in immersion theme dining experiences.

The musical show Disney's Steps in Time is presented several times each day. This is a wonderful and totally original family-oriented show featuring singing, dancing, colorful costumes, and a touch of Disney magic. As you wander throughout the outside areas of the Hollywood Backlot, the music you hear will likely be theme songs from your favorite ABC T.V. shows, like *Home Improvement*.

⊕ HOT SPOT

In the Hollywood Pictures Backlot area of DCA, it's hard to miss the Hyperion Theater, a large indoor theater that seats more than 2,000 guests. This is the home of DCA's live stage musical, *The Power of BLAST!*

Disney Animation

Ages 2–4:	★
Ages 5–10:	★★★
Ages 11–15:	★★★
Ages 16–Adult:	★★★
Senior Citizens:	★★★

The phrase, "It all started with the mouse," is a popular one at The Walt Disney Company. Disney Animation is really four attractions in one. By experiencing them all, you'll discover how Disney animation is created, be reunited with classic Disney characters, and get a sneak peak at animated Disney films that are currently in production. This attraction involves a series of walk-through exhibits, hands-on interactive activities (designed primarily for young people), and several different live shows and demonstrations.

If you've ever wondered what Disney character you are the most like, you can take an easy quiz and make this determination during your visit to Disney Animation. Plan on spending at least one hour exploring the various areas of this indoor attraction, where much of what's offered is self-paced.

When you enter into the Disney Animation building, you'll find yourself in the **Animation Courtyard.** Be sure to look up as well as all around you. Surrounded by colorful drawings, you'll feel as if you've stepped into one of Disney's animated adventures. The artwork will change right before your eyes, so be sure to take a moment to enjoy the sights.

The **Drawn to Animation** area offers both a movie and a live animation demonstration. The best seats in this 230-seat theater are in the fourth row (toward the center of the room). No matter which seat you wind up in, however, you'll see and hear everything.

Your hosts are Mushu (the animated dragon from Disney's *Mulan*) and an actual Disney animator. From this ten-minute presentation, you'll discover how Disney characters are created and learn where the animators get their ideas. The presentation is highly enjoyable, whether you're six or sixty.

The **Sorcerer's Workshop** area includes a handful of interactive activities, primarily designed for young people who want to explore their own creative talents. This area features several technology-based interactive kiosks that teach about the various steps in the animation process. Here you can determine which Disney character you're the most like.

When you enter Disney Animation, you're not required to participate in every presentation, movie, and demonstration. You can roam freely though many of the exhibits and decide what demonstrations or presentations you'd like to participate in. The entire attraction is housed in a large, air-conditioned building.

⊕ HOT SPOT

For a detailed look at how the entire animation process works, check out *Back to Neverland,* a film that's hosted by Water Cronkite and Robin Williams. This movie is educational, as well as extremely funny and worth seeing. You'll certainly develop a new appreciation for the work that goes into producing a full-length animated motion picture.

*Jim Henson's Muppet*Vision 3D*

Ages 2–4:	★★
Ages 5–10:	★★★
Ages 11–15:	★★★
Ages 16–Adult:	★★★
Senior Citizens:	★★★

Fans of the classic television series *The Muppet Show* will get a touch of comic nostalgia when Kermit, Miss Piggy, and the rest of the Muppet gang present a fun-filled 3-D movie in an interactive theater that was custom-designed for this presentation. This is definitely a family-oriented movie attraction. Directly across from this attraction is a small shop, called Rizzo's Prop Shop, that offers Muppet-related products and souvenirs.

This attraction features a 2-D, twelve-minute preshow that's followed by a comical and rather bizarre twelve-minute 3-D movie. The theater itself was custom-designed to look like the set from *The Muppet Show* television series. During the movie, the theater itself actually becomes part of the show. Muppet fans of all ages will truly love this attraction. Special 3-D glasses are provided, but be sure to wait until you're comfortably seated in the main theater before putting them on. These special glasses can be placed over prescription eyewear.

 This is a must-see attraction.

Superstar Limo

Ages 2–4:	N.S.
Ages 5–10:	★★
Ages 11–15:	★★
Ages 16–Adult:	★★
Senior Citizens:	★★

Step into a cartoonlike re-creation of Los Angeles as you experience what life is like for a famous celebrity riding a stretch limo through Tinsel Town on the way to a big movie premier at Mann's Chinese Theater.

You'll see famous Hollywood landmarks and you might even be discovered as Hollywood's next superstar. This ride offers a spoof of Hollywood and depicts the utter superficiality of show business. It's a lighthearted (indoor and air-conditioned) adventure that's suitable for the entire family. In a word, it's cute. You'll see moving mannequins of Hollywood stars—like Whoopi Goldberg, Tim Allen, Jackie Chan, Jim Carrey, and Cher—and hear other celebrities, like Joan Rivers, as you ride through the colorful sets that make up this attraction.

The limo holds six people (three rows of two people each). On the left side of each row is a T.V. monitor that features a video-phone connection to your agent as you explore Hollywood. Sitting in a left-most seat provides the best view of this small monitor.

As you visit each area of Hollywood, your car will move relatively slowly. This is by no means a thrill ride. At the very end, don't forget to look up to see your photo on a giant monitor. If the line isn't too long for this ride, it's well worth checking out, but this certainly isn't the most amazing ride or attraction in the park.

Who Wants to Be a Millionaire—Play It!

Ages 2–4:	N.S.
Ages 5–10:	★
Ages 11–15:	★★★
Ages 16–Adult:	★★★
Senior Citizens:	★★★

America's attention has been captivated by a television game show that asks the simple question, "Who wants to be a millionaire?" Well, Who Wants To Be a Millionaire—Play It! is one of DCA's most popular interactive attractions. Due to its popularity, you'll definitely want to take advantage of FASTPASS to experience it.

As soon as you step into the soundstage that houses this attraction, you'll find yourself in the midst of a faithful re-creation of the *Who Wants to Be a Millionaire* T.V. studio set. While Regis is in New York hosting the actual game show, a stand-in host is on-hand as you experience what it would be like to watch a taping of the real-life show.

The big difference, however, is that every seat in the theater is interactive, which means you can play along! And, if you're quick (and accurate) when it comes to providing answers, you may find yourself in the famous "hot seat" competing for prizes. (Sorry, in this version of the game, no cash is awarded.)

Who Wants To be A Millionaire—Play It! is well worth experiencing. It's fun, challenging, and highly entertaining. In a word, this attraction is impressive . . . and yes, that's my final answer!

👍 This is a must-see attraction.

FAST FACT

This interactive attraction lasts about thirty minutes (the length of the actual T.V. show) and is extremely faithful to the game-show format, with a few minor exceptions that allow the entire "studio audience" to be involved in the game.

Golden State

The various rides and attractions in this area of DCA provide a look at the heritage of the state of California. As you explore, you'll learn about the cultural diversity and exciting history of this state. You'll also learn about some of the industries that have thrived throughout the history of California. The Golden State area successfully combines education and fun.

The Boudin Bakery

Ages 2–4:	N.S.
Ages 5–10:	★
Ages 11–15:	★
Ages 16–Adult:	★★
Senior Citizens:	★★

San Francisco is known for many things including its soft sourdough bread. This short walk-through attraction demonstrates how this bread is made. A short video (starring Rosie O'Donnell) is shown and samples are given out at the end. The lines for this attraction are typically short, and adults in particular will find it interesting.

Bountiful Valley Farm

Ages 2–4:	N.S.
Ages 5–10:	★
Ages 11–15:	★
Ages 16–Adult:	★
Senior Citizens:	★★

This outdoor exhibit showcases many plants, trees, and shrubs that are native to California. You'll find yourself in a parklike environment that you can walk through at your own pace. There are also several outdoor eating/resting areas nearby.

For kids (ages twelve and under), head for the nearby picnic tables where various supervised arts and crafts activities are offered. There's also a small stage (called Mickey's Garden) where live shows and demonstrations are held throughout the day. Near the stage is a sign listing show times.

Don't plan on spending too much time in this area. It does, however, provide a scenic, pleasant walk as you head toward an attraction, like *It's Tough to Be a Bug*. In the heart of this area is the Fresh Fruit Stand that sells healthy snacks, like apples, bananas, oranges, watermelon, nuts, and drinks. Other nearby food selections include BBQ chicken, peanut butter and jelly sandwiches, and salads.

Golden Dreams

Ages 2–4:	N.S.
Ages 5–10:	★
Ages 11–15:	★
Ages 16–Adult:	★★★
Senior Citizens:	★★★

This twenty-minute documentary movie will appeal mainly to adults. It offers a brief history of California using stunning movie footage and still photography. Narrated by Whoopi Goldberg, this movie takes you on a whirlwind tour through time. Golden Dreams is shown throughout the day and evening in an air-conditioned, indoor theater.

Golden Vine Winery

Ages 2–4:	N.S.
Ages 5–10:	N.S.
Ages 11–15:	N.S.
Ages 16–Adult:	★★
Senior Citizens:	★★★

Designed for adults, this attraction features a seven-minute movie exploring the history and growth of the California wine industry. You'll see how wine is made and learn about the famous Napa Valley wine country. At the end, you'll be invited to sample some of California's best-known wines during a wine tasting (for adults only). If you're traveling with kids, you'll want to skip this attraction. Adults who enjoy sampling wine, however, will find Golden Vine Winery to be informative and mildly entertaining, that is if you're not put off by the infomercial-like quality of the overall presentation that promotes California wines.

The lines for this attraction are always short. The movie portion of the attraction holds fifty people at a time and is shown continuously throughout the day and evening. In addition to a wine tasting, you'll also find a fine-dining restaurant that is part of this attraction, along with a wine shop that sells a large selection of California wines.

 TRAVEL TIP

If you purchase wine at this shop, you must take advantage of the Package Express service and have it delivered either to the front of the park (to be picked up on your way out) or directly to your room (if you're staying at a Disney hotel). You're not allowed to carry wine bottles around the park.

Grizzly River Run

Ages 2–4:	N.S.
Ages 5–10:	★★
Ages 11–15:	★★★
Ages 16–Adult:	★★★
Senior Citizens:	★

Get ready to experience the thrill of white-water rafting. As you climb aboard a circular raft (which holds six people), be prepared to get wet as you weave around the man-made and sometimes turbulent river. If you're carrying a camera or any other electronics, make sure they're protected. Especially if you're traveling with kids, you might want to have dry clothing to change into after experiencing this wet and sometimes wild ride.

Grizzly River Run is suitable for people of all ages and is truly a lot of fun and not too scary, except when you experience the river's two drops (one of which is a 21-foot drop). Because the river has many twists and turns, it's often hard to see what thrills are coming next, which adds to the excitement.

Yes, you're going to get wet, but chances are you'll dry quickly in the California sun. It's best to avoid experiencing this ride before lunch or dinner if you plan on eating in an air-conditioned restaurant and don't have a change of clothes.

It's Tough to Be a Bug!

Ages 2–4:	N.S.
Ages 5–10:	★★★
Ages 11–15:	★★★
Ages 16–Adult:	★★★
Senior Citizens:	★★★

Featuring characters from the popular computer animated movie *A Bug's Life*, this 3-D movie, entitled *It's Tough to Be a Bug!*, is shown in a custom-built theater that actually becomes part of the show, making for an interactive experience. If you thought being a human was difficult, you're about to discover what life is like as a bug. This attraction will appeal to everyone, but primarily to kids and teens. It's lighthearted, visually stunning, and the 3-D effects are extremely realistic.

In fact, because of the realism, both on the movie screen and in the theater itself, the eight-minute movie may scare young children (under the age of six). This is one of the few DCA attractions that actually has a Disney theme and features Disney characters.

Mission Tortilla Factory

Ages 2–4:	★
Ages 5–10:	★
Ages 11–15:	★★
Ages 16–Adult:	★★
Senior Citizens:	★★

This short walk-through attraction offers a demonstration of how flour and corn tortillas are made. At the end of the exhibit, you'll be given a free taste. Mission Tortilla Factory is a self-paced indoor attraction. You can get through the entire thing in three to five minutes, and the lines are typically short. Kids and teens might find the working machinery somewhat fascinating.

Redwood Creek Challenge Trail

Ages 2–4:	★★★
Ages 5–10:	★★★
Ages 11–15:	N.S.
Ages 16–Adult:	N.S.
Senior Citizens:	N.S.

Designed for kids, this interactive (outdoor) play area is modeled after California's redwood forests. Here, young people will find all kinds of places to climb up, slide down, and explore as they explore this playground/obstacle course. Parents are encouraged to watch from a nearby area. If you have some time, this is a great place to allow your child to run around and burn off excess energy.

Soarin' over California

Ages 2–4:	N.S.
Ages 5–10:	★★
Ages 11–15:	★★★
Ages 16–Adult:	★★★
Senior Citizens:	★★★

Combining motion simulator and Omnimax movie technology, you'll feel as if you're soaring over California as you're given a beautiful airborne tour of historic landmarks and national parks. As you experience this realistic movie on the giant screen in front of you, you'll be suspended 45 feet in the air in what's designed to feel like a hang glider. Your movements are perfectly synchronized with the movie.

While there is a mild thrill element to this attraction, it's relatively calm and visually stunning. It's well worth experiencing this four-minute "flight" across California, which allows you to see a full 180 degrees around you. Unless you're prone to motion sickness, this attraction is suitable for everyone (except young kids).

 This is a must-see attraction.

TRAVEL TIP

The best seats available for Soarin' over California are in the front row of each vehicle. The calmest ride is offered in the backseats of each vehicle.

Paradise Pier

 This area of DCA has a "fun in the sun" theme. If you enjoy traditional amusement park thrill rides, that's exactly what's in store for you here. Some of the rides are suitable for people of all ages (including young kids), but some of the more intense thrill rides are much better suited for thrill-seeking teens and adults. Of course, if you want a totally mellow experience, you can always skip the rides and check out the carnival games and shopping area (Games of the Boardwalk). While you'll have to pay for each game of skill and chance you play, you could win carnival prizes, like plush toys.

TRAVEL TIP

Near the main entrance area of Paradise Pier, you'll find an Information Kiosk/Wait Board, which will give you accurate estimates for how long the wait is for each attraction within the park. There will also be a cast member on-hand to answer your questions.

California Screamin'

Ages 2–4:	N.S.
Ages 5–10:	N.S.
Ages 11–15:	★★★
Ages 16–Adult:	★★★
Senior Citizens:	★

One of DCA's premier thrill rides for adults, California Screamin' is a fast-moving roller coaster that goes from zero to 55 miles per hour in 4.7 seconds. The track includes a series of steep drops, tight turns, and a 360-degree loop. This is a traditional outdoor roller coaster and one of the scariest rides you'll find anywhere in The Disneyland Resort. Teens and adults in particular will really enjoy it. For the most beautiful view of DCA, ride California Screamin' in the evening or at night when the park is lit up.

Due to its popularity, you'll probably experience a long line. To cut down on the wait, be sure to take advantage of FASTPASS. As you experience this ride, a souvenir photo will automatically be taken. Upon exiting the ride, you can preview the picture and choose whether to purchase an 8" × 10" color print ($16.95) or four postcards ($19.95).

 This is a must-see attraction.

Games of the Boardwalk

Ages 2–4:	N.S.
Ages 5–10:	★★
Ages 11–15:	★★
Ages 16–Adult:	★★
Senior Citizens:	★★

Throughout this area of the park, you'll find a handful of skill- and luck-based carnival games, priced between $1 and $2 per play. Prizes include plush toys. This is a fun way to spend some time, if you don't mind spending a bit more money.

Golden Zephyr

Ages 2–4:	★★
Ages 5–10:	★★
Ages 11–15:	★★
Ages 16–Adult:	★★
Senior Citizens:	★★

Experience the thrill of soaring through the air in a large, silver rocket ship. Each ship holds fourteen people (seven rows with two people per row). The rockets spin around in the air for about two minutes before coming to a safe landing. This is a mildthrill ride for young people.

Jumpin' Jellyfish

Ages 2–4:	★★
Ages 5–10:	★★
Ages 11–15:	★★
Ages 16–Adult:	★★
Senior Citizens:	★★

This attraction is a mild thrill ride that lifts riders up into the air and slowly lowers them. This happens several times in a one-minute time frame. Two people can ride per seat. Jumpin' Jellyfish isn't scary, unless you're afraid of heights. It's most suitable for children between the ages of five and twelve.

King Triton's Carousel

Ages 2–4:	★★
Ages 5–10:	★★
Ages 11–15:	★★
Ages 16–Adult:	★★
Senior Citizens:	★★★

As you can guess from its name, this beautiful carousel has a water theme. Instead of riding on horses, guests ride on colorful creatures from the sea, such as fish, dolphins, and sea horses. Some of the creatures are stationary, while others move up and down as you go around. The ride lasts about two minutes. Parents can stand next to the sea creature their child is riding on, or ride with them.

 TRAVEL TIP

> There's also a viewing area for people who don't actually experience the ride itself. From this area, you can take great pictures of your kids on the ride. While this is a kid-oriented ride, parents should never leave their children unsupervised.

Maliboomer

Ages 2–4:	N.S.
Ages 5–10:	N.S.
Ages 11–15:	★★★
Ages 16–Adult:	★★★
Senior Citizens:	★

What goes up must come down—in this case, extremely fast. Maliboomer is very much like the Free Fall thrill ride found at other amusement parks. You're strapped onto a benchlike vehicle (four people per bench), raised 180 feet into the air, and then dropped. The fall lasts about two seconds, but for many, that's long enough. Avoid this ride if you've just eaten. It's most suited for teens and adults (at least 52 inches tall). The view from Maliboomer is definitely better at night, but the thrill is offered anytime. To save time, be sure to utilize FASTPASS.

Mulholland Madness

Ages 2–4:	N.S.
Ages 5–10:	★★★
Ages 11–15:	★★★
Ages 16–Adult:	★★
Senior Citizens:	★

Designed for kids, and those not brave enough to experience California Screamin', Mulholland Madness is a traditional roller coaster, but one designed for young people. It offers a much tamer, although fun, experience as you race along the track. To reduce the wait, be sure to use FASTPASS for this attraction.

Orange Stinger

Ages 2–4:	★
Ages 5–10:	★★★
Ages 11–15:	★★★
Ages 16–Adult:	★★
Senior Citizens:	★

You'll know when you've reached this ride because it's shaped like a giant orange. Inside the oversized piece of fruit are single-person swings that rise into the air and spin around. This is a family-oriented ride that's most suitable for kids over the age of seven (and over 48 inches tall). Orange Stinger is a mild thrill ride that spins relatively quickly. It's probably best to avoid experiencing it right after eating.

S.S. Rustworthy

Ages 2–4:	★★★
Ages 5–10:	★★★
Ages 11–15:	★★
Ages 16–Adult:	N.S.
Senior Citizens:	N.S.

This kid-oriented play area looks like an old fireboat and offers all sorts of activities for kids to experience. There are things to climb and fire hoses to squirt. Kids under the age of twelve will enjoy this attraction. Chances are anyone who experiences the S.S. *Rustworthy* is going to get wet, so it's best to have a change of clothes on hand.

Sun Wheel

Ages 2–4:	★★★
Ages 5–10:	★★★
Ages 11–15:	★★★
Ages 16–Adult:	★★★
Senior Citizens:	★★★

This giant Ferris wheel looks like a sunburst but contains colorful and totally enclosed gondolas that guests ride in. Four adults can ride in each gondola. You'll go around in this ride twice and be able to see a spectacular view of DCA (and beyond) from 150 feet in the air. To add a small thrill, each gondola is on a small track that allows it to slide around and rock. You can, however, request a gondola that doesn't slide if you want to experience a somewhat mellower ride. This is not for people who are afraid of heights!

TRAVEL TIP

On busy days, the wait for the Sun Wheel can be long. Unfortunately, while waiting, you'll be outside with no cover overhead, so you'll be exposed to the direct sun (or rain). Be sure to wear sunblock and bring a drink with you as you wait.

Dining in DCA

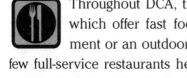 Throughout DCA, there are many dining areas, most of which offer fast food in an indoor food court environment or an outdoor setting with tables. There are only a few full-service restaurants here, such as **Avalon Cove** (a seafood restaurant that overlooks the lake within DCA and features an outdoor bar). Celebrity chef Wolfgang Puck created this restaurant.

Within the Hollywood Backlot Area, there's also the **ABC Soap Opera Bistro,** which is a theme-dining experience that no soap opera fan will want to miss. You'll dine among re-creations of sets from *General Hospital, All My Children, One Life to Live,* and *Port Charles,* plus see costumes and props from these soaps. This is a full-service and somewhat pricey restaurant, but soap opera fans won't be disappointed.

For a more formal dining experience, the **Vineyard Room** offers indoor and outdoor dining areas and serves fine American cuisine along with a large selection of California wines. Although there are entrées suitable for children, this is definitely a more adult-oriented restaurant.

Most people visiting DCA prefer a less expensive and less formal lunch or dinner experience. For this, the park offers several food court environments that offer a wide range of food selections, like burgers, chicken, and Chinese dishes. The **Lucky Fortune Cookery** in the Golden State area serves a teriyaki chicken or teriyaki beef bowl for $7.49, an egg roll on a stick for $3.00, or California roll (sushi) (six pieces) for $6.49.

Hollywood & Dine (in the Hollywood Pictures Backlot area) and the **Taste Pilot's Grill** (in the Condor Flats area) are both great places to stop with the family for lunch or dinner. In addition, throughout the park, food stands sell burgers, corn dogs, pizza, and other quick food items. For snacks, cotton candy, shaved ice, hot dogs, and other items can also be found. In the Paradise Pier, however, is the **Burger Invasion** (serving McDonald's food), definitely a familiar favorite among kids.

█ TRAVEL TIP

Don't forget, just a short walk away from DCA is Downtown Disney, which offers an even greater selection of theme-oriented, sit-down restaurants suitable for the entire family.

DCA's Shopping Opportunities

 Just like Disneyland, DCA offers a wide range of shops where guests can purchase all kinds of souvenirs. Whether you're looking for plush toys, Disney clothes, toys, or other items, there are plenty of shopping opportunities within this park.

Some of the specialty shops include **ABC SoapLink** (offering soap opera–themed souvenirs), **Rizzo's Prop Shop** (offering Muppet-themed items), **Golden Vine Winery** (a wine shop that sells a vast selection of California vintages), and **Treasures in Paradise** (offering a broad selection of DCA merchandise as well as toys).

The **Off the Page Shop** (found near the Disney Animation attraction) sells mid- to high-priced collectibles, such as limited edition Disney animation cells, posters suitable for framing, and collectible character statues, plus the usual Disney-themed souvenir merchandise.

Throughout DCA (as well as Disneyland), you'll find many shops and kiosks that are **Disney Collector Pins Trading Centers.** Here, you can purchase hundreds of different collectible pins (many of which are limited editions). You can also trade with cast members or other guests. Many collectors proudly wear their pins on baseball hats, on specially made lanyards, or on their clothing. The pin collector lanyards are priced at $10 each. The cost of the actual enamel pins begins at $6.50 each and goes up from there.

For $14.95, a special photo pin is available. Your picture is taken, placed on a Disney-themed backdrop you select, and then transformed into a stunning pin. This is a wonderful addition to any collection because it's personalized.

Somewhat less expensive collectibles you'll find throughout the park are crushed pennies imprinted with Disney-related designs commemorating a specific attraction, ride, character, or event. In many of the shops, you'll find small machines in which you insert a penny (along with two quarters for payment). Right before your eyes, the penny will be flattened and imprinted with the design of your choice.

Each machine allows you to choose from three different designs, and there are many different machines located throughout the park. For an additional $5, you can also purchase a small imprinted binder in which to store and display your penny souvenirs. This is a relatively inexpensive collectible for kids (ages eight and up).

CHAPTER 12

DCA's Parades, Shows, and Special Events

IN ADDITION TO THE MANY ATTRACTIONS and rides that pay tribute to the state of California, Disney's California Adventure features live family-oriented entertainment in the form of shows, parades, and special events. All of these events add to the overall experience you'll have as you explore this theme park.

Disney's Electrical Parade

Ages 2–4:	★★
Ages 5–10:	★★★
Ages 11–15:	★★★
Ages 16–Adult:	★★★
Senior Citizens:	★★★

When the sun sets, DCA becomes the stage for a classic Disney parade that was a staple for decades at Disneyland. Guests of all ages will enjoy this charming presentation featuring many of the classic Disney characters and dozens of parade floats covered in thousands of colorful sparkling lights.

Disney's Electrical Parade creates a truly magical entertainment experience that's presented nightly along DCA's parade route, which begins in Sunshine Plaza and concludes in Paradise Bay.

For the best viewing location, be sure to stake out your spot along the parade route at least thirty minutes before the scheduled show time. While Disney parades come and go, this one continues to be a favorite. It's definitely worth seeing, even if it means leaving the park in the afternoon, taking a nap, and returning after dark for the parade. On nights when Disney's Electrical Parade is presented twice, the later show is always the least crowded.

══FAST FACT

DCA has arranged for a limited number of guests each night to enjoy an elegant meal while watching **Disney's Electrical Parade** from an exclusive viewing location. Advance reservations are required. Call ✆(714) 781-4400.

The Power of BLAST!

Ages 2–4:	★
Ages 5–10:	★★★
Ages 11–15:	★★★
Ages 16–Adult:	★★★
Senior Citizens:	★★

Located in the heart of The Hollywood Pictures Backlot area is The Hyperion Theater, a large indoor theater which is currently the home of *The Power of BLAST!*, a musical show based on the Tony-award winning Broadway show. While not based on any Disney characters, TV show or movie, this live show is an unusual musical performance.

Although the shows themselves are very different, *The Power of BLAST!* can loosely be compared to the Broadway shows *Blue Man Group* and *Stomp!* in terms of its unique, high-energy musical performance. Although a bit loud at times, this show appeals to people of all ages.

Shows are presented throughout the day (except Tuesdays) within The Hyperion Theater, which seats 2,000 guests in a comfortable and air conditioned environment. While all of the seats within the theater are excellent, for the best seats, arrive to the theater between 20 and 30 minutes prior to the posted show time.

Checking out this show in the middle of the afternoon to break up a hectic day provides for a relaxing and enjoyable break. The show itself lasts about 30 minutes. For an additional fee (in addition to DCA park admission), a special dinner show package is available. For details about this dinner/show package, call ☎ (714) 781-DINE.

Disney's Eureka! A California Parade

Ages 2–4:	★★
Ages 5–10:	★★★
Ages 11–15:	★★★
Ages 16–Adult:	★★
Senior Citizens:	★★

Just as Disneyland offers a daytime character parade, the streets of DCA become the parade route for Disney's Eureka! A California Parade. While not a character-based parade, this kid-oriented presentation features dozens of performers, acrobats, live musicians, dancers, and oversize puppets—all wearing colorful costumes and riding on elaborate parade floats. The parade celebrates the "Spirit of the Golden Dream" and the energy, vitality, and diversity of the people, cultures, and heritage of California.

≡FAST FACT

This park is always evolving, and the parades and shows are subject to change. So, don't be surprised if the live entertainment is different from what's described here.

Although this parade probably won't become a classic, like Disney's Electrical Parade, and does not feature the Disney characters, it is nevertheless entertaining for the younger set. If you're on a tight schedule, your best bet is to skip this parade and take advantage of the shorter lines for the rides and attractions while the parade is under way. If you have time to spare and you're traveling with kids, however, this parade is worth checking out.

Disney's Eureka! A California Parade is presented once or twice per day (typically in the afternoon) and follows the same route as Disney's Electrical Parade.

Goofy's Beach Party Bash

Ages 2–4:	★★★
Ages 5–10:	★★★
Ages 11–15:	★★
Ages 16–Adult:	★
Senior Citizens:	★

Located in the Hollywood Pictures Backlot, across from the Superstar Limo attraction, is a relatively small outdoor stage where Goofy's Beach Party Bash is presented several times throughout the day. This is a kid-oriented musical show that is special because of its intimate setting (there are benches that surround the stage that offer a close-up view) and the fact that the Disney characters stick around after the show to meet and greet guests. It is an excellent photo opportunity with the popular Disney characters.

In this twenty-minute show, Donald Duck directs Goofy and his son Max in a spoof of a beach movie. Special guest stars include Mickey and Minnie Mouse. The show is presented at least six times per day. If you arrive early, try to get your kids seated in the first row or two for the best view of the characters.

≡FAST FACT

Along with the parades and shows, throughout the day and evening, chances are you'll experience other live entertainment in the form of street performers, musicians, and entertainers, all of whom contribute to the overall upbeat atmosphere of the park.

The Junior Explorer Program

Ages 2–4:	★★★
Ages 5–10:	★★★
Ages 11–15:	★
Ages 16–Adult:	N.S.
Senior Citizens:	N.S.

If you're traveling with children, be sure to stop by the Junior Explorer kiosk in the Sunshine Plaza area. Here, you can pick up a free Junior Explorer Game & Guidemap, which encourages kids to embark on a scavenger hunt as they experience the theme park. At predefined locations, kids who participate are given special stickers. Only by collecting all six stickers is the child awarded the title "Junior Explorer." Upon presenting a guide map with all six stickers at the Engine-Ears Toys shop, a special ID card will be presented to the young guest.

TRAVEL TIP

> By following the guidebook, you'll be directed to the best kid-oriented attractions and rides within the park. This is a great activity for kids under the age of twelve and their parents. Best of all, it's free!

Ahwahnee Camp Circle Story Theater

Ages 2–4:	★★★
Ages 5–10:	★★★
Ages 11–15:	★
Ages 16–Adult:	N.S.
Senior Citizens:	N.S.

In the Redwood Creek Challenge Trail area of the park, a special live show is presented several times each day. This show shares the legends and myths of California's indigenous Americans, the Miwoks. This kid-oriented show (which will appeal to kids under the age of twelve) also includes traditional campfire ghost stories. Show times are posted within the Redwood Creek Challenge Trail area.

Disney's LuminAria

Ages 2–4:	★★
Ages 5–10:	★★★
Ages 11–15:	★★★
Ages 16–Adult:	★★★
Senior Citizens:	★★★

During the holiday season (early November through early January), DCA features a special holiday presentation, called Disney's LuminAria. Featuring innovative pyrotechnic effects set to a stirring soundtrack, Disney's LuminAria encourages guests to actually become part of the heartwarming show.

Before watching the show, guests are invited to the LuminAria Holiday Art Card Center (located within the park), where they can create personalized Art Cards. For each performance of LuminAria, more than a hundred cards are selected and included in the show. Within the cards, guests are encouraged to write down a holiday wish or remembrance. These special wishes will ultimately shine as thousands of points of candlelight during the show's grand finale.

 TRAVEL TIP

This is just one of the special events presented as part of DCA's seasonal holiday celebration. For more information, check out the *Souvenir Map and Guide to Disney's California Adventure.*

CHAPTER 13

Special Services at the Disney Theme Parks

OVER THE YEARS, more than 450 million people have visited The Disneyland Resort. In order to cater to the needs of its guests, the Disney theme parks offer a wide range of special services. This chapter describes many of these services and how to take advantage of them.

ATMs

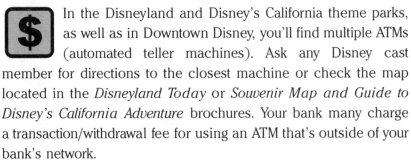 In the Disneyland and Disney's California theme parks, as well as in Downtown Disney, you'll find multiple ATMs (automated teller machines). Ask any Disney cast member for directions to the closest machine or check the map located in the *Disneyland Today* or *Souvenir Map and Guide to Disney's California Adventure* brochures. Your bank many charge a transaction/withdrawal fee for using an ATM that's outside of your bank's network.

Near the main entrance of Disneyland, along Main Street, U.S.A., you'll find the Bank of Main Street, which offers basic banking services as well as an ATM. With proper identification, you can cash a check for up to $100, made payable to "Disneyland," at the Bank of Main Street and at the main entrance of each theme park. A similar check-cashing service is available at the front desks of the Disney hotels (for hotel guests only).

Throughout The Disneyland Resort, cash (U.S. currency), traveler's checks, Disney Dollars, personal checks, Visa, MasterCard, American Express, JCB, the Disney Credit Card, and Discover Card are accepted. Credit cards are not accepted at the various food and merchandise kiosks located throughout the parks.

≡FAST FACT

Foreign currency exchange services are available at the Bank of Main Street and at the Thomas Exchange (in Downtown Disney).

Child Care

Baby Centers can be found in both Disney theme parks. Clean facilities for preparing formulas, warming bottles, nursing, and changing diapers are provided. For a small fee, you can buy various baby products at these locations. Changing tables can also be found in almost all of the public restrooms in the theme parks. In Disneyland, you'll find the Baby Care Center on the northeast end of Main Street, U.S.A. (in an alley). In Disney's California Adventure, the Baby Care Center can be found next to the Mission Tortilla Factory.

Baby-Sitting Services

Although The Disneyland Resort doesn't officially offer baby-sitting services to guests, if you're staying at one of the Disney hotels, you can coordinate private baby-sitting services by contacting the concierge or front desk. Disney's Grand Californian Hotel offers Pinocchio's Workshop, a child activity center that's open from 5:00 P.M. to midnight.

In the Anaheim area, there are two independent **Kinder Care Learning Centers,** located at ⌨ 2515 East South Street, ✆ (714) 774-5141, and ⌨ 2560 E. La Palma Avenue, ✆ (714) 991-5443.

Stroller Rentals

Both theme parks offer stroller rentals for $7 per day (or $12 for two strollers per day). The rental locations are near the entrance of each theme park. When renting a stroller, be sure to keep the receipt with you at all times. If you park your stroller to experience an attraction, and your stroller is gone when you return, simply go to a stroller replacement center or the main rental area for a replacement. Ask any Disney cast members for the location of the nearest replacement center.

 TRAVEL TIP

Because you'll be leaving the stroller unattended (parked outside of each attraction you experience), it's an excellent idea to rent a stroller when you get to one of the theme parks. Do not plan on bringing your own. Also, never leave anything valuable within the storage compartments of the stroller.

Emergency and Health-Related Services

No matter what type of emergency you experience, medical or otherwise, contact the nearest Disney cast member immediately. Those who work at Disneyland are highly trained to deal with virtually any type of emergency, such as lost children, medical-related problems, and lost or stolen items.

Disneyland and Disney's California Adventure have fully equipped first aid stations. Various amenities, such as pain relievers, sunblock, and bandages, can be purchased at many of the gift shops, including those along Main Street, U.S.A. (in Disneyland).

If a child gets lost in one of the theme parks, report it immediately. Children (under age eleven) who are found are taken to Disney's Child Services office, while people over the age of twelve are taken to City Hall in Disneyland or Guest Services in Disney's

California Adventure. To contact **Disney's Child Services,** call ✆ (714) 781-4210.

When adults get separated, messages can be left at either City Hall (Disneyland) or Guest Relations (Disney's California Adventure). It's highly recommended, however, that you predetermine a location and time to meet if you get separated within the theme parks.

Health-Related Services

The closest pharmacy to The Disneyland Resort, located about one mile away, is **Sav-On Drugs** at ▢ 1660 West Katella Avenue, ✆ (714) 530-0500. This pharmacy is open until 10:00 P.M. on weekdays, 8:00 P.M. on Saturdays, and 6:00 P.M. on Sundays. Another Sav-On Drugs, open twenty-four hours a day, is located about 5 miles from **The Disneyland Resort** at ▢ 12031 Brookhurst Street in Garden Grove. The telephone number is ✆ (714) 530-5280.

Refrigeration facilities for prescription medications (such as insulin or antibiotics) are available, free of charge, in both theme parks and in the Disney hotels. Contact the First Aid office or Guest Relations for more information.

 **TRAVEL TIP**

Before leaving on vacation, make sure to obtain copies of any prescriptions you might need to take with you, along with contact information for your doctor and medical insurance company. Then, if you need to have your prescription refilled, it will be much less of a hassle.

In-Room Medical Care

If during your stay in Anaheim or anywhere in the Los Angeles area you need medical attention, you can arrange to have a doctor come directly to your hotel room for a consultation, twenty-four hours a day. If the doctor you see prescribes medication, that prescription will be delivered directly to your hotel room as part of the service.

House Call Physicians is covered by most medical insurance

plans and major credit cards are accepted. It is not operated by or affiliated with The Walt Disney Company. For information about **House Call Physicians,** call ☏ (800) DOCS-911. This is a licensed medical practice, not a telephone referral service.

Services for the Disabled

The Disneyland Resort offers a wide range of services for physically disabled guests. Manually operated wheelchairs and Electric Convenience Vehicles can be rented (for a small daily fee) near the entrance of either theme park. If you're staying at a Disney hotel, complimentary wheelchairs are available from the hotel. See the front desk for details.

For guests with visual disabilities, a special Braille guidebook is available, free of charge, from City Hall (in Disneyland) or Guest Relations (in Disney's California Adventure). For those with hearing impairments, closed captioning is available on many of the movie/video-based attractions, written storylines are available for virtually all of the rides and attractions, and some of the rides and attractions use Assistive Listening Systems. (The receiver is available from City Hall in Disneyland or DCA's Guest Relations.)

For additional information about the various services available for disabled guests, call **Guest Relations** at ☏ (714) 781-4773. A free publication, called *The Guidebook for Guests with Disabilities,* offers information about accessibility to the various rides, shows, attractions, shops, and restaurants in the theme parks. This guide is available from Guest Relations.

If you have special dietary needs, speak with the chef at any of the sit-down restaurants in The Disneyland Resort. Whenever possible, your special needs will almost always be met.

All of the Disney hotels also offer special accommodations for the disabled. These accommodations must be reserved in advance, when making your actual reservation. Guests with almost any type of disability will find that their needs are met. In some cases, however, you may need to plan ahead to ensure that the proper accommodations and/or services will be available at the time of your visit.

≡FAST FACT

In Downtown Disney, the First Aid center is located between Ralph Brennan's Jazz Kitchen and Island Charters.

Religious Services

 To find a house of worship or nearby religious services, check any local Anaheim/Orange County telephone book or ask the front desk (or concierge) at your hotel. Synagogues, churches (Baptist, Catholic, Episcopal, Lutheran, and United Methodist), and a variety of other houses of worship are located in the Anaheim area. In many cases, free shuttle service is available from The Disneyland Resort to the house of worship of your choice.

Lockers

 Lockers are available for rent in both Disney theme parks. While visiting the parks, you'll want to keep your hands as free as possible. Storing items you bring into the park or that you purchase (souvenirs) is an excellent strategy. You can store an extra change of clothing, jackets, or camera equipment until you need it. Renting a locker is a lot more convenient than running back and forth to your parked car or hotel room, which will typically require a long walk and/or a tram ride.

Depending on the size of the locker, rental rates range from $1 to $5 per day. Locker space is somewhat limited. On busy days, they tend to be totally filled by noon at the latest.

Lost and Found

 There's a Lost & Found office located in both theme parks. If you lose an item, report it missing as quickly as possible. If someone returns the item quickly, you can pick it up at the Lost & Found office. If the item is found after your departure from the park, the Walt Disney Company will mail it to you at whatever address you provide. If you find someone else's lost item, bring it to one of the park's Lost & Found offices. If the item is not claimed in sixty days, you have the option of keeping it.

═FAST FACT

You'll find the Lost & Found office just off Main Street, U.S.A. (in Disneyland) behind the Market House. In Disney's California Adventure, the Lost & Found is located across from Guest Services.

Package Express Service

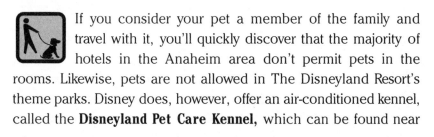 If you're staying at one of the Disney hotels, one of the perks is that whenever you purchase a souvenir, for example, you can have it delivered directly to your hotel room, free of charge. This means you won't have to carry around your purchases or store them in lockers.

If you aren't staying at one of the Disney hotels, you can arrange to have your purchases delivered and held at the Package Express Pickup Window, located just outside the main entrance to the theme parks. You can pick up your items at the end of the day. This is a complimentary service.

Pet Care

If you consider your pet a member of the family and travel with it, you'll quickly discover that the majority of hotels in the Anaheim area don't permit pets in the rooms. Likewise, pets are not allowed in The Disneyland Resort's theme parks. Disney does, however, offer an air-conditioned kennel, called the **Disneyland Pet Care Kennel,** which can be found near the main parking structure. For $10, pets can be boarded during the day, but they must be picked up at night. For more information about rates and availability, call ☎ (714) 781-4565.

 TRAVEL TIP

Although Disney provides kennel facilities, the cast members who work at the kennels do not handle the pets. Guests must place their pet in an assigned cage and are encouraged to visit their pet several times during the day/night to walk and feed it. If you're interested in a full-service kennel facility, there are several located outside Disney property.

Public Telephones

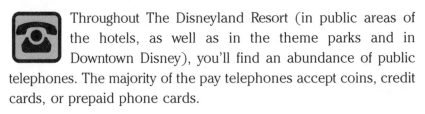 Throughout The Disneyland Resort (in public areas of the hotels, as well as in the theme parks and in Downtown Disney), you'll find an abundance of public telephones. The majority of the pay telephones accept coins, credit cards, or prepaid phone cards.

≡FAST FACT

Even if you're over the age of twenty-one, Disneyland does not permit alcoholic beverages anywhere in the theme park. Alcohol, however, is served at several dining locations in Disney's California Adventure, as well as in Downtown Disney. It's important to remember, however, that Disney security will not tolerate disorderly conduct from people under the influence of alcohol.

Virtually all of the nationwide cellular services work in the Anaheim area (and in The Disneyland Resort). Depending on your cellular service or digital PCS contract, however, you may be charged per-minute roaming fees, so contact your cellular service provider for details.

When using a public phone, local calls cost thirty-five cents. Long-distance rates vary. If you can find a good deal on a calling card (with no per-call surcharge and only a per-minute rate), this will probably be the least expensive option when using a pay phone or making calls from a hotel room.

Before making calls from your hotel room, determine what the surcharges will be. Some hotels charge $1 or more every time you pick up the phone to make an outgoing call, even if you're calling locally or using a toll-free phone number.

CHAPTER 14

Exploring Downtown Disney

WHETHER YOU'RE LOOKING for Disney-oriented nightlife or an alternative to spending time during the day in the Disney theme parks, Downtown Disney can provide many hours of entertainment, with shopping, dining, and activities designed for people of all ages. Adults will enjoy the boutiques, bars, and cafés, while younger people will appreciate the toy shops, novelty stores, candy shops, and theme restaurants.

The Lowdown on Downtown Disney

 Operating hours are from 7:00 A.M. to 2:00 A.M. For more information, call **General Information** at ✆ (714) 300-7800 or visit ✍ *www.Disneyland.com.*

While The Disneyland Resort is known for its theme parks, Downtown Disney adds a fun, theme parklike twist to the dining and shopping experience during the day or late into the evening. Conveniently located about a one-minute walk from the main entrances of Disneyland and Disney's California Adventure (as well as several Disney-owned hotels), Downtown Disney offers a wide range of family-oriented dining options, plenty of upscale shopping, plus a handful of attractions and activities. Checking out Downtown Disney is a great way to spend several hours when you're not exploring the theme parks.

Whether you're looking to relax and enjoy breakfast before spending a day at one of the Disney theme parks, you want to enjoy a sit-down lunch or dinner, or you're in the mood for a late-night snack, Downtown Disney offers many dining options, including several theme restaurants, such as ESPN Zone and the Rainforest Café.

If you don't find the perfect gifts and souvenirs in the Disney theme parks, chances are you'll find exactly what you're looking for in the many shops of Downtown Disney. Some of these shops are exclusive to Downtown Disney, while others (like Illuminations and Sephora) are more common chain stores you'd find at an upscale mall.

TRAVEL TIP

When leaving either Disney theme park, be sure to have your hand stamped at the exit and keep your Disney Passport (admission ticket) handy. You'll need both the passport and a hand stamp to re-enter the park. You're welcome to enter and exit the Disney theme parks as often as you wish on the day your passport is valid.

When it comes to entertainment, the AMC Theaters offer a dozen state-of-the-art theaters showing the latest movies, and many of the restaurants offer live entertainment. The House of Blues, for example, contains an indoor theater where concerts and special events featuring well-known recording artists are regularly held.

Lovely landscaping that includes fountains and waterfalls surrounds the shops, restaurants, and attractions. Near the AMC Theaters, various entertaining attractions, such as a live interactive exotic bird show, are presented throughout the day.

Getting to Downtown Disney

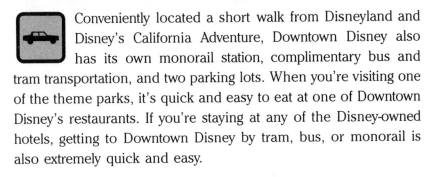

Conveniently located a short walk from Disneyland and Disney's California Adventure, Downtown Disney also has its own monorail station, complimentary bus and tram transportation, and two parking lots. When you're visiting one of the theme parks, it's quick and easy to eat at one of Downtown Disney's restaurants. If you're staying at any of the Disney-owned hotels, getting to Downtown Disney by tram, bus, or monorail is also extremely quick and easy.

Parking

If you're planning to drive to The Disneyland Resort and spend the day at one of the theme parks, it's definitely cheaper to park in one of the theme park's parking lots (for a flat rate of $7 per day). There is no separate admission charge to visit Downtown Disney.

Downtown Disney also has two conveniently located parking lots (off Disneyland Drive). The parking fees, however, can be significantly higher than the fees for the less convenient Mickey & Friends theme park parking lot (depending on how much time you plan to spend in this area).

══FAST FACT

Located near the Disney monorail station is a ticket booth where you can buy theme park tickets. The line at this booth is typically significantly shorter than the ticket booths located directly in front of the two Disney theme parks.

For self-parking, the first three hours are free of charge with validation from any shop or restaurant in the area. After that, there's a $6 per hour parking fee (billed in twenty-minute increments). The maximum daily parking fee is $30. If you prefer valet parking, drop your car off right in front of Downtown Disney for an additional $6 flat fee, plus the regular self-parking rates.

Complimentary bicycle parking is available. Complimentary and conveniently located guest drop-off areas are available at Magic Way and Downtown Drive (near Rainforest Café) and on Harbor Boulevard, just south of the Esplanade intersection.

Driving Directions

Whether you're driving your own car or a rental, there's plenty of parking available at The Disneyland Resort. If you're staying at one of the Disney-owned hotels, you'll often save time and money by parking at your hotel and taking the complimentary bus, tram, or monorail transportation to Downtown Disney. Some independent hotels, motels, and resorts also offer complimentary shuttle bus transportation to and from Downtown Disney (and the theme parks).

The following are basic driving directions to Downtown Disney from Interstate-5:

- From the Southbound 5 freeway, take the Disneyland Drive/Ball Road exit. At the end of the exit ramp, turn left on Disneyland Drive; then stay in one of the two right-hand lanes. Follow the Downtown Disney signs. After passing Ball Road, turn right onto Magic Way; then get into the left-most lane. As you approach the Downtown Disney North Parking Lot, turn left into the lot.
- From the Northbound 5 freeway, take the Katella/Disney Way exit. At the traffic light (at the end of the exit ramp), turn left onto Katella. Pass through the Cross Harbor Boulevard intersection. The following intersection will be Disneyland Drive. Turn right at this intersection (onto Disneyland Drive), and take an immediate left into the Downtown Disney South parking lot.

Taking the Tram

The Disney Tram service operates continuously between Downtown Disney, Disneyland, Disney's California Adventure, the Mickey & Friends Parking Lot, and the Timon Parking Lot. The tram operates for two hours after the Disneyland and Disney's California Adventure theme parks close.

Transportation from the Disney-Owned Hotels

A complimentary Disney double-decker shuttle bus service is available between all of the Disney-owned hotels and Downtown Disney. This bus also makes a stop at the Mickey & Friends Parking Lot. In less than five minutes, however, you can easily walk from The Disneyland Hotel and Disney's Grand Californian Hotel.

Taking the Monorail

The Disneyland Monorail operates between Downtown Disney and Disneyland. You must have a valid Disneyland Passport (or annual pass) to ride the monorail.

 TRAVEL TIP

As soon as you arrive at Downtown Disney, pick up a free Downtown Disney Show Schedule, available from any information kiosk or ticket counter. This will provide you with special event show times and keep you apprised of what's happening the week of your trip at ESPN Zone, House of Blues, AMC Theaters, Ralph Brennan's Jazz Kitchen, and Y Arriba Y Arriba.

Activities and Attractions

 Shopping and dining are definitely the main offerings at Downtown Disney. However, in addition to the live entertainment offered at many of the restaurants within this area, you can also experience the following activities and attractions:

AMC Theaters

☏ (714) 769-4AMC for show times and information
Noon to 11:00 P.M. (hours of operation)

After a fun-filled day at one of the Disney theme parks, or perhaps to fill the time during a rainy day or evening, you can catch a movie at the AMC Theaters located in the heart of Downtown Disney. Each of the twelve screens offers a state-of-the-art THX sound system, plus stadium seating. This is a 60,000-square-foot movie theater complex, complete with multiple concession stands. Matinee and late-night showings of the various movies are typically available to accommodate your vacation schedule.

ESPN Zone

  📞 (714) 300-ESPN for reservations and information
  ✎ *http://espn.go.com/espninc/zone*

    The restaurant and gift shop are open on:
        Monday–Thursday: 11:30 A.M. to midnight
        Friday: 11:30 A.M. to 1:00 A.M.
        Saturday: 9:00 A.M. to 1:00 A.M.
        Sunday: 9:00 A.M. to midnight

    The Bar & Sports Arena (arcade) is open:
        Monday–Thursday: 11:30 A.M. to midnight
        Friday: 11:30 A.M. to 2:00 A.M.
        Saturday: 9:00 A.M. to 2:00 A.M.
        Sunday: 9:00 A.M. to midnight

Based on the popular sports-oriented cable network (owned and operated by the Walt Disney Company), the ESPN Zone offers a theme-dining experience combined with a state-of-the-art sports bar (for adults) and a tremendous arcade for sports fans of all ages. In the main dining room, there's also a working T.V. studio where *ESPN Up Close with Gary Miller* is taped on weekdays. This T.V. show often features special guests, including well-known professional athletes.

Located near the main entrance of ESPN Zone is also an ESPN Radio studio, where you'll often find live radio broadcasts taking place. In addition to watching the live sports programming that originates from this location, you can also check out virtually any televised sporting event that's currently taking place on the dozens of large T.V. screens located throughout the complex. There's even a movie screen–size T.V. in the main bar area. If you need to use the restroom during a televised sports event, don't worry—you won't miss a second of the game or event. There are even video monitors located in the restrooms.

Upstairs, on the second floor, is a giant arcade that features dozens of sports-oriented arcade games and interactive activities, such as the Xtreme Glacier indoor rock-climbing facility. As with any arcade, guests pay for each arcade game or activity separately. Game cards (used instead of quarters or tokens for the arcade games) are available in $5 increments.

During the NFL season, ABC-T.V.'s post–Monday Night football show, *Monday Night Live*, broadcasts live from the ESPN Zone. This show features sportscasters Bill Weir, Rob Fukuzaki, and Curt Sandoval, who offer game highlights, interviews, contests, and post-game analysis. Former Los Angeles Ram and NFL Hall of Famer Jackie Slater and former NFL great Bob Golic often join the hosts.

Of course, there's also an ESPN gift shop located in the complex. You'll find a wide range of ESPN logo merchandize and other sports-oriented memorabilia.

⊕ HOT SPOT

RPM 2 Night is one of the ESPN Zone's most popular interactive experiences. Prepare yourself to enter the pits and climb aboard a Formula One race car for a four-minute thrill ride. Take the race car for a spin around the virtual track and test your driving skills against another driver. Feel the wind in your face as you reach 200 miles per hour.

Exotic Bird Show

As you walk through Downtown Disney and enjoy the lush landscaping and upscale shops, you may come across one or two people training several exotic birds. Just outside the AMC Theaters and near Rainforest Café, you'll find a small stage where an exotic bird show is presented at various times throughout the day. Not only is this a chance to learn about the exotic birds and see them perform tricks, you can have your picture taken with one of the birds. It makes for an awesome photo opportunity and an inexpensive souvenir. Kids, in particular, will enjoy this interactive show.

House of Blues

✆ (714) 781-4560 for reservations and information

✍ *www.HOB.com* or ✍ *www.ticketmaster.com*

This popular theme restaurant often features live entertainment in the main dining room. However, within the House of Blues theater, big-name recording artists perform in an intimate setting. Don't be fooled by the name of this establishment. Pop, R & B, hip-hop, and rock-and-roll acts are often featured.

Ticket prices for the evening concerts range from $5 to $30. Although tickets can be purchased in advance from Ticketmaster, you can often pick up day-of-show tickets at the House of Blues box office. Keep in mind, for all shows and concerts at House of Blues, doors open one hour prior to show time.

🧳 TRAVEL TIP

The Downtown Disney area lights up at night and offers a festive atmosphere for a romantic evening stroll or a less romantic evening shopping spree. Consider leaving your young children with a baby-sitter if you plan to enjoy Downtown Disney's nightlife.

Shopping in Downtown Disney

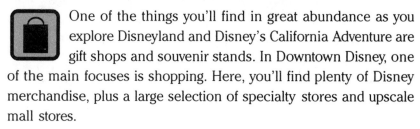 One of the things you'll find in great abundance as you explore Disneyland and Disney's California Adventure are gift shops and souvenir stands. In Downtown Disney, one of the main focuses is shopping. Here, you'll find plenty of Disney merchandise, plus a large selection of specialty stores and upscale mall stores.

The following descriptions of the stores you'll find within Downtown Disney are listed in alphabetical order. A complimentary map of Downtown Disney can be obtained from any Disneyland information kiosk, the Compass Newsstand, or any Disney-owned hotel.

 TRAVEL TIP

Even in special play areas designed for kids, like the one you'll find in the LEGO Imagination Center, never leave your children unsupervised anywhere in Downtown Disney.

Basin

Transform your bathroom at home (or even your hotel room) into a lavish spa when you purchase any of the fancy soaps, shampoos, body and bath products available from this upscale store. The prices aren't cheap, but the products are among the best from around the world. Indulge yourself or pick up some gifts for friends or loved ones who enjoy pampering themselves.

Build-A-Bear Workshop

One of the newest shops is a teddy bear factory where kids (and adults) can actually create their own teddy bear, choose an outfit for it, and then adopt it. Kids in particular will enjoy creating their own, one-of-a-kind teddy bear. For more information, visit ✐ *www.buildabear.com*.

Compass Books & Café

If you're looking for a bestseller to read by the pool, or want to browse this bookshop's large selection of travel books, Compass Books & Café is an upscale bookstore that also offers an impressive children's book section. In addition to the latest book releases, the café area serves gourmet coffees and bakery products. Limited seating is available both inside and outdoors.

Department 56

Inside this store, Christmas is celebrated 365 days per year. Here, you'll find an extensive selection of holiday decorations and collectibles, plus many miniature Christmas village displays. This is a wonderful store for adults to browse through. A visit here will definitely help get you into the Christmas spirit, even if it's mid-July. At home, if you need a touch of Disney magic combined with a taste of the holiday season, visit the **Department 56** Web site at ✍ *www.department56.com.*

Hoypoloi

This gallery and gift shop offers a wonderful selection of exotic art, some of which has an Eastern inspiration. If you're shopping for unique housewarming or wedding gifts, or want something nice for your own home, check out the unusual offerings at Hoypoloi. This upscale store will appeal to adults and features breakable items that should be kept away from kids.

≡FAST FACT

Located near ESPN Zone and the AMC Theaters, you'll find the Compass Newsstand, a newsstand (offering a wide selection of newspapers and magazines) that doubles as an information booth. This is a great meeting place for family members who separate when exploring Downtown Disney.

Illuminations

Scented candles of all shapes and sizes are available from Illuminations. This is the same chain store found in many upscale malls. In addition to the candles themselves, you'll find a wide selection of candleholders and accessories that can help you create a beautiful candlelit ambiance in any setting. After a long day at the theme parks, you might want to pick up a soothing aromatherapy candle to relax with in your hotel room. To see a sampling of what Illuminations offers before leaving home, check out the company's Web site at ✍ *www.illuminations.com.*

Island Charters

Clothing and accessories for adults with a nautical and aviation theme are offered here. Whether you're looking for casual wear or beachwear, you'll find popular designer labels in this shop. As you browse, you'll be entertained by upbeat beach music, such as "Surfing USA" from the Beach Boys.

Kiosks

Throughout Downtown Disney, you'll find a selection of kiosks that sell a wide range of products and souvenirs. One of the more popular kiosks sells Balzac toys (colorful and lightweight balls that are perfect for the pool or beach). Another popular kiosk offers hair wraps, which is the perfect "fashion statement" for anyone looking to add a touch of color and fun to their medium-length to long hair. Colored threads are interwoven with beads and your hair to create simple or complex designs and styles. Hair wraps are a favorite among kids and teens. Be sure to get a price quote before the hair wrap is done. The average price is between $8 and $20 per strand, depending on the length and bead selection.

LEGO Imagination Center

Kids of all ages will enjoy exploring this large and colorful store that offers everything related to LEGO. In addition to life-size LEGO statues of Darth Vader and R2-D2 from *Star Wars*, for example, you'll discover that this shop sells every current LEGO set in existence. There are also play areas for young people to build small LEGO projects. In addition to LEGO sets, the LEGO Imagination Center sells a wide range of LEGO accessory products and logo merchandise, such as watches and T-shirts.

Liquid Planet

Do you like to surf? Whether you're a surfer dude or simply looking for beach attire that will help you look stylish as you soak up the sun near your hotel's pool, you'll find a colorful selection of beach, tropical, and surf attire for both men and women available here.

Mainspring

Are you always running late? Well, this shop offers nothing but wristwatches in every style and from virtually every designer you can think of. Whether you're looking for something sporty or elegant, you'll find watches from Swatch, Armitron, Timex, Casio, Fossil, Nike, Armani, and many others.

▮ TRAVEL TIP

Surprisingly enough, what was not on display at Mainspring when this book was being written were Mickey Mouse or Disney inspired watches.

Marceline's Confectionery

Any sweet tooth can be satisfied with a visit to this upscale candy store that offers prepackaged candies and gourmet jelly beans, along with homemade treats, such as caramel apples, fudge, and cookies. The price of a caramel apple with various toppings, such as nuts, ranges from $3 to $4. This is the perfect place to stop for dessert on the go.

Petals

Designer women's purses and pocketbooks, along with a selection of leather wallets and other leather products from Coach, Guess, Jill Stuart, and other designers are what you'll find in this upscale boutique.

Sephora

Some of the world's best-known skincare products, cosmetics, fragrances, and soaps (for both men and women) are available at this relatively large Sephora store. You'll find this retail chain, which is staffed by knowledgeable sales associates, at many upscale malls. Indulge yourself or pick up a gift for a friend or loved one who enjoys pampering themselves. For a preview of what you'll find in the store, visit the company's Web site at ✑ *www.Sephora.com.*

Soliton

Here in Southern California, the sun can get pretty intense. If you accidentally forgot your sunglasses or you're shopping around for a pair that's more stylish, you'll find an incredibly large selection of designer sunglasses for men, women, and children at Soliton. See the latest styles and find sunglasses that enhance your image while protecting your eyes.

Something Silver

As the name suggests, this store offers a large selection of silver jewelry, including bracelets, earrings, necklaces, and charms. The prices are pretty reasonable.

Starabilias

Located across from the Rainforest Café, this unusual antique and collectibles showroom and store allows you to take home valuable pieces of pop culture and history. Whether you consider yourself a collector, Starabilias is a fun place for adults and teens to explore. Here, you'll find genuine items, such as an antique Coca-Cola vending machine (which can be yours for $8,995), a

1930s Texaco gas pump (suggested retail price $10,000), and a Ty Cobb autographed baseball bat (which you can own for $10,000).

A wide range of autographed memorabilia from politicians, recording artists, Hollywood's superstars, and historical figures are also available. The inventory of this store changes regularly. In addition to high-priced collectibles, you'll find a selection of inexpensive toys and collectibles.

⟹FAST FACT

For a preview of the items you'll find at **Starabilias** or to place an order online, you can visit the company's Web site at ✍ www.Starabilias.com.

Tin Pan Alley

Toys and trinkets symbolizing today's pop culture can be purchased. At Tin Pan Alley, you'll find a large assortment of collectible refrigerator magnets, posters, and other inexpensive toys, such as a collection of toys based on storybook character Curious George. This is a fun place to explore with kids, although you'll find few (if any) Disney-themed items.

World of Disney

Prepare yourself to experience the ultimate collection of Disney merchandise. In fact, this store offers the world's second largest collection of Disney clothing, jewelry, household items, toys, collectibles, artwork, sporting goods, plush toys, Disney movie merchandise, costumes, and many other items featuring Mickey, Minnie, and all of the other Disney characters.

Like a regular department store, World of Disney is divided into departments, each featuring its own type of Disney-themed merchandise. For example, there's a separate men's, women's, and children's clothing section, a toy department, and an area where household merchandise is showcased. This is the perfect one-stop shop for all of your Disney vacation souvenirs.

 TRAVEL TIP

If you're a member of the Disney Club, you can save up to 10 percent on all of your purchases at World of Disney. Also, if you're staying at a Disney-owned hotel, you can arrange to have your purchases delivered to your hotel room, so you don't need to carry them around as you explore Downtown Disney and beyond.

The Downtown Disney Dining Options

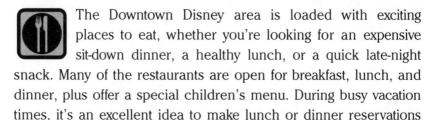 The Downtown Disney area is loaded with exciting places to eat, whether you're looking for an expensive sit-down dinner, a healthy lunch, or a quick late-night snack. Many of the restaurants are open for breakfast, lunch, and dinner, plus offer a special children's menu. During busy vacation times, it's an excellent idea to make lunch or dinner reservations at the more popular restaurants.

At night, many of the restaurants with a club atmosphere (that offer full bars), such as House of Blues, aren't necessarily suitable for young children. However, during breakfast, lunch, and dinner times, virtually all of the restaurants within Downtown Disney offer special children's menus or money-saving dining options if you're traveling with kids.

Virtually all of the restaurants here at Downtown Disney could be considered theme-dining experiences. Thus, in most cases, you'll be paying a premium to experience the atmosphere. In addition to the restaurants you'll find in Downtown Disney, the various Disney-owned hotels, such as The Disneyland Hotel, offer a handful of dining options at several different price ranges.

As you'll quickly discover, your dining choices are extensive. If you have a car, an abundance of dining options are just off The

Disneyland Resort property, throughout the Anaheim area. Some of the more popular off-property dining options are described elsewhere in the book. Because these aren't Disney-owned and operated (or on Disney property), the prices are often cheaper.

 TRAVEL TIP

If you're a Disneyland Annual Pass Holder or a member of the Disney Club, you can save 10 percent when you dine at many of the participating restaurants in Downtown Disney. Discounts at some restaurants are also available to American Express cardholders.

To help you find a restaurant that fits your dining budget, the following symbols are used to describe the price range of an overall per-person meal.

> **$:**   Under $10 per person
> **$$:**   Under $20 per person
> **$$$:**   Over $20 per person

Catal Restaurant & Uva Bar

✎ (714) 781-4560 or ✎ (714) 774-4442 for reservations

Price Range: $$/$$$

This lovely restaurant and bar offers outdoor seating, allowing you to enjoy the ambiance of Downtown Disney. The menu, however, is limited to a handful of Mediterranean dishes. Some of the house specialties include Greek chicken and lemon kabobs, North African steamed mussels, and Moroccan tuna skewers. A variety of vegetarian entrées is also available.

World-renowned chef Joachim Spilchal created the Catal Restaurant & Uva Bar. This more adult-oriented restaurant is an excellent place to enjoy an elegant lunch, dinner, late-night snack, or drinks.

Compass Books & Café

✎ (714) 774-4442

Price Range: $

This bookstore/coffee shop combination offers a selection of freshly brewed gourmet coffees and teas, plus an assortment of snacks. A limited amount of outdoor seating is available. While this is a great place for adults to take a breather and enjoy a cup of java, you won't find too many menu selections suitable for children.

ESPN Zone

✎ (714) 300-3776 for reservations

✐ *http://espn.go.com/espninc/zone*

Price Range: $$/$$$

This is the perfect dining experience for sports fans of all ages. This 35,000-square-foot complex includes a full-service restaurant, plus a state-of-the-art sports bar (for adults only). The restaurant offers a family dining experience with main entrées including cedar plank salmon, grilled chops, and New York strip steak. As you enjoy your lunch or dinner (brunch is served on weekends), you might catch a live broadcast of *ESPN Close- Up with Gary Miller*, which originates from an actual T.V. studio located in the main dining room on weekdays.

══FAST FACT

You can also visit the ESPN Zone in Atlanta, Baltimore, Chicago, Las Vegas, New York, and Washington, D.C.

Häagen-Dazs

✎ (714) 533-0070

Price Range: $

If you're in the mood to cool off with a scoop of gourmet ice cream, check out the selection of tasty treats offered at Häagen-Dazs. On the menu, you'll also find frozen yogurt, sorbet, and gelato, plus brownies, cookies, and specialty coffee drinks. The prices aren't cheap, but the snacks are delicious! A limited amount of outdoor seating is available.

House of Blues

☎ (714) 778-BLUE for reservations

✎ *www.HOB.com*

Price Range: $$/$$$

In addition to offering live musical entertainment at the House of Blues theater, this establishment features a full-service restaurant. Since this is a popular, family-oriented restaurant, you'll probably want to make lunch or dinner reservations, or be prepared to wait for a table. A full menu, including vegetarian dishes, and a children's menu is served daily. House specialties include Memphis-style ribs, cedar plank salmon with watercress-jicama salad, and Voodoo shrimp.

 **TRAVEL TIP**

Near the entrance of every restaurant you'll find the menu posted. Be sure to review the menu to ensure the restaurant you choose fits within your budget and offers a selection of foods that will appeal to everyone you're dining with. Some of the fine-dining restaurants will accommodate special requests. Be sure to check with the host or hostess.

La Brea Bakery Café

☎ (714) 490-0233

Price Range: $/$$/$$$

Open between 7:00 A.M. and midnight, seven days per week, this is the perfect place for the family to enjoy an affordable breakfast, lunch, dinner, or late-night snack. La Brea Bakery Café is really two dining establishments in one. Here, you can obtain a quick snack, which you can enjoy while on the go or sitting outside. The more formal dining area, however, includes both indoor and outdoor seating, plus a full menu that includes freshly baked breads and pastries, gourmet coffee drinks, sandwiches, and full entrées.

La Brea Bakery Café is located between Disneyland and Disney's California Adventure, right at the entrance of the Downtown Disney area. The main dining area offers a somewhat elegant and expensive, albeit limited, menu. Main entrées range from $10.75 to over $20. Soups and salads are priced between $6.50 and $12.75. One of the house specialties, a roasted half-chicken with crushed potatoes and bitter greens, is priced at $17.25. Despite the convenient location, this probably isn't the best place to dine with kids or teens, due to the limited menu and high prices.

Marceline's Confectionery
☏ (714) 300-7918
Price Range: $

In addition to offering a large selection of prepackaged candies and chocolates, Marceline's Confectionery can satisfy anyone's sweet tooth with its homemade caramel apples, fudge, and cookies.

Naples Ristorante e Pizzeria
☏ (714) 776-6200 for reservations
Price Range: $$/$$$

Gourmet pizza, made from the freshest available ingredients and baked in old-style wood-burning ovens, is the house specialty at this family-oriented restaurant that serves lunch, dinner, and late-night snacks. In addition to pizza, however, you'll find an assortment of Italian entrées.

TRAVEL TIP

> When The Disneyland Resort is crowded, during the peak vacation times, for example, make lunch or dinner reservations at any of the more formal or theme-oriented restaurants within Downtown Disney to avoid long waits.

Rainforest Café

📞 (714) 772-0413 for reservations

✎ *www.rainforestcafe.com*

Price Range: $$/$$$

This popular chain of award-winning theme restaurants has established its largest location in Downtown Disney. The Rainforest Café offers a theme parklike dining experience, complete with Audio-Animatronics animals (from the rain forest), lush trees, waterfalls, large saltwater fish tanks, and even an indoor lightning and rain storm. You and your family will feel as if you're dining in a rain forest thanks to a wide range of audio and visual special effects. Don't worry, while the décor may appear real, you won't get wet.

Rainforest Café is one of the most popular family-oriented dining destinations in Downtown Disney, in part because of its awesome atmosphere and extensive menu, which boasts over 117 items, plus a full bar. The restaurant is open for breakfast, lunch, and dinner. Sandwiches, burgers, soups, salads, steaks, chicken dishes, and vegetarian dishes are available. According to the chefs, the menu is inspired by Mexican, Italian, Cajun, and Caribbean flavors but also offers plenty of all-American fare.

Prepare yourself to enjoy extremely friendly and attentive service. Reservations are definitely recommended, especially during peak travel periods. If you're a member of the Rainforest Café's Safari Club (annual membership is $10), you can greatly reduce your wait time. In addition to the excellent food, the dessert menu will make your mouth water.

When it comes to dessert, the house specialty is the Volcano, a chocolate fudge brownie that erupts with caramel, vanilla ice cream, and plenty of hot fudge. This $10.99 dessert is delicious and is big enough for two (or more) people.

For a complete lunch for two (excluding alcohol), be prepared to spend around $40. A children's menu is available. As with any theme-dining experience, be prepared to exit the dining room area by walking though a gift shop that offers a selection of toys and gifts, all with a rain forest and wildlife theme. If your child is celebrating a birthday during your visit to The Disneyland Resort, the Rainforest Café is an excellent place to host a child's birthday party.

≡FAST FACT

The restaurant promotes saving the world's rain forests. In the gift shops of every Rainforest Café, one of the souvenirs available is the Rain Forest Preservation Kit. Every kit purchased saves 3,540 square feet of endangered rain forest. Proceeds are earmarked for the Sierra Nevada de Santa Marta Adopt-an-Acre program coordinated through the Nature Conservancy.

Ralph Brennan's Jazz Kitchen

✆ (714) 781-4560 for reservations

✆ (714) 776-5200

Price Range: $$/$$$

Experience the atmosphere of Bourbon Street (Disney style) in the heart of Anaheim. If you're a jazz music fan and enjoy fine Louisiana cuisine, this is the place to stop for lunch, dinner, or a late-night snack. Live music is performed as you enjoy a fine-dining experience or something off the less expensive quick-service menu. Between 8:00 A.M. and 11:00 A.M. daily, you can also enjoy coffee and beignets. This is a fun place for young adults and adults. The restaurant also offers a full-service bar.

Wetzel's Pretzels

✆ (714) 535-5994

✍ www.wetzels.com

Price Range: $

When you're in the mood for a quick, inexpensive snack or a drink (soda or lemonade, for example), then drop by Wetzel's Pretzels. This is the same shop you'll find at most local malls. All pretzels are homemade and served within thirty minutes after leaving the oven. Some of the special toppings available for the pretzels include cheese, sour cream, butter, salt, cinnamon, and almonds. Keep in mind that soon after enjoying a pretzel, especially one topped with salt and/or butter, you'll be craving a cold drink, so plan accordingly. Wetzel's Pretzels is open 8:00 A.M. to midnight. Nearby outdoor seating is available; however, this is not a sit-down eating establishment.

Y Arriba Y Arriba

✆ (714) 781-4560 for reservations

✑ *www.yarriba.com*

Price Range: $$/$$$

Open until 2:00 A.M., this full-service Latin restaurant offers a full bar and ongoing live entertainment. The main dining room contains a stage where musical and dance acts perform. Designed in response to the growing international influence of Latin culture, the menu features tapas (the appetizer dishes that are a favorite throughout the Latin world) with a selection from every Latin country. A children's menu is also available.

This family dining–style restaurant is designed for groups of people to share multiple entrées, giving everyone at the table an opportunity to sample new dishes, or to order a meal-size portion of their own.

According to one of the restaurant's founders, "This is far from being just another theme restaurant. We believe our dining experience is unique, with universal appeal, and it adds to that with an ever-changing mix of live Latin entertainment and imagery."

The name Y Arriba Y Arriba has a secure place in musical history as the rousing cry in the middle of the song "La Bamba." Although its literal translation is about "overcoming" or "conquering," today it means almost anything you want it to. "That is exactly what we want our new concept to be," says Jorge Currais, fifth-generation descendant of the founder of La Zaragozana, the historic first family restaurant in Cuba. "We want everybody to get something different from a visit to Y Arriba Y Arriba—whether it be the food, drink, décor, or entertainment; whether they just have fun or learn something about Latin history and culture."

Additional Services

All of the usual amenities, including pay telephones, restrooms, and ATM machines, can be found in various places throughout the Downtown Disney area. In addition, the Walt Disney Travel Company (the travel agency owned and operated by the Walt Disney Company) has an office in this area to assist guests in making (or changing) their travel arrangements. For international travelers, there's also a Thomas Cook Currency Exchange located around the corner from the AMC Theaters and Compass Books & Café. There are two Union Bank of California ATM machines. One ATM is near the AMC Theaters, and the second is near the Häagen-Dazs ice-cream shop. For additional information about the guest services available in Downtown Disney, visit the information kiosks located near the main east and west entrances of the area.

TRAVEL TIP

Throughout Downtown Disney, shirts and shoes must be worn at all times. Smoking is prohibited inside all stores, dining areas, and restrooms. Skateboards, in-line skates, bicycles, and scooters cannot be ridden in the public areas of Downtown Disney.

CHAPTER 15

Six Flags Magic Mountain

ASIDE FROM THE DISNEYLAND RESORT, there are many other tourist attractions in and around the Los Angeles area, including several major theme parks. In this chapter, you'll learn about Six Flags Magic Mountain, which offers roller coasters and other more traditional amusement-park rides.

Park Information

This park is the home of fifteen world-class coasters, plus a handful of other thrill rides, which make it particularly suited to teens and thrill-seeking adults. What you'll also find in Six Flags Magic Mountain, however, is a new and expanding kids area, called Bugs Bunny World, containing over a dozen rides designed for young people, including a kids-only coaster. This themed area, based on the Loony Tunes, will entertain kids for a full day's worth of fun.

Six Flags Magic Mountain is open seven days per week during the spring and summer. Otherwise, unlike the Disney theme parks, it operates year-round, but is open only on weekends and holidays. For an exact schedule and hours of operation, call ✆(818) 367-5965 or visit the **Six Flags** Web site (✉ *www.sixflags.com*).

Attractions

Every year, Six Flags is known for adding at least one or two new rides. Some of the most recent additions include X, Déjà Vu, and GOLIATH, Jr. (all roller coasters). Other roller-coaster additions over the years have included: Gold Rush (1971), Revolution (1976), Colossus (1978), Ninja (1988), Viper (1990), Psyclone (1991), Batman: The Ride (1994), and Superman: The Escape (1996).

Each coaster offers a totally different type of experience. Yet, each combines fast motion with drops, loops, corkscrews, and other thrilling elements designed to provide the ultimate high-speed rush.

During peak times of the year, Magic Mountain can get pretty crowded, with the longest lines forming for the newest and most thrill-oriented rides. Even when the park isn't too crowded, you could still wait between an hour and ninety minutes, especially for some of the newer coasters, like Déjà Vu. To minimize the waits, a special FASTLANE ticket upgrade is available.

 TRAVEL TIP

By purchasing the optional FASTLANE ticket upgrade (for an additional $15 over the cost of standard admission into the park), you can avoid lines for up to four major attractions of your choice. Only a limited number of FASTLANE tickets are sold each day, so be sure to take advantage of this opportunity as early in the day as possible.

Virtually all of the rides and attractions that make up Magic Mountain are outdoor-based. Thus, while visiting this park, you'll be exposed to the day's weather conditions, so dress accordingly and wear sunblock and sunglasses. No matter what you choose to wear, be sure comfortable shoes are part of your outfit. Plenty of walking is required.

Six Flags Magic Mountain is also where you'll find Six Flags Hurricane Harbor, a large water park (open seasonally) containing water slides, a wave pool, a lazy river, and three large activity areas designed to provide a full day's worth of water-based fun for people of all ages. Hurricane Harbor is open weekends only, beginning May 12, but opens on weekdays as well starting in late May through early September, before returning to the weekends-only schedule for the majority of September. The park remains closed for the fall and winter. There is a separate admission charge for Hurricane Harbor, although an all-inclusive (discounted) ticket is available. See Chapter 6 for details.

Divisions

Like most theme parks, Magic Mountain is divided into several distinctly themed areas, all of which offer plenty of thrill rides and various other attractions. The park contains the following areas:

- Baja Ridge
- Bugs Bunny World
- Colossus County Fair
- Cyclone Bay
- Gotham City Backlot
- High Sierra Territory
- The Movie District
- Rapids Camp Crossing
- Samurai Summit
- Six Flags Plaza

To maximize your time, it's best to explore one area at a time, experience each ride in that area, and then move on to the next area. Otherwise, you'll spend a considerable amount of extra time walking around. A free tram that circles much of the park offers an alternative to walking, but you will have to wait to board the tram.

≡FAST FACT

No matter where you explore, you'll hear the screams of guests as they ride the various coasters. Everywhere you go, just look up (or to the side) to see coaster tracks winding above and around the park's many walkways and paths.

Six Flags Guest Services

When you arrive at Six Flags Magic Mountain, you'll be directed into the park's extremely large parking lot. Be sure to remember exactly where you park. Parking costs $7 per day for cars. Once parked, walk to the nearest tram station for transportation directly to the park's main entrance. The walk between the parking lot and the entrance can take more than fifteen minutes, so taking the tram is worthwhile.

At the main entrance, you'll come upon the row of ticket counters. When facing the ticket counters, to the right you'll find several ATM machines.

After purchasing your tickets, you'll be directed through a security area, where guests walk through metal detectors and are subject to having their personal items searched. Once you're through security (which could take up to fifteen minutes, depending on the crowds), you'll find the Guest Services office and Ticket Will Call windows. To the left will be the park's main entrance.

Inside the park itself, ATM machines, baby-changing facilities, first-aid stations, telephones, water fountains, lockers, wheelchair rentals, and stroller rentals are all available. There are also free (daily) kennels for your pet adjacent to the parking lot, and there are multiple picnic areas in the parking area (outside the park) where families can enjoy food they bring to the park. No food from outside can be brought into the park itself. Visit Guest Services for details.

As soon as you arrive at the park (and pay for parking), you'll be given a full-color park map and guide. Review this map before entering the park so that you obtain a basic understanding of the park's layout and can determine where the various attractions are. Each ride's height restrictions are listed in this free booklet, as is information about the park's various shows and dining options. The Mooseburger Lodge is the most formal dining experience in the park.

There are no formal restaurants at Six Flags Magic Mountain. There are, however, many fast-food options, which offer designated indoor and/or outdoor seating. You'll find a wide assortment of food options, including burgers, pizza, hot dogs, chicken, tacos and burritos, Chinese food, ice cream, corn dogs, chilidogs, and candy.

 TRAVEL TIP

Many of the park's main thrill rides have age and/or height restrictions and are not suitable for young kids. For most thrill rides, guests must be at least 42, 48, or 54 inches tall. Signs are posted near the entrance to each ride where restrictions apply.

Getting to Six Flags Magic Mountain

 The following basic driving directions to Six Flags Magic Mountain are from Anaheim (Disneyland) and the Hollywood/Universal City (Universal Studios Hollywood) area. For more customized directions, call ✆ (818) 367-5965.

- From Anaheim (The Disneyland Resort), take the Interstate 5 (I-5) freeway north and exit at Magic Mountain Parkway. At the end of the ramp, take a left at the traffic signal and travel under the freeway overpass. Follow Magic Mountain Parkway to the main parking lot and the main entrance to Six Flags California.

- From the Hollywood/Universal City area, take the 101 freeway north to the 170 freeway north. Next, take the 170 freeway (north) to the Interstate 5 (I-5) freeway north. Follow the I-5 north to Magic Mountain Parkway. At the end of the ramp, take a left at the traffic signal and travel under the freeway overpass. Follow Magic Mountain Parkway to the main parking lot and the main entrance to Six Flags California.

The Rides, Shows, and Attractions

 This section describes the rides, shows, and attractions you'll find in each area of Magic Mountain. Be sure of the age groups for each ride. As you're planning your day, you may want to break away with the young kids for several hours to explore Bugs Bunny World, while the other teens and adults you're traveling with experience the thrill rides.

When waiting for people to experience the thrill rides, kids can explore the rides, shows, and attractions in Bugs Bunny World. In addition, there are other shows throughout the park suitable for people of all ages. There are also carnival games to play (that cost extra) where prizes are awarded, shops to visit, and snacks to be purchased and consumed.

▌ TRAVEL TIP

Many of the thrill rides at Six Flags Magic Mountain are not for kids, nor are they suitable for expectant mothers, anyone with a heart or back condition, or people who suffer from motion sickness or other physical ailments. If you have any questions or concerns, be sure to consult the ride's signage or ask a park employee before experiencing any of the thrill rides.

BAJA RIDGE

X

Ages 2–4:	N.S.
Ages 5–10:	N.S.
Ages 11–15:	★★★
Ages 16–Adult:	★★★
Senior Citizens:	N.S.

RIDE RESTRICTIONS: Guests must be at least 48 inches tall.

This is one of Magic Mountain's newest rides. It's also one of the most high-tech coasters you'll find anywhere in the world. Dubbed as the first "4th dimensional thrill," riders will fly, flip, spin, and rotate 360 degrees forward, backward, upside down, and headfirst as they experience the closest thing possible to actually flying through the air at high speeds.

Riders are strapped into the ride in a standing position (each car holds twenty-eight passengers—seven rows of four people across). Riders will ultimately experience four G-forces as they glide along the ride's 3,610 feet of twisting track at speeds up to 76 miles per hour. To kick off the excitement, there's a 200-foot drop right at the start.

Be prepared for long waits to experience X. To avoid the longest lines, check out this ride during peak mealtimes or first thing in the morning. On weekdays, when the park is less crowded, the lines for this ride are a bit shorter, but waits between thirty and ninety minutes are typical.

👍 This is a must-see attraction.

Viper

Ages 2–4:	N.S.
Ages 5–10:	N.S.
Ages 11–15:	★★★
Ages 16–Adult:	★★★
Senior Citizens:	N.S.

RIDE RESTRICTIONS: Guests must be at least 54 inches tall.

For over eleven years, this coaster has been thrilling people of all ages, bringing them 188 feet into the air, then having them travel at 70 miles per hour along the coaster's 3,830 feet of track.

The ride lasts two minutes and is famous for offering the world's tallest vertical loop (140 feet). Each train holds twenty-eight people, with people sitting in pairs. As with most coasters, the best seats are always in the front of the train.

 This is a must-see attraction.

Revolution

Ages 2–4:	N.S.
Ages 5–10:	N.S.
Ages 11–15:	★★★
Ages 16–Adult:	★★★
Senior Citizens:	N.S.

RIDE RESTRICTIONS: Guests must be at least 48 inches tall.

The Revolution, which opened during America's bicentennial in 1976, brings riders along 3,457 feet of track at speeds up to 55 miles per hour. The ride lasts about two minutes, includes a 90-foot-high vertical loop, and positive G-forces up to 4.4. Each train holds twenty riders (in five cars, with passengers sitting in pairs).

 This is a must-see attraction.

≡FAST FACT

The Revolution was the world's first giant looping coaster and was inspired by the old-fashioned wooden coasters of yesteryear.

Bugs Bunny World

In addition to over a dozen kid-oriented rides you'll find when you pass through the giant tree that marks the entrance to Bugs Bunny World, there's also the Warner Bros. Kids' Club Stage (featuring live entertainment) and popular characters that roam the park greeting guests (taking pictures and signing autographs).

One of the attraction highlights of this area is the interactive petting zoo, where young people (and those traveling with them) can come face-to-face and play with goats, see exotic birds (including flamingos), plus view an assortment of other animals. Pony rides are available.

This area of Magic Mountain is really a stand-alone theme park for kids (and their parents). If you're visiting Magic Mountain with kids under the age of twelve, this is where they'll have the most fun. Plan on spending at least several hours here.

COLOSSUS COUNTY FAIR

GOLIATH

Ages 2–4:	N.S.
Ages 5–10:	N.S.
Ages 11–15:	★★★
Ages 16–Adult:	★★★
Senior Citizens:	N.S.

RIDE RESTRICTIONS: Guests must be at least 48 inches tall.

The name of this coaster says it all— GOLIATH is big . . . very big . . . and very fast. Riders reach a top speed of 85 miles per hour as they race along the coaster's 4,500 feet of track. The ride lasts a full three minutes and includes a near vertical (61-degree) drop into a 120-foot long underground tunnel. The highest point of this ride is 255 feet.

 This is a must-see attraction.

Buccaneer

Ages 2–4:	N.S.
Ages 5–10:	N.S.
Ages 11–15:	★★
Ages 16–Adult:	★★
Senior Citizens:	N.S.

RIDE RESTRICTIONS: Guests under 48 inches must be accompanied by an adult.

Riders climb aboard a land-based old pirate ship that "sails" out of control during a turbulent adventure cruise.

Swashbuckler

Ages 2–4:	N.S.
Ages 5–10:	N.S.
Ages 11–15:	★★
Ages 16–Adult:	★★
Senior Citizens:	N.S.

RIDE RESTRICTIONS: Guests must be at least 42 inches tall.

This spinning swing set lifts guests high into the air, then goes around, and around, and around at a pretty quick rate. It's best to avoid this ride just after eating.

Colossus

Ages 2–4:	N.S.
Ages 5–10:	N.S.
Ages 11–15:	★★★
Ages 16–Adult:	★★★
Senior Citizens:	N.S.

RIDE RESTRICTIONS: Guests must be at least 48 inches tall.

Bringing riders 125 feet into the air, this 2.5 minute ride travels at speeds upwards of 62 miles per hour. Riders experience fourteen hills, one with a drop height of 115 feet.

 This is a must-see attraction.

⊕ HOT SPOT

Colossus is a traditional wooden coaster that opened back in 1978. It is, however, the tallest and fastest wooden dual-track coaster on the West coast.

Metro "Colossus County Fair Station"

Ages 2–4:	★★
Ages 5–10:	★★
Ages 11–15:	★★
Ages 16–Adult:	★★
Senior Citizens:	★★

The Magic Mountain Metro System (which is the transit system within the park) has a stop in this area. The Metro offers an alternative to walking if you need to get from one area of the park to another.

Circus Wheel

Ages 2–4:	N.S.
Ages 5–10:	N.S.
Ages 11–15:	★★
Ages 16–Adult:	★★
Senior Citizens:	N.S.

RIDE RESTRICTIONS: Guests under 42 inches tall must be accompanied by an adult.

This ride is all about spinning and twisting. It's a traditional amusement park thrill ride that's moderately turbulent.

Center Ring Games

Ages 2–4:	N.S.
Ages 5–10:	★
Ages 11–15:	★
Ages 16–Adult:	★
Senior Citizens:	★

In this area of the park you'll find a collection of skill and luck-based carnival games. Prizes, such as plush toys, are awarded. The cost is between $1 and $2 per play.

Boardwalk Arcade

Ages 2–4:	N.S.
Ages 5–10:	★
Ages 11–15:	★
Ages 16–Adult:	★
Senior Citizens:	★

A collection of classic and new video games and pinball machines can be found in this indoor arcade. The cost of each game varies.

Magic Moments Theater

Ages 2–4:	N.S.
Ages 5–10:	★★
Ages 11–15:	★★
Ages 16–Adult:	★★
Senior Citizens:	★★

This show typically runs throughout the year and showcases nonstop visual laser effects. Loud music and sound effects accompany the visual effects.

TRAVEL TIP

This show is suitable for the entire family; however, young children may get frightened. Also, be sure to check with Guest Relations for show times for the day of your visit.

CYCLONE BAY

Déjà Vu

Ages 2–4:	N.S.
Ages 5–10:	N.S.
Ages 11–15:	★★★
Ages 16–Adult:	★★★
Senior Citizens:	N.S.

RIDE RESTRICTIONS: Guests must be at least 54 inches tall and under 6 feet 4 inches tall.

Whether you're traveling forward or backwards along this ride's 1,203 feet of track, you're in for a major thrill. Featuring ski-lift-style seating, you'll find yourself traveling up to 65 miles per hour along a seemingly endless array of twists and turns. Déjà Vu is one of Magic Mountain's newest rides, having opened in 2001. Because it's new, expect longer than normal lines; however, if you love coasters, it's worth the wait.

 This is a must-see attraction.

Psyclone

Ages 2–4:	N.S.
Ages 5–10:	N.S.
Ages 11–15:	★★★
Ages 16–Adult:	★★★
Senior Citizens:	N.S.

RIDE RESTRICTIONS: Guests must be at least 48 inches tall.

Based on the wooden coaster found at Coney Island (and built in 1927), Psyclone was added to Magic Mountain's famous coaster collection back in 1991. It's a classic wooden coaster with over a half-mile of steel track. The ride includes eleven hills, five high-speed bank turns, and a 183-foot long tunnel. Travel at speeds up to 50 miles per hour in a train holding twenty-four passengers (two people per row). For a classic coaster experience, this is the one to choose.

 This is a must-see attraction.

Arrowhead Splashdown

Ages 2–4:	N.S.
Ages 5–10:	N.S.
Ages 11–15:	★★
Ages 16–Adult:	★★
Senior Citizens:	N.S.

RIDE RESTRICTIONS: Guests under 42 inches must be accompanied by an adult.

Enjoy what starts off as a calm and relaxing log flume water ride, but don't think you'll be staying dry for too long. This ride ends with a dramatic 57-foot plunge and a giant splash.

Dive Devil

Ages 2–4:	N.S.
Ages 5–10:	N.S.
Ages 11–15:	★★
Ages 16–Adult:	★★★
Senior Citizens:	N.S.

RIDE RESTRICTIONS: Guests must be at least 48 inches tall.

This ride nicely combines the thrill of skydiving and hang gliding as you're hoisted 150 feet into the air (strapped in a harness), then dropped. You'll ultimately reach a speed of 60 miles per hour as you ride alone or strapped together with up to three people.

 TRAVEL TIP

Reservations are required to experience Dive Devil, which also has an additional cost associated with it. This is the closest thing you'll experience to skydiving without actually jumping out of an airplane.

Sharkey's Shooting Gallery

Ages 2–4:	N.S.
Ages 5–10:	★
Ages 11–15:	★★
Ages 16–Adult:	★
Senior Citizens:	★

Using electronic replicas of rifles, test your aim at a old-fashioned shooting gallery.

Cyclone Bay Arcade and Games

Ages 2–4:	N.S.
Ages 5–10:	★
Ages 11–15:	★★
Ages 16–Adult:	★
Senior Citizens:	★

This area offers a collection of coin-operated arcade games, pinball machines, and other carnival-like tests of skill and luck. An additional fee applies to experience the various games. Prizes are awarded at some of the games.

Cyclone 500

Ages 2–4:	N.S.
Ages 5–10:	N.S.
Ages 11–15:	★★
Ages 16–Adult:	★★
Senior Citizens:	★★

RIDE RESTRICTIONS: Guests must be at least 58 inches tall.

For an additional fee, you can strap yourself into a go-cart and race around a nearly mile long track. Each car holds a driver and (optional) passenger.

GOTHAM CITY BACKLOT

Batman: The Ride

Ages 2–4:	N.S.
Ages 5–10:	N.S.
Ages 11–15:	★★★
Ages 16–Adult:	★★★
Senior Citizens:	N.S.

RIDE RESTRICTIONS: Guests must be at least 54 inches tall.

While suspended from the track, riders sit in ski-lift-style chairs that travel at speeds upwards of 50 miles per hour along 2,700 feet of track. This ride originally opened in 1994 and features a series of hairpin turns, vertical loops, a corkscrew, and a "one-of-a-kind heartline spin with a zero gravity force producing a feeling of weightlessness."

 This is a must-see attraction.

Grinder Gearworks

Ages 2–4:	N.S.
Ages 5–10:	N.S.
Ages 11–15:	★★
Ages 16–Adult:	★★
Senior Citizens:	N.S.

RIDE RESTRICTIONS: Guests must be at least 42 inches tall.

Prepare to be lifted into the air and plastered against the wall of this ride that's positioned at a 45-degree angle as it spins quickly.

The Batman & Robin Live Action Show

Ages 2–4:	N.S.
Ages 5–10:	★★
Ages 11–15:	★★★
Ages 16–Adult:	★★★
Senior Citizens:	★★

Batman and Robin are the stars of this live action stunt show featuring an elaborate set and impressive special effects, including lasers and pyrotechnics. While this is a family-oriented show based on the popular *Batman* movies, young kids may be frightened by the loud explosions.

 This is a must-see attraction.

≡FAST FACT

The Batman Action theater, where this show takes place, offers outdoor, stadiumlike bench seating with good visibility to the stage area no matter where you sit. On busy days, arrive at the theater twenty to thirty minutes before the posted show time. During off-peak times of the year, this show may not be presented. Check the theater marquee and nearby signage for show times and details.

HIGH SIERRA TERRITORY

Metro "High Sierra Territory Station"

Ages 2–4:	★★
Ages 5–10:	★★
Ages 11–15:	★★
Ages 16–Adult:	★★
Senior Citizens:	★★

The Magic Mountain Metro System (which is the transit system within the park) has a stop in this area. The Metro offers an alternative to walking if you need to get from one area of the park to another.

Yosemite Sam Sierra Falls

Ages 2–4:	N.S.
Ages 5–10:	N.S.
Ages 11–15:	★★
Ages 16–Adult:	★★
Senior Citizens:	N.S.

RIDE RESTRICTIONS: Guests under 42 inches tall must be accompanied by an adult.

This white-water rafting simulation ride takes you on a twisting and turning journey along a man-made river. Be prepared to get a bit wet, although this ride is much tamer than the majority of the thrill rides offered within the park.

Granny Gran Prix

Ages 2–4:	N.S.
Ages 5–10:	★
Ages 11–15:	★
Ages 16–Adult:	★
Senior Citizens:	★

RIDE RESTRICTIONS: Guests must be at least 48 inches tall or 42 inches if accompanied by an adult.

Ride in electronically powered re-creations of antique cars. This is a good ride for parents to experience with their children and preteens. Older people, however, will probably want to pursue more thrill-oriented rides.

GOLIATH, Jr.

Ages 2–4:	N.S.
Ages 5–10:	★★★
Ages 11–15:	★★
Ages 16–Adult:	N.S.
Senior Citizens:	N.S.

For young people who enjoy coasters, but aren't old enough to experience the adult-oriented thrills of the park's large coasters, Magic Mountain now offers GOLIATH, Jr., which takes riders a mere 10 feet into the air and travels at 10 miles per hour. The ride lasts about ninety seconds. Riders must be *under* 54 inches tall.

Sierra West

Ages 2–4:	N.S.
Ages 5–10:	N.S.
Ages 11–15:	★
Ages 16–Adult:	★
Senior Citizens:	N.S.

RIDE RESTRICTIONS: Guests must be at least 42 inches tall.

While riding in a sled-shaped vehicle, you'll be spun around on a fast moving track.

The Animal Action Show

Ages 2–4:	★
Ages 5–10:	★★★
Ages 11–15:	★★
Ages 16–Adult:	★★
Senior Citizens:	★★

This live show stars a cast of trained animals that perform tricks. It's suitable for the entire family and offers a touch of humor. The Animal Action Show is a great way to break up the day, especially if you're visiting the park with kids.

⊕ HOT SPOT

The Golden Bear Theater is where a wide range of concerts and special events are held throughout the year. For details on events during the time of your visit, contact Guest Relations or check the signage located near the theater entrance. This amphitheater holds 3,200 guests.

SAMURAI SUMMIT

Superman: The Escape

Ages 2–4:	N.S.
Ages 5–10:	N.S.
Ages 11–15:	★★★
Ages 16–Adult:	★★★
Senior Citizens:	N.S.

RIDE RESTRICTIONS: Guests must be at least 48 inches tall.

You'll go from a total standstill to virtually flying at 100 miles per hour in less than seven seconds when you experience the awesome thrills of Superman: The Escape, which first made its debut at Magic Mountain back in 1997. You'll feel like Superman as this ride soars forty-one stories into the air and offers 6.5 seconds of weightlessness as you plummet downward. You'll probably wish your stomach was made of steel if you experience this ride too soon after eating.

 This is a must-see attraction.

Ninja

Ages 2–4:	N.S.
Ages 5–10:	N.S.
Ages 11–15:	★★★
Ages 16–Adult:	★★★
Senior Citizens:	N.S.

RIDE RESTRICTIONS: Guests must be at least 42 inches tall.

For ninety seconds, you'll experience a true sense of speed as you race along nearly a half-mile of coaster track while traveling at 55 miles per hour. The trains on this coaster swing freely from side to side (with 180 degrees of movement) as you experience the sharp turns, drops, and twists.

👍 This is a must-see attraction.

Sky Tower

Ages 2–4:	★
Ages 5–10:	★★
Ages 11–15:	★★
Ages 16–Adult:	★★
Senior Citizens:	★★

For the ultimate aerial view of Magic Mountain, this ride takes you up twenty-eight stories, spins slowly around, and then brings you calmly back to ground level. It's the perfect family-oriented, non-thrill ride.

Metro "Samurai Summit Station"

Ages 2–4:	★★
Ages 5–10:	★★
Ages 11–15:	★★
Ages 16–Adult:	★★
Senior Citizens:	★★

The Magic Mountain Metro System (which is the transit system within the park) has a stop in this area. The Metro offers an alternative to walking if you need to get from one area of the park to another.

SIX FLAGS PLAZA

Flashback

Ages 2–4:	N.S.
Ages 5–10:	N.S.
Ages 11–15:	★★★
Ages 16–Adult:	★★★
Senior Citizens:	N.S.

RIDE RESTRICTIONS: Guests must be at least 48 inches tall.

Promoted by the park as the world's only "hairpin drop roller coaster," Flashback offers yet another alternative to the traditional high-speed coaster experience you'll find at other parks. Along the one-third mile of track, you'll experience six steeply banked vertical dives, plus a handful of spirals. The ride lasts about ninety seconds and can be found in the northeast area of the park.

👍 This is a must-see attraction.

Grand Carousel

Ages 2–4:	★★
Ages 5–10:	★★★
Ages 11–15:	★★
Ages 16–Adult:	★★
Senior Citizens:	★★

RIDE RESTRICTIONS: Guests under 42 inches must be accompanied by an adult.

Originally built in 1912, this lovely carousel has been fully restored. It's the perfect attraction for young people and adults alike who want to enjoy a classic amusement park ride experience.

Orient Express

Ages 2–4:	N.S.
Ages 5–10:	★
Ages 11–15:	★
Ages 16–Adult:	★
Senior Citizens:	★

This is a people mover that travels up to the top of Samurai Summit.

Log Jammer

Ages 2–4:	N.S.
Ages 5–10:	N.S.
Ages 11–15:	★★
Ages 16–Adult:	★★
Senior Citizens:	★

RIDE RESTRICTIONS: Guests under 42 inches must be accompanied by an adult.

For a water-based long ride that's a bit wet and wild, check out Log Jammer. It's less thrill-oriented than a coaster, but certainly offers its own entertaining experience.

Palace Games

Ages 2–4:	N.S.
Ages 5–10:	★★
Ages 11–15:	★★
Ages 16–Adult:	★★
Senior Citizens:	★★

Skeeball, games of skill, classic arcade games, and pinball machines are what you'll find in this area. There's an additional fee to play the various games.

Looney Tunes Nights

Ages 2–4:	★
Ages 5–10:	★★★
Ages 11–15:	★★
Ages 16–Adult:	★
Senior Citizens:	★★

Presented on predetermined dates between late May and early September, this live action musical parade stars many of the popular Looney Tunes characters along with popular DC Comics superheroes. The parade concludes with a fireworks presentation over Six Flags Plaza (that's visible from anywhere in the park where you can see the Sky Tower).

THE MOVIE DISTRICT

Tidal Wave

Ages 2–4:	N.S.
Ages 5–10:	N.S.
Ages 11–15:	★★
Ages 16–Adult:	★★
Senior Citizens:	N.S.

RIDE RESTRICTIONS: Guests must be at least 42 inches tall.

Have you ever wondered what it would be like to travel down a 50-foot waterfall? Well, you're about to find out. This ride ends with a splash!

The Riddler's Revenge

Ages 2–4:	N.S.
Ages 5–10:	N.S.
Ages 11–15:	★★★
Ages 16–Adult:	★★★
Senior Citizens:	N.S.

RIDE RESTRICTIONS: Guests must be at least 54 inches tall.

Since 1998, The Riddler's Revenge has offered yet another alternative for coaster fanatics looking for the ultimate thrill. This ride is based around Batman's arch enemy, The Riddler, and features a fast-moving coaster where riders stand up for the entire experience as they travel along 4,370 feet of track at speeds up to 65 miles per hour. The ride includes six inversions, one 360-degree vertical loop, one 360-degree oblique loop, and two over-the-top diving loops, plus two 150-foot-long barrel rolls.

 This is a must-see attraction.

Freefall

Ages 2–4:	N.S.
Ages 5–10:	N.S.
Ages 11–15:	★★
Ages 16–Adult:	★★
Senior Citizens:	N.S.

RIDE RESTRICTIONS: Guests must be at least 42 inches tall.

What goes up, must come down. That's the basic concept behind this classic theme park ride which takes riders up a ten-story tower then drops at 55 miles per hour. The actual drop lasts about two seconds.

Gold Rusher

Ages 2–4:	N.S.
Ages 5–10:	N.S.
Ages 11–15:	★★
Ages 16–Adult:	★★
Senior Citizens:	N.S.

RIDE RESTRICTIONS: Guests must be at least 48 inches tall.

The concept behind this coaster is a runaway mining train. It travels at 35 miles per hour and lasts about 2.5 minutes. It's somewhat less turbulent than a traditional coaster, but, nevertheless, offers plenty of excitement.

Sandblasters

Ages 2–4:	N.S.
Ages 5–10:	N.S.
Ages 11–15:	★★
Ages 16–Adult:	★★
Senior Citizens:	N.S.

RIDE RESTRICTIONS: Guests must be at least 42 inches tall.

This is a traditional bumper car ride.

Scrambler

Ages 2–4:	N.S.
Ages 5–10:	N.S.
Ages 11–15:	★
Ages 16–Adult:	★
Senior Citizens:	N.S.

RIDE RESTRICTIONS: Guests must be at least 36 inches tall.

This ride is all about spinning, twisting, turning, and getting dizzy. It's a staple amusement park ride you'll find at many parks.

RAPIDS CAMP CROSSING

Roaring Rapids

Ages 2–4:	N.S.
Ages 5–10:	N.S.
Ages 11–15:	★★
Ages 16–Adult:	★★
Senior Citizens:	N.S.

RIDE RESTRICTIONS: Guests must be at least 42 inches tall.

This ride was the first man-made white-water rafting ride. It offers a splashing good time, but is far less scary than the park's various coasters. Oh, and plan on getting wet! People over the age of ten will enjoy Roaring Rapids.

⊕ HOT SPOT

Roaring Rapids is a great ride for cooling off on a particularly hot day or when you need to take a break from the coasters. You might want to have a dry change of clothes on hand.

Mining Town Games

Ages 2–4:	N.S.
Ages 5–10:	★★
Ages 11–15:	★★
Ages 16–Adult:	★★
Senior Citizens:	★

These carnival-style games test your skill and luck. Prizes are awarded, but you have to pay as you play. The cost is $1 or $2 per game.

Mining Town Arcade

Ages 2–4:	N.S.
Ages 5–10:	★★
Ages 11–15:	★★
Ages 16–Adult:	★★
Senior Citizens:	★

Here you'll find over fifty pinball machines and coin-operated arcade games. There's an additional charge to play each game.

Special Events

 Throughout the year, Six Flags Magic Mountain is known for hosting an array of special events. For example, the July 4th Fireworks Spectacular is one of the most impressive fireworks displays you'll see in southern California. During most of October, the theme park transforms into a Halloween Fright Fest, with special attractions and events. In late summer, the park is also the host to Festival Latina (a festival of Latin culture).

Season Pass Savings

 It is possible to experience this entire park in a single day. However, if you're traveling with kids and spend the majority of your time in the Bugs Bunny World area, you may want to break up your visit to make it a two-day excursion.

For slightly more than the cost of a single-day admission ticket, you can purchase a season pass, which allows you to return as often as you wish in a twelve-month period. This is an incredible deal if you can stay in the Valencia area for two days or so and enjoy the various coasters at your leisure.

Nearby Lodging

 Within a mile of Six Flags Magic Mountain, there are a handful of hotels and motels. Keep in mind, you get what you pay for in this area. Expect to stay in a no-frills motel room for between $50 and $75 per night. If you decide to spend the night, it's always a good idea to ask to see a room before paying for it.

Nearby hotels, motels, and RV parks include:

Airtel Plaza Hotel

⊞ 7277 Valjean Avenue
Van Nuys, CA 91406

✆ (818) 997-7676

Best Western Valencia Inn

⊞ 27413 N. Tourney Road
Valencia, CA 91355

✆ (661) 255-0555

Castaic RV Park

⊞ 31540 Ridge Route Road
Castaic, CA 91384

✆ (661) 257-3340

Comfort Inn

⊞ 31558 Castaic Road
Castaic, CA 91384

✆ (661) 295-1100

Comfort Suites

⊞ 25380 The Old Road
Stevenson Ranch, CA 91381

✆ (661) 254-7700

The Hampton Inn

⊞ 25259 The Old Road
Stevenson Ranch, CA 91381

✆ (661) 253-2400

Hilton Gardens Inn

⊞ 27710 The Old Road
Valencia, CA 91355

✆ (661) 254-8800

Hyatt Valencia

⊡ 24500 Town Center Drive
Valencia, CA 91355

✆ (661) 799-1234

Marriott's Fairfield Inn

⊡ 25340 The Old Road
Stevenson Ranch, CA 91381

✆ (661) 290-2828

Marriott's Residence Inn

⊡ 25320 The Old Road
Stevenson Ranch, CA 91381

✆ (661) 290-2800

Motel 6

⊡ 12775 Encinitas Avenue
Sylmar, CA 91342

✆ (818) 362-9491

Ramada Inn

⊡ 300 West Palmdale Boulevard
Palmdale, CA 93551

✆ (661) 273-1200

Valencia Travel Village RV Park

⊡ 27946 Henry Mayo Road, Hwy 126
Valencia, CA 91355

✆ (661) 257-8047

CHAPTER 16

Knott's Southern California Resort

THE KNOTT'S SOUTHERN CALIFORNIA RESORT, located in Buena Park, California (just ten minutes away from The Disneyland Resort and 30 miles south of downtown Los Angeles), is comprised of the world-famous Knott's Berry Farm theme park, the much newer Knott's Soak City U.S.A. water park, a shopping area, and the nearby Radisson Resort hotel.

Resort Information

Knott's Berry Farm is one of the oldest tourist attractions in this part of California. In the 1930s, people traveled from Los Angeles and the surrounding area to Buena Park to buy Walter and Cordelia Knott's fried chicken and boysenberry pie, which they sold from their farm.

Since then, Knott's Southern California Resort has expanded into a 160-acre vacation destination designed for the entire family. The Knott's Berry Farm theme park offers a large selection of teen- and adult-oriented thrill rides, a large kids-only area (offering more than twenty rides for young people), and a slew of family-oriented attractions and shows suitable for the entire family.

The park's teen- and adult-oriented rides provide a more traditional amusement park experience than Disneyland and Disney's

California Adventure and are far less roller coaster–oriented than Six Flags Magic Mountain. The park does, however, feature several coasters, including the GhostRider (which many believe is the world's best wooden roller coaster).

Snoopy and Charles Schultz's Peanuts characters are the mascots of Camp Snoopy, the kids' section of Knott's Berry Farm. Actually a theme park within a theme park, Camp Snoopy offers more than twenty rides specifically for young people, plus a wide range of attractions and shows for the young at heart.

While Six Flags Magic Mountain focuses on offering the very latest and most modern thrill rides, Knott's Berry Farm is older and more traditional. It was built in a country farm setting.

When you're traveling with kids, the Knott's Berry Farm theme park can easily provide a full day's worth of amusement park entertainment. If you want to see and do everything at a somewhat casual pace, you could fill two days. If your focus is on entertaining young kids (under the age of twelve), Camp Snoopy will provide one day's worth of entertainment.

Located next to Knott's Berry Farm is Knott's Soak City U.S.A., a totally separate water-based theme park that requires a separate admission and offers more than twenty-one water rides and attractions with a 1950s California theme. This park is more suitable for teens and adults, but there are a few kid-oriented rides. Soak City U.S.A. easily provides from six hours to a full day's worth of entertainment.

For families planning to turn their visit to Knott's Southern California Resort into a weekend getaway or several-day stay, the nearby **Radisson Resort** hotel has teamed up with Knott's to provide a complete vacation package. For specially priced package deals, which include hotel accommodations and admission to the Knott's theme parks, call ✆ (800) 333-3333. The Radisson Resort extends the Peanuts theme of the parks into the hotel setting, so character appearances (by Snoopy and the Peanuts) are common.

Rounding out the Knott's Southern California Resort complex is a small shopping and dining area. Here you'll find **Mrs. Knott's**

Chicken Dinner Restaurant, which continues to serve the famous fried chicken and pies that made the Knott name famous throughout Southern California. No admission is required to visit where this family-oriented restaurant is located (three hours of free parking is provided).

In addition, you'll find a handful of souvenir, clothing, and other shops within the California Marketplace area. Kids in particular will enjoy shopping at **Snoopy Headquarters,** which offers toys, clothing, and other souvenirs—all featuring the Peanuts characters. Homemakers, however, will enjoy browsing through **D'Vine Home & Candle,** a lovely store showcasing home accessories, gifts, candles, crafts, and collectibles. During the holiday season, a portion of the Marketplace Emporium (which typically offers gifts and collectibles) transforms into a Christmas shop, offering ornaments, decorations, and other festive items.

⊕ HOT SPOT

If you're planning to dine at Mrs. Knott's Chicken Dinner Restaurant, be prepared for a wait. This continues to be a favorite among local residents as well as tourists, so during peak mealtimes, a one-hour or longer wait is not uncommon.

Hours of Operation

The Knott's Berry Farm theme park is open everyday (except Christmas). Call or visit the Web site as hours are subject to change ✆ (714) 220-5200 ✉ *www.knotts.com.*

Knott's Soak City U.S.A. is a seasonal park, open daily between late May and early September, plus on weekends only through late September. Hours of operation vary. The remainder of the year, the water park is closed.

Historical Moments

In 1920, decades before Walt Disney founded Disneyland in

Anaheim, the Knott family moved to Buena Park, California, and founded a twenty-acre farm on rented land. Eight years later, the family built Cordelia Knott's tearoom, plus maintained a berry farm and plant nursery. Around this time, the Knott family purchased ten acres of the land it was previously renting.

When 1932 rolled around, Walter Knott began growing a new type of berry. It was a cross between a red raspberry, a blackberry, and a loganberry. The berries were called "boysenberries" after one of Walter's closest friends. In 1934, to help support the family during the Depression, Cordelia Knott started serving chicken dinners in her tearoom. A few years later, the couple opened a full-service restaurant.

Over the years that followed, the family opened a souvenir shop and saloon near their restaurant as guests came from all over to taste Cordelia's famous chicken and dessert pies.

≡FAST FACT

Within the Marketplace area, you'll also find an ice-cream parlor, a fast-food Mexican restaurant, the Farm Bakery, a candy store, and the Berry Market, which sells the famous Knott's preserves and other gourmet foods.

In 1952, the family purchased the still-operational narrow-gauge railroad and built tracks for this train around the farm area. In 1955, Cordelia and Walter attended the grand opening of Disneyland. That visit planted the idea in the couple's head to transform their property into a theme park. By 1968, the park contained several rides and began charging an admission fee. Since then, new rides, shows, and attractions have been added each year as Knott's Berry Farm has expanded into a full-size theme park for the entire family.

Cordelia died in 1974 at the age of eighty-four; Walter followed in 1981, just shy of his ninety-second birthday. But the couple left a legacy for people of all ages to enjoy. In 1997, Knott's Berry Farm was acquired by Ohio-based Cedar Fair, L.P., a national family of amusement parks and resorts. Since then, the park has continued to grow into a resort complex.

Getting to the Resort

From the I-5, 91, 22, or 405 freeways, take the Beach Boulevard exit in Buena Park and follow the signs to the park's main entrance. The ride between Knott's Southern California Resort and The Disneyland Resort is about ten minutes, and many non-Disney hotels in Anaheim offer a shuttle service to this park. The drive between the Los Angeles area and Knott's Southern California Resort will take forty-five minutes to one hour (possibly a bit more) depending on traffic.

Plenty of parking is available at the resort. If you're coming from Anaheim or a hotel in the Southern California area, both **Pacific Coast Sightseeing** and **Airport Bus** provide shuttle service directly to the park. Call ☎ (714) 636-7433 for details.

Guest Services

Like all theme parks in the area, Knott's Berry Farm and Knott's Soak City U.S.A. offer many guest services designed to make your visit to the park more enjoyable. On the premises you'll find lockers, public telephones, restrooms, baby changing/nursing areas, ATM machines, first aid, a lost and found, stroller rentals, wheelchair rentals, and shops that sell sundries (including sunblock, film, etc.) Each park has an Information Center with a helpful staff on hand to answer any questions.

A Guided Tour

Because this park is really two distinct parks in one, how you spend your time will depend on the ages of the people you're traveling with. The main Knott's Berry Farm theme park is designed for teens and adults. These areas of the park offer dozens of thrill rides and other attractions.

Camp Snoopy is just for kids (and their parents). If you're traveling with kids under the age of twelve, plan on spending the majority of your day in this area. Many of the shows presented at Knott's Berry Farm are family-oriented.

For adults traveling with young kids (too young to experience the thrill rides), the Parent Swap program offers a way for all adults in your group to enjoy the thrill rides, yet not leave young children unattended. While utilizing this option cuts wait times, adults with kids can't enjoy the thrill rides together. The Parent Swap program requires one adult to stay behind (near the exit of a thrill ride) with the kids, while the other adults wait in line and experience each thrill ride. Immediately after the adults finish their ride, the adult who was left behind with the kids can enter the ride (through the exit). He or she does not wait in line and is able to experience that ride immediately. One additional person (of the appropriate height) can accompany the adult who waited, providing the kids are not left unattended. For details, contact Guest Services.

 TRAVEL TIP

Keep in mind that many of the thrill rides have height and/or weight restrictions, making them unsuitable for kids. Many of these restrictions are listed in this chapter; however, signs are also posted at the entrance to each attraction if any restrictions apply.

While Knott's Berry Farm is known for its rides, this park also offers a wide range of theme-oriented shops, dining options, shows, and activities for people of all ages. Throughout the park, you'll also see artisans and craftspeople showcasing their skills and creations, offering live demonstrations, and interacting with park guests. Woodcarvers, glassblowers, candle makers, blacksmiths, gemologists, and silversmiths are just a few of the artisans and craftspeople you'll see. These demonstrations are both informative and entertaining, especially for adults.

Like all theme parks, this one requires lots of walking, so be sure to wear comfortable shoes. Also, the spring, fall, and winter evenings tend to get chilly, so having a jacket or sweatshirt on hand (which can be stored in a car or locker during the day) is a good idea. On hot days, be sure to wear comfortable clothes and apply plenty of sunblock. Sunglasses are also advisable. Since you'll probably want to keep your hands as free as possible throughout the day, consider using a waist pack to store your camera, cell phone, sunblock, and sunglasses, when these items are not in use.

You'll quickly discover that throughout the Marketplace area, as well as in the park, there are many shops and souvenir stands. Whether you're shopping for a child, or yourself, it's typically best to save the shopping for the end of the day, unless you plan on storing your purchases in the lockers. Carrying around your purchases will get cumbersome and inconvenient, especially if you plan on experiencing the various thrill rides.

≡FAST FACT

Knott's Berry Farm's areas all interconnect. The park itself takes on a large oval shape. Within the park, however, you'll find many paths to follow and out-of-the-way places to explore. If you're visiting this theme park for the overall experience, be sure to take some time to explore the various paths and exhibits.

As soon as you arrive at the park, pick up a free copy of the *Knott's Berry Farm Map & Fun Guide* booklet. It's available at all the ticket counters, at Guest Relations, and at many of the shops. Also, be sure to pick up a separate show schedule. Become acquainted with the layout of the park and choose a place to meet in case you're separated from the people you're traveling with. The fountain near the Grand Entrance area of the park is a central meeting location. If you'd like to get a bird's-eye view of the entire park, go directly to the Sky Cabin ride. This family-oriented ride will take you on a three-minute flight up one of the tallest towers in the park. You'll be riding in an enclosed cabin that rotates slowly, giving you an excellent view of the entire park.

Knott's Berry Farm is divided into several unique themed areas, including Ghost Town, Indian Trails, Camp Snoopy (the kids area), Fiesta Village, The Boardwalk, and Wild Water Wilderness. Each area offers its own set of rides, attractions, shops, dining options, and unique things to see and do.

Ghost Town

 The Ghost Town area is where you'll find the world-famous GhostRider coaster, along with a handful of other rides. For a taste of the old west, you can also experience an authentic stagecoach ride. The following sections highlight some of the major rides and attractions within this area of the park.

Butterfield Stagecoach

Ages 2–4:	N.S.
Ages 5–10:	★★
Ages 11–15:	★★
Ages 16–Adult:	★★
Senior Citizens:	★★

RIDE RESTRICTIONS: Guests under 46 inches tall must be accompanied by an adult.

Climb aboard a classic horse-drawn stagecoach for a ride around the perimeter of Ghost Town. This is a slow-paced ride, but one that's enjoyable for the entire family.

Calico Mine Ride

Ages 2–4:	N.S.
Ages 5–10:	N.S.
Ages 11–15:	★★
Ages 16–Adult:	★★
Senior Citizens:	★★

RIDE RESTRICTIONS: Guests under 46 inches tall must be accompanied by an adult.

This train ride takes guests through the depths of a gold mine. It's a somewhat fast-paced journey that could be considered a mild thrill ride. It's suitable for people over the age of ten.

Ghost Town Calico Railroad

Ages 2–4:	N.S.
Ages 5–10:	N.S.
Ages 11–15:	★★
Ages 16–Adult:	★★
Senior Citizens:	N.S.

RIDE RESTRICTIONS: Guests under 46 inches tall must be accompanied by an adult.

Take a leisurely train ride around the perimeter of the theme park on the world's last operational narrow-gauge steam train.

GhostRider

Ages 2–4:	N.S.
Ages 5–10:	N.S.
Ages 11–15:	★★★
Ages 16–Adult:	★★★
Senior Citizens:	N.S.

RIDE RESTRICTIONS: Guests must be at least 48 inches tall.

GhostRider is one of the best-known wooden roller coasters in the world. It looms 118 feet over the Ghost Town area and is the largest ride in the entire park. The ride itself follows 4,533 feet of twisting track that includes a 108-foot (banked) drop, plus thirteen additional drops, sudden dips, twists, and banked turns. For coaster fans, this ride shouldn't be missed.

👍 This is a must-see attraction.

Timber Mountain Log Ride

Ages 2–4:	N.S.
Ages 5–10:	N.S.
Ages 11–15:	★★
Ages 16–Adult:	★★
Senior Citizens:	N.S.

RIDE RESTRICTIONS: Guests must be at least 48 inches tall.

This water-based log ride follows a predefined track along a simulated 2,100-foot river. Much of this ride is experienced in the dark as you travel between 8 and 10 feet per second. The ride, however, ends with a huge splash (and a large drop). Chances are you'll get wet, so be prepared.

VertiGo

Ages 2–4:	N.S.
Ages 5–10:	N.S.
Ages 11–15:	★★★
Ages 16–Adult:	★★★
Senior Citizens:	N.S.

RIDE RESTRICTIONS: Guests must be at least 48 inches tall.

One of the newest rides in the park, VertiGo sends riders (strapped to a special seat) 300 feet into the air at 50 miles per hour. Before launch, you can choose four different ways to experience this ride. In addition to the park's standard admission fee, each "flight" is priced between $8 and $10. VertiGo is like a reverse bungee jump.

Knott's Wild West Stunt Show

Ages 2–4:	N.S.
Ages 5–10:	★★
Ages 11–15:	★★
Ages 16–Adult:	★★
Senior Citizens:	★★

This family-oriented live show transports you back to the Old West for a comical stunt show. The show is presented in an outdoor amphitheater several times each day (weather permitting). See the sign in front of the theater for show times.

≡ FAST FACT

By teaming up with Knott's Southern California Resort, the nearby Radisson Resort offers a two-park package, which includes a two-night stay at the hotel, one full-day admission to Knott's Berry Farm, and one full-day admission to Knott's Soak City U.S.A (all for two adults and two children). Free hotel parking, free gifts for the kids, and one buffet breakfast round out the package for about $300.

Indian Trails

 This area of Knott's Berry Farm showcases the native American civilizations of the Pacific Northwest, Great Plains, Southwest, and West. Here you'll find handcrafted totem poles, authentic architecture, and a wide range of crafts and other artifacts on display. Indian Trails is a wonderful place to explore during the day or evening, while digesting after a meal, and before returning to the thrill rides. The area will be of particular interest to adults.

Camp Snoopy

 Camp Snoopy is a separate theme park for kids located inside Knott's Berry Farm. Here, you'll find more than twenty rides for young people, plus a handful of shows and attractions designed to entertain the under-twelve crowd (and their parents). If you're traveling with kids, be prepared to spend at least several hours in this area.

Many of the rides are scaled-down versions of adult rides. For example, there's the mini-scrambler, Woodstock's Airmail (similar to the Supreme Scream described in the Boardwalk section), and the Timberline Twister roller coaster. One of the popular attractions in the six-acre Camp Snoopy area is a fully interactive petting zoo, where kids can spend time with various farm animals.

TRAVEL TIP

This is where you're most apt to come across Snoopy and friends meeting and greeting guests, so have your camera ready.

Fiesta Village

 Fiesta Village is one of the larger areas of Knott's Berry Farm. Here, you'll find the greatest collection of rides (most of which are thrill rides), suitable for teens and adults. Some of the highlights in this area include:

Dragon Swing

Ages 2–4:	N.S.
Ages 5–10:	N.S.
Ages 11–15:	★★
Ages 16–Adult:	★★
Senior Citizens:	N.S.

RIDE RESTRICTIONS: Guests under 42 inches tall must be accompanied by an adult.

Climb aboard a giant pirate ship that rocks back and fourth, traveling high into the air.

Gran Slammer

Ages 2–4:	N.S.
Ages 5–10:	★★
Ages 11–15:	★★
Ages 16–Adult:	★★
Senior Citizens:	★★

RIDE RESTRICTIONS: Guests under 42 inches tall must be accompanied by an adult; to ride alone, guests must be over 48 inches tall.

Somewhat similar to the Dragon Swing, the Gran Slammer offers an excellent view of the entire park as you swing back and forth, up and around high in the air.

Hat Dance

Ages 2–4:	N.S.
Ages 5–10:	★
Ages 11–15:	★★
Ages 16–Adult:	★★
Senior Citizens:	N.S.

RIDE RESTRICTIONS: Guests under 36 inches tall must be accompanied by an adult; to ride alone, guests must be taller than 42 inches.

This ride can best be compared to the "teacups" at Disneyland. In this case, however, passengers sit inside a colorful, oversize sombrero as they spin quickly around.

Jaguar!

Ages 2–4:	N.S.
Ages 5–10:	★★
Ages 11–15:	★★★
Ages 16–Adult:	★★
Senior Citizens:	N.S.

RIDE RESTRICTIONS: Guests must be at least 42 inches tall.

This medium-thrill coaster takes riders through the ancient Temple of the Jaguar as well as around and above it. This kid-oriented coaster is suitable for young people (over the age of eight). It's far less scary and less turbulent than a full-size coaster.

Merry Go Round

Ages 2–4:	★★
Ages 5–10:	★★★
Ages 11–15:	★★
Ages 16–Adult:	★★
Senior Citizens:	★★

This classic carousel is over 100 years old and features forty-eight hand-carved wooden animals, including lions, tigers, camels, zebras, and horses.

Montezooma's Revenge

Ages 2–4:	N.S.
Ages 5–10:	N.S.
Ages 11–15:	★★★
Ages 16–Adult:	★★★
Senior Citizens:	N.S.

RIDE RESTRICTIONS: Guests under 48 inches tall must be accompanied by an adult.

This high-tech coaster shoots riders around two giant (seven-story) loops, both forward and backward. You go from full stop to 60 miles per hour in less than three seconds.

 This is a must-see attraction.

Tampico Tumbler

Ages 2–4:	N.S.
Ages 5–10:	N.S.
Ages 11–15:	★★
Ages 16–Adult:	★★
Senior Citizens:	N.S.

RIDE RESTRICTIONS: Guests must be at least 48 inches tall.

Tampico Tumbler is a classic amusement park ride. You sit in a small vehicle, rise into the air, and spin around.

WaveSwinger

Ages 2–4:	N.S.
Ages 5–10:	★
Ages 11–15:	★★
Ages 16–Adult:	★★
Senior Citizens:	N.S.

RIDE RESTRICTIONS: Guests under 47 inches tall must be accompanied by an adult.

In a single-person swing, you rise into the air and then fly around in circles, relatively quickly. WaveSwinger is a classic amusement park ride offering a moderate thrill (in terms of the rapid spinning).

Edison International Electric Nights

Ages 2–4:	★
Ages 5–10:	★★★
Ages 11–15:	★★★
Ages 16–Adult:	★★★
Senior Citizens:	★★★

After dark, throughout the summer, the lake area of Fiesta Village becomes the stage for a colorful light, laser, and fireworks show. It's a visual spectacle suitable for the entire family that shouldn't be missed. Standing anywhere around the Reflection Lake area provides an excellent viewing point. This show changes each year; however, the accompanying music includes American classics mixed with Peanuts musical favorites.

≡FAST FACT

Located near Reflection Lake is the Church of Reflection, an old church (historic landmark) that is still used by guests as a memorable place to exchange marriage vows. Contact Guest Relations for details.

The Boardwalk

 In addition to offering a wide selection of carnival-style games of skill and luck (prizes are awarded, but there's an additional fee of $1 or $2 per game to play), this area features a handful of thrill rides.

Boomerang

Ages 2–4:	N.S.
Ages 5–10:	N.S.
Ages 11–15:	★★★
Ages 16–Adult:	★★★
Senior Citizens:	N.S.

RIDE RESTRICTIONS: Guests must be at least 48 inches tall.

This roller coaster was developed in Europe and is one of the most popular thrill rides in the park, so be prepared for a wait. You're strapped into the coaster's train (two people per row), and then in just under two minutes', frame, you'll fly around a 360-degree loop forward, then reverse direction, and ride around in reverse. One minute of this ride is a slow lift, which greatly builds anticipation for the big drop, loop, and corkscrew.

This is a must-see attraction.

HammerHead

Ages 2–4:	N.S.
Ages 5–10:	N.S.
Ages 11–15:	★★
Ages 16–Adult:	★★
Senior Citizens:	N.S.

RIDE RESTRICTIONS: Guests must be at least 48 inches tall.

This ride is somewhat like the Dragon Swing ride, except the vehicle you ride in goes 82 feet into the air and spins a full 360 degrees, which means you go upside down.

Perilous Plunge

Ages 2–4:	N.S.
Ages 5–10:	N.S.
Ages 11–15:	★★★
Ages 16–Adult:	★★★
Senior Citizens:	N.S.

RIDE RESTRICTIONS: Guests must be at least 48 inch tall.

Perilous Plunge isn't your typical water flume ride. In reality, it's just 34 feet shorter than the real-life Niagara Falls waterfall. This ride takes you in a boatlike vehicle 127 feet into the air and then drops you at a 75-degree angle. The result is a big splash at the bottom. Plan on getting wet! Each vehicle holds four people per row.

 This is a must-see attraction.

Sky Cabin

Ages 2–4:	★★
Ages 5–10:	★★
Ages 11–15:	★★
Ages 16–Adult:	★★
Senior Citizens:	★★

For the ultimate view of the entire park, enjoy this slow-moving journey up one of the park's tallest towers as the totally enclosed cabin spins around (slowly). The entire journey lasts about three minutes. The view is incredible.

Supreme Scream

Ages 2–4:	N.S.
Ages 5–10:	N.S.
Ages 11–15:	★★★
Ages 16–Adult:	★★★
Senior Citizens:	N.S.

RIDE RESTRICTIONS: Guests must be at least 52 inches tall.

Much like the popular Freefall amusement park ride, the Supreme Scream takes you 254 feet straight up and then drops you straight down. During the three-second drop, you travel at 50 miles per hour.

Wheeler Dealer Bumper Cars

Ages 2–4:	N.S.
Ages 5–10:	★★
Ages 11–15:	★★
Ages 16–Adult:	★★
Senior Citizens:	★★

RIDE RESTRICTIONS: Guests must be at least 54 inches tall to ride alone or between 36 inches and 53 inches to ride with an adult.

Wheeler Dealer Bumper Cars offers classic bumper car excitement. One adult rides per car. A child can accompany an adult, but space will be tight.

TRAVEL TIP

Eating, drinking, or taking pictures (or videotaping) is not permitted on any of the thrill rides. While alcohol cannot be brought into the park, alcoholic beverages can be ordered by guests over the age of twenty-one in many of the park's sit-down restaurants.

Charles M. Schultz Theatre

Ages 2–4:	★★
Ages 5–10:	★★★
Ages 11–15:	★★★
Ages 16–Adult:	★★★
Senior Citizens:	★★★

This Broadway-style musical ice show stars Snoopy, the Peanuts characters, plus a handful of human singers and dancers, all dressed in colorful costumes. Various other shows are also presented here during the holiday season and throughout the summer. Check the Entertainment Schedule or the theater marquee for show times and show details. The Charles M. Schultz Theatre is an air-conditioned theater (with traditional theater-style seating). The theater holds 2,100 guests.

Laser Invaders!

Ages 2–4:	N.S.
Ages 5–10:	★★★
Ages 11–15:	★★★
Ages 16–Adult:	★
Senior Citizens:	★

At the start of this interactive attraction, you're given a laser rifle and special vest, and directed into a dark, mazelike area for hand-to-hand laser-tag combat. There's a small additional fee to participate. At the end of each session, you'll be given a scorecard that rates your skill. A five-minute session costs $3 per person. A ten-minute session is priced at $5. This is a favorite among preteen boys in particular.

Wild Water Wilderness

 This area houses only one major ride, but it is where you'll encounter the Mystery Lodge. Here, a storyteller gives you a multimedia look at Native American culture. This is an entertaining, family-oriented ride/attraction.

Bigfoot Rapids

Ages 2–4:	N.S.
Ages 5–10:	★★★
Ages 11–15:	★★★
Ages 16–Adult:	★★★
Senior Citizens:	★★

RIDE RESTRICTIONS: Guests must be at least 46 inches tall.

This area of Knott's Berry Farm was established to be the home of California's longest man-made whitewater river. Six riders at a time ride in circular rafts that spin around as they proceed along the somewhat turbulent river and over small waterfalls. You're going to get wet on this ride because it's turbulent, although not at all scary. Make sure your belongings are secured so they remain dry during this white-water adventure.

Ranger Station

The Ranger Station is a small "zoo" where young guests in particular can get an up close look at spiders, insects, and other creatures and check out sightings of Sasquatch (a.k.a. Bigfoot) in the California High Sierra. This is a walk-through attraction that's self-paced. "Rangers" are on-hand to answer questions.

Special Events

 Throughout the year, Knott's Berry Farm hosts a wide range of special events, many of which are based on holidays. Between late November and late December, for example, the **Knott's Christmas Crafts Village** opens in Ghost Town (and is hosted by Santa). Carolers, community choirs, and dozens of artisans create a festive atmosphere. The park also offers several different holiday-oriented shows, including the **It's Christmas, Snoopy** ice spectacular.

Kids can celebrate the spring season with a bunch of different special activities that take place in Camp Snoopy between late March and late April. These events are all hosted by the Peanuts characters.

For adults, Knott's Berry Farm is also the host to the annual **Spring Crafts festival,** a month long showcase and sale of hand-crafted works of art, including jewelry, pottery, country crafts, and dolls.

Throughout the summer months (June through September), The Peanuts gang hosts **Snoopy's Rockin' Summer,** which offers a handful of new shows and activities for kids.

One of the biggest events of the year, however, happens in the fall, when Knott's Berry Farm is transformed into **Knott's Scary Farm.** This interactive haunted theme park is for kids, teens, and adults alike and offers a wide range of live entertainment and frights.

For kids, Camp Snoopy is transformed into **Camp Spooky** to celebrate the Halloween season. All of the Halloween season events are included in the standard cost of admission into the park. During the times when these events are taking place, plan on staying late into the evening.

TRAVEL TIP

To maximize your time, it's best to explore one area of the park at a time. This strategy will save a lot of walking. For example, if you were to experience Super Scream and then Bigfoot Rapids, you'd find yourself walking across the entire park.

CHAPTER 17

Exploring the Rest of Anaheim

IN ADDITION TO ITS WORLD-FAMOUS theme parks, Anaheim is also the home to a handful of theaters, shopping centers, museums, sports and recreation facilities, an ice-skating rink, hundreds of restaurants, and many other tourist attractions. This chapter offers details on just a few of the family-oriented attractions located in the Anaheim area.

Overview of Anaheim

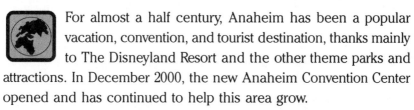 For almost a half century, Anaheim has been a popular vacation, convention, and tourist destination, thanks mainly to The Disneyland Resort and the other theme parks and attractions. In December 2000, the new Anaheim Convention Center opened and has continued to help this area grow.

Located about 28 miles south of downtown Los Angeles and 90 miles from San Diego, Anaheim had a population of 306,298 in 2001, making it the second-largest city in Orange County, California. The year-round tourist traffic, however, makes the population much larger. In fact, the Anaheim area alone houses over 150 hotels and motels, offering over 20,000 rooms (almost half of which are within walking distance of Disneyland). The average year-round occupancy of these hotels is approximately 86.5 percent.

For complete details on special events happening in Anaheim during the time of your visit, be sure to call the **Anaheim/Orange County Visitor Information Line** at ℘ (714) 765-8899, ext. 9888, or the **Anaheim/Orange County Visitor & Convention Bureau** at ℘ (714) 765-8888. For a free fax-on-demand service that offers information about area attractions and events, call ℘ (888) 440-4405 from any fax machine.

═FAST FACT

Before becoming a tourist destination, Anaheim was the wine capital of California. In the late 1880s, however, a blight wiped out all the vineyards, shutting down the wine industry in this area. After that, Anaheim was the home to many orange groves and thrived as an agricultural community until just after World War II.

Shopping Centers

 Do you like to shop? No matter what you're looking to purchase or what the weather is like, you'll find plenty of nearby malls and shopping centers to explore in the Anaheim area.

Downtown Disney

Located in The Disneyland Resort, Downtown Disney offers a collection of upscale shops, boutiques, and themed restaurants. Check out Chapter 14 for details about this unique shopping and family entertainment complex.

The Anaheim Indoor Marketplace

This indoor outlet mall/swap meet contains more than 200 shops offering mostly brand-name merchandise at discounts typically ranging 50 to 70 percent below retail. The marketplace is open from 10:00 A.M. to 7:00 P.M. on Wednesdays through Monday and closed on Tuesdays. It is located less than a mile from The Disneyland Resort. A **free shuttle bus** is available by calling ☎ (714) 999-0952. For more information, check out the Web site at ✍ *www.anaheimindoormarketplace.com.*

Anaheim Plaza Shopping Center

This newly built outdoor shopping center features stores like Old Navy, CompUSA, Ross Dress for Less, and Wal-Mart.

The Block at Orange

More than 100 shops and restaurants are featured in this outdoor shopping plaza. The Virgin Megastore, Starbucks Coffee, Borders Books, Mars Music, Vans Skate Park, Ron Jon Surf Shop, Saks Fifth Avenue Outlet, and Off 5th are just a few of the stores you'll find. There's also an AMC thirty-screen movie theater. The mall is located about ten minutes from Disneyland.

Buena Park Mall

Located one block east of Knott's Berry Farm (about ten minutes from Disneyland), this two-level mall features more than 160 stores and a food court.

Shoe City

This is the Los Angeles area's largest shoe store, featuring brands like Adidas, Converse, Reebok, Vans, Sketchers, New Balance, Nike, and Fila. A free shuttle bus service to the store (from Anaheim) is offered.

🧳 TRAVEL TIP

To receive a free copy of the *Official Visitors Guide for Anaheim/Orange County,* call ☎ (888) 598-3200.

Museums

You'll find a handful of family-oriented museums in and around Anaheim. For special events and exhibit information, call each museum directly.

Anaheim Museum

This museum showcases the history of Anaheim, starting with the German settlers. Call ☎ (714) 778-3301 for more information.

The Bowers Museum of Cultural Art and Kidseum

With over 70,000 objects in its collection, this is one of the largest cultural institutions in California. The Kidseum is an indoor, 11,000-square-foot interactive, hands-on center where kids can experience the beauty, ceremony, and history of several cultures through storytelling, puppet shows, and other activities. This museum is located in nearby Santa Ana. Call ☎ (714) 567-3600 for more information.

Discovery Science Center

Called by its creators "an amusement park for the mind," this science museum offers more than 100 interactive exhibits. This museum is located in nearby Santa Ana. Call ☎ (714) 542-2823 for more information.

Doll & Toy Museum

Check out the doll collection of Bea DeArmond, who has been acquiring her dolls for more than seventy years. On display are more than 5,000 dolls and toys from around the world. The collection includes in excess of 500 Barbies. You'll find this museum located 4 miles from Disneyland. Nearby are several hobby, crafts, and collectors shops. Admission is a mere $2 (per adult) and $1 (per child). Call ☎ (714) 527-2323 for more information.

Sports and Recreation

 Anaheim is also the home to several professional sports teams, including the **Anaheim Angels** (Major League baseball) and the **Mighty Ducks** (National Hockey League).

The 45,050-seat **Edison International Field** is where you can catch the Anaheim Angels between April and October. Call (714) 634-2000 for more information. The Mighty Ducks call the 19,200-seat **Arrowhead Pond of Anaheim** home between October and April. For information on their schedule, call ✆ (714) 704-2500.

Throughout Orange County, you'll also find forty-five public and private golf courses. The **Anaheim Hills Golf Course** can be reached at ✆ (714) 998-304.) Tee times at the **Dad Miller Golf Course** can be obtained by calling ✆ (714) 765-3481. Or try the **Islands Golf Center** at ✆ (714) 630-7888.

For ice skating (open to the public), visit the **Glacial Garden Ice Arena** in Anaheim. Call ✆ (714) 502-9023 for its hours of operation. The **Disney Ice Arena** can be reached at ✆ (714) 735-7465, or you can visit the Web site at ✐ *www.disneyice.com.*

TRAVEL TIP

When purchasing your tickets for Disneyland or Disney's California Adventure, ask about discounted tickets for Anaheim Angels or Mighty Ducks home games. Special offers are available directly from the Disneyland ticket booths at the park.

Day Spas

 Whether you're looking for a massage, facial, body wrap, mineral bath, or some other luxurious way to pamper yourself, you'll find it at one of the day spas located in Anaheim. The Hilton Anaheim offers the **Hilton Sports & Fitness Center,** which is open daily between 6:00 A.M. and 10:00 P.M.

Call ✆ (714) 750-4321 or check out the Web site at ✑ *www.ana heim.hilton.com* for details. Other day spas in the area include:

Burke Williams Day Spa: ✆(714) 769-1360
Spa & Fitness Club: ✆(714) 850-0050)
Glen Ivy Hot Springs Spa: ✆(909) 277-3529)

Tourist Attractions

 In addition to Disneyland, Disney's California Adventure, and Knott's Berry Farm, Anaheim also offers a handful of other (albeit smaller) family tourist attractions. Here's a sampling of the activities you can enjoy outside of the well-known theme parks in Anaheim.

Adventure City

✆ (714) 236-9300

Designed especially for kids between the ages of two and twelve, this outdoor, two-acre theme park offers eleven rides and attractions, a snack shop, game area, and some live entertainment.

Joey & Maria's Comedy Italian Wedding

✆ (800) 944-5639

This dinner comedy show (suitable primarily for teens and adults) re-creates a classic Italian wedding. As you eat dinner, you're one of the guests at this elaborate affair. This show is presented every Friday and Saturday evening at the Anaheim Plaza Hotel, located across from Disneyland.

Medieval Times Dinner & Tournament

✆ (714) 521-4740 or ✆ (800) 899-6600

✑ *www.medievaltimes.com*

Inside this giant castle, you and your family can step back in time and enjoy a meal while knights in armor participate in an eleventh-century jousting tournament right before your eyes. Matinee performances are presented during certain times of the year. This attraction is located about ten minutes away from Disneyland and one block from Knott's Berry Farm. The cost is about $40 per adult and $27 per child. While the show is highly entertaining and exciting, the "eat with your hands only" food is just so-so.

Movieland Wax Museum

☎ (714) 522-1154

✉ www.movielandwaxmuseum.com

The Movieland Wax Museum features life-size wax figures of more than 400 celebrities and historical figures. You can easily spend at least two hours exploring here.

Admission is $12.95 per adult and $6.95 per child. Senior citizens can visit for $10.55. Hours of operation are typically 10 A.M. to 7:30 P.M.; however, the hours are extended during the summer and holidays. This is an indoor attraction, so it's something the whole family can enjoy on a rainy or chilly day. This attraction is located one block north of Knott's Berry Farm and about ten minutes from Disneyland.

The Rib Trader Merlin's Magic Dinner Show

☎ (714) 744-9288

✉ www.ribtrader.com

Enjoy a complete dinner along with a comedy and magic show. This two hours' worth of quality entertainment is suitable for the entire family. Ticket prices are $24.95 for adults and $12.95 for children. Look for the money-saving coupon in the *Welcome to Southern California* magazine, distributed free of charge at many area hotels.

Ripley's Believe It or Not!

☎ (714) 522-1152

✉ www.movielandwaxmuseum.com/rippage

Located next to the Movieland Wax Museum, this is another family-oriented attraction that examines the weird and unusual and puts it on display. The museum features 10,000 square feet of jungle-themed entertainment and houses hundreds of rare and unusual artifacts.

Open between 11:00 A.M. and 5:00 P.M. (weekdays) and 10:00 A.M. to 6:00 P.M. (weekends) with extended hours during the summer months and on holidays, admission to this museum is priced at $8.95 per adult and $5.25 per child.

 **TRAVEL TIP**

A special combo admission ticket for the Movieland Wax Museum and Ripley's Believe It or Not! is available for $16.95 (adults), $9.75 (children), and $13.95 (seniors). These tickets are available at either box office. Together, these attractions offer a complete half-day's worth of indoor entertainment.

The Soprano's Last Supper
📞 (800) 944-5639

This dinner comedy show is a funny interactive spoof on the top-rated HBO television series. Performances are held every Friday evening at the Anaheim Plaza Hotel. This show will appeal mainly to adults, including college students.

Wild Bill's Wild West Dinner Extravaganza
📞 (800) 883-1546

Located two blocks from Knott's Berry Farm (about ten minutes from Disneyland), this family-oriented dinner show features singing, dancing, acrobatics, and a variety of other acts with a Western theme. Ticket prices are $39.95 for adults and $18 for children. Look for the money-saving coupon in the *Welcome to Southern California* magazine, distributed free of charge at many area hotels.

TRAVEL TIP

The Entertainment Book for Orange County has two-for-one and other discount admission offers for many of the tourist attractions in the Anaheim area. For details, visit *www.entertainment.com* or call 📞(800) 933-2605.

CHAPTER 18

Universal Studios Hollywood

LOCATED IN THE HEART of Universal City, California, Universal Studios Hollywood is one of the best-known working motion picture and television studios in the world. Although this facility continues to be a working studio, it's also become one of Hollywood's most popular theme park attractions.

Park Information

Operating hours for **Universal Studios Hollywood** theme park are from 8:00 A.M. to 10:00 P.M. during the summer, Thanksgiving, Easter, and Christmas, and 9:00 A.M. to 7:00 P.M. during all other times. Keep in mind that hours may vary during peak holidays' seasons. For general information, call ✆ (800) UNI-VERSAL or visit ✍ *www.UniversalStudiosHollywood.com.*

With rides, shows, and attractions all based on blockbuster motion pictures and popular T.V. shows, the Universal Studios Hollywood theme park allows you to experience some of your favorite movies, like *Jurassic Park, Terminator 2, Back to the Future, E.T. – The Extraterrestrial,* and others, in a whole new way. This is a family-oriented theme park, with a combination of quasi-thrill rides and a wide range of shows, attractions, dining options, and shops.

The Universal Studios Hollywood theme park is divided into three main areas: the Upper Lot, the Lower Lot, and CityWalk. The Upper and Lower Lots are where you'll find all of the rides, shows, and attractions.

One of the most interesting offerings at Universal Studios Hollywood is the famous backlot tour. While riding on a tram, you'll get an up close look at Hollywood history and see actual movies and television shows that are in production. You'll also see sets from well-known movies, and even experience a few surprises.

In addition to the actual theme park, Universal Studios Hollywood also features CityWalk, an exciting place to dine, shop, and catch a movie. With so much to see and do, Universal Studios Hollywood easily offers a full day (or two days) of entertainment. To see and do just about everything on a day with average crowds in the park, you'll need between eight and ten hours.

▮ TRAVEL TIP

At the entrance of Universal Studios Hollywood, before you reach the ticket booths, all guests must pass through metal detectors. Security personnel will inspect purses and other items. During busy periods, waiting in line for this process could delay your entry into the park by between ten and thirty minutes.

Guest services include lockers, restrooms, ATMs, first aid, stroller rentals, wheelchair rentals, and public telephones. If you've been to Universal Studios Florida, you'll quickly notice that this theme park is somewhat smaller; however, the actual working studio aspect of this park is bigger. After all, this was originally a major motion picture studio. Likewise, in terms of the rides, shows, and attractions, you'll find a lot of similarities between the two parks. For example, both Universal Studios Hollywood and Universal Studios Florida (in Orlando) offer Back to the Future: The Ride, Terminator 2: 3D, and E.T. Adventure.

The biggest complaint most guests have is that the music that is pumped through speakers throughout the park is too loud and it can't be avoided.

Getting to Universal Studios Hollywood

Universal Studios Hollywood is located between Hollywood and the San Fernando Valley, just off the Hollywood 101 Freeway. Take the Universal Center Drive or Lankershim exits and follow the signs.

If you're staying in Anaheim and spending several days at The Disneyland Resort, you can still visit Universal Studios Hollywood without having to rent a car. Free round-trip shuttle bus transportation between Anaheim and Universal Studios is available for each adult admission pass to **Universal Studios Hollywood** purchased. To use this bus service, you must buy your tickets by calling ✆ (800) UNIVERSAL. The prepurchased tickets need to be picked up at the Airport Bus Transportation Center located near Disneyland.

The shuttle bus takes approximate forty-five minutes each way and operates seven days a week. Departures from Anaheim to Universal City occur at 7:30, 9:00, 10:30 A.M., and noon. Return trips (Universal City to Anaheim) depart at 4:00, 5:30, 7:00, and 8:30 P.M. During peak travel seasons, the bus service is extended. Reservations are required. This bus service is also available without purchasing park admission tickets. The round-trip adult fare is $18, and $9 for children, ages three to eleven.

Admission

Admission to Universal Studios Hollywood is based on a full-day ticket, which allows unlimited access to all rides, shows, and attractions. There's an additional daily parking fee of $7 for regular parking or $12 for "Preferred Parking" (which is more conveniently located at the park's entrance). RV parking is $10 per day.

Type of Pass	Adult	Child*	Senior**
1-Day Pass	$43	$33	$37
CityWalk Nightime Party Pass with Single-Day Ticket	$58	N/A	N/A

Type of Pass	Adult	Child*	Senior**
Front of the Line Pass	$79	N/A	N/A
Director's Pass	$69	N/A	N/A
Southern California Value Pass	$75	N/A	N/A
Celebrity Annual Pass	$49	$39	$44
Deluxe Celebrity Annual Pass	$72	$62	$67
* (Ages 3 to 11), **(Ages 60 and up)			

The CityWalk Nightime Party Pass with Single-Day Ticket allows you to enjoy the theme park during the day and the CityWalk night-clubs at night, all for one price.

The Front of the Line Pass allows you to go right to the front of the lines, plus get the best seats for the shows. This is a one-day pass.

The Director's Pass allows you to participate in aftershow demonstrations and special character meet-and-greet events. This is a one-day pass.

The Southern California Value Pass is a fourteen-day pass (good on consecutive days only) that offers admission to Universal Studios Hollywood and the clubs in CityWalk.

For a mere $6 more than the price of a one-day park pass, anyone can purchase a Celebrity Annual Pass to Universal Studios Hollywood. In addition to offering unlimited admission to the theme park on 333 preselected days, annual pass holders also receive a handful of special discounts, including:

- 15 percent discount on admission for up to six additional guests purchasing one-day passes
- 25 percent discount on merchandise at most of the theme park's shops
- 20 percent discount on food and beverages purchased in the theme park and many participating CityWalk restaurants
- Discounts when purchasing tickets to events held at the Universal Amphitheater or admission tickets to the Movieland Wax Museum (in Hollywood)

- Special hotel discounts, ranging from 10 to 25 percent off standard room rates at nearby participating hotels, including the Hilton Universal City & Towers, the Anabelle Hotel, Beverly Garland Holiday Inn, Hyatt West Hollywood, Le Park Suite Hotel, Le Reve Hotel, Nite Inn Studio City, Safari Inn, and the Sportman's Lodge.

For more information about **Celebrity Annual Passes,** call ✆ (888) 309-9625. For an additional $30 per year, unlimited parking is also available.

📣 TRAVEL TIP

The prices listed in this book are subject to change. In addition, all of the admission tickets to Universal Studios Hollywood have expiration dates (typically one year from the date purchased), so don't buy passes you won't be using during your stay in Southern California.

The Backlot Tram Tour

Ages 2–4:	N.S.
Ages 5–10:	★
Ages 11–15:	★★★
Ages 16–Adult:	★★★
Senior Citizens:	★★★

Departing every five to fifteen minutes throughout the day and evening (with the final tram leaving the Upper Lot at around 4:00 P.M.), this 55-minute tour provides an up close, fun-filled look at how a major motion picture studio operates. As you ride in a tram, a tour guide offers lots of information and facts, not to mention a few too many corny jokes as you travel around the studio's 415 acres.

You'll see famous movie sets (from movies like *Jurassic Park III*, *Psycho*, *Back to the Future*, and *The Grinch*) and working soundstages and learn a bit about the studio's history. You might even catch a glimpse of a famous celebrity at work. In the backlot area are over 500 famous sets from movies and T.V. shows.

Universal Studios was originally opened in 1912, so you'll get a glimpse of the rich history of this studio, which has produced over 8,000 movies along with countless T.V. shows, infomercials, television commercials, and music videos.

In addition to just seeing the working studio, the Backlot Tram Tour offers a few surprises, so keep your camera ready! For example, you'll explore a mummy's tomb, experience an earthquake (Hollywood style), and even confront King Kong and Jaws.

The Backlot Tour is suitable for people of all ages. If you're truly interested in experiencing a behind-the-scenes look at the studios, a special VIP Experience package is available for $125 per person. This package includes admission to the theme park, front- of-the-line access to all rides and attractions, plus a personalized guided tour of the studio's lot. You'll actually visit working soundstages where T.V. shows or movies are being filmed. This special tour gives you much greater access than the regular Backlot Tram Tour.

TRAVEL TIP

Especially in the evening, be sure to bring a jacket along on this tour. The trams are open and constantly moving, so if the temperature drops, you will be cold if you're not dressed appropriately.

The Upper Lot

 The theme park area of Universal Studios Hollywood is divided into two main areas: the Upper Lot and the Lower Lot. You can travel between these two areas freely by taking a series of escalators (the journey takes about five minutes). An elevator is also available. About halfway between the two areas, where you switch escalators, there's a large terrace area that offers a wonderful view of the Universal Studios' soundstages and backlot (where the T.V. shows and movies are actually filmed). You can also see the Warner Bros. Studios in the distance. The view is spectacular; this is a wonderful picture-taking spot.

Animal Planet Live!

Ages 2–4:	★★
Ages 5–10:	★★★
Ages 11–15:	★★★
Ages 16–Adult:	★★
Senior Citizens:	★★★

SHOW LENGTH: twenty minutes

Based on programming from the Animal Planet television cable network, as the name suggests, this is a totally live stage show that features actual animal trainers and a cast of animals you've seen on popular television shows and movies. Exotic birds, trained monkeys, snakes, and famous dogs are among the animals that perform in a show that can best be described as both extremely cute and enjoyable.

⚏FAST FACT

Discover Card offers a special promotion when you use your Discover credit card to purchase admission passes to the park. For each adult one-day pass you buy, you get a second day of park access for free. Special hotel accommodations and park admission packages are also available. For more information, call **Universal Studios Vacations** at ☎(800) 711-0080.

This is a highly entertaining and rather humorous show that young kids in particular will enjoy. However, it's definitely suitable for and appealing to people of all ages. The theater in which this show is presented is large, so there's seldom a wait—assuming you arrive about fifteen minutes before a scheduled show time. Show times are posted in front of the theater, on the information boards located throughout the park, and in the printed park schedule available from the ticket booths. The theater itself is covered, so you'll be sheltered from direct sunlight or light rain.

After each performance, some of the animals and their trainers remain on stage to meet and greet young audience members. This provides for an excellent photo opportunity.

Back to the Future: The Ride

Ages 2–4:	N.S.
Ages 5–10:	★★★
Ages 11–15:	★★★
Ages 16–Adult:	★★★
Senior Citizens:	★★★

RIDE RESTRICTION: Guests must be at least 40 inches tall.

When the ads for Universal Studios Hollywood explain that you can "ride the movies," this ride is definitely what they're talking about. Although it has been around for a few years now, Back to the Future: The Ride continues to be an extremely popular attraction, so be prepared to wait to experience it. (The good news is, the waiting area is mostly covered, so you'll be sheltered from direct sun or rain during most or all of your wait.)

Once you get inside the massive building that houses this ride, you'll see a video preshow that sets the stage for your turbulent adventure. This preshow features Doc Brown and Biff from the original *Back to the Future* movie trilogy. (Michael J. Fox's character is noticeably absent but that doesn't impact the fun you'll have experiencing this attraction.)

After the preshow, you'll be divided into groups and led into a small room, where you'll watch an additional four-minute video that continues to provide the background story for your upcoming adventure. Next, you'll be directed to board the actual ride and step into your time-traveling vehicle, which is Doc Brown's latest invention. Each vehicle holds eight passengers.

Using a state-of-the-art flight simulator, audio, and Omnimax movie technology, your vehicle will move and bounce around in a way that's perfectly synchronized with the Omnimax movie shown on a massive 80-foot-tall projection screen in front of you. You'll hear (and feel) the realistic sound effects through the 300 speakers that surround you.

To make the experience even more realistic, smoke and other special effects are utilized. Back to the Future: The Ride was two years in the making and cost over $16 million to create. This ride is as turbulent as a roller coaster; although there are no real drops, it feels as if there are. The closest thing to this attraction at The Disneyland Resort is the Star Tours ride, although this one is better.

With the exception of the steep drop at the end of Jurassic Park: The Ride (which offers a very different type of experience), this is the closest thing to a thrill ride you'll experience at Universal Studios Hollywood.

 This is a must-see attraction.

TRAVEL TIP

Keep in mind, throughout the year, special promotions are offered. For example, around Halloween, a special "Buy 1 Adult Ticket, Get 2nd Day Free" promotion takes place. Ask the ticket booth for details, or call the park's general information number.

The Blues Brothers

Ages 2–4:	N.S.
Ages 5–10:	N.S.
Ages 11–15:	★★
Ages 16–Adult:	★★
Senior Citizens:	★★★

SHOW LENGTH: twenty minutes

Presented several times a day in an outdoor stage area located on the Upper Lot, this live musical performance stars the Blues Brothers, Jake and Elwood, who perform a handful of popular musical numbers. Grab a snack at a nearby refreshment kiosk, then kick back and get ready to clap along or dance to the upbeat music.

The Mummy Returns: Chamber of Doom

Ages 2–4:	N.S.
Ages 5–10:	N.S.
Ages 11–15:	★★
Ages 16–Adult:	★★
Senior Citizens:	★★

Based on the popular *The Mummy Returns* motion picture, this is a self-paced, walk-through attraction that re-creates actual sets and props from the movie, yet creates a truly haunting experience as you're transported into an ancient Egyptian tomb. Like the movie, this attraction is not suitable for young kids.

Unlike other attractions within Universal Studios Hollywood, this one is somewhat temporary. At some point in the future, it may very well be replaced with an interactive, walk-through experience based on another popular movie.

Nickelodeon Blast Zone

Ages 2–4:	★★★
Ages 5–10:	★★★
Ages 11–15:	★★
Ages 16–Adult:	N.S.
Senior Citizens:	N.S.

This is basically a kids-only attraction that features a tremendous, colorful interactive play area complete with shooting fountains and other water-based activities for young people to enjoy on hot days. Although kids will find this attraction extremely enjoyable, they're going to be completely soaked when they're done. Part of this attraction involves the excitement of having 500 gallons of water dumped on your head.

In addition to the water-based activities, this is where you'll encounter a handful of characters from Nickelodeon's most popular T.V. shows. This entire area is extremely interactive and offers a multitude of photo-taking opportunities. This attraction also features The Wild Thornberrys Adventure Temple (containing over 25,000 foam balls and other activities) and Nick Jr. Backyard (designed for kids under the age of six), which are totally dry areas for children to explore.

Ideally, you'll want to have a full change of clothes on hand for anyone who experiences the Nickelodeon Splash area of this attraction. A wet child will be uncomfortable walking around the rest of the park and entering into some of the air-conditioned attractions and restaurants.

Save this attraction for particularly hot days unless you have a change of clothes available. While you probably won't want to enter into this area, you should stay in the viewing area and maintain a close eye on your children as they experience the Nickelodeon Blast Zone.

TRAVEL TIP

When making any purchases at Universal Studios Hollywood (excluding the food and souvenir kiosks), be sure to show your AAA membership card to receive a 10 percent discount. Discounts are offered on admission passes and most souvenirs and food items. Discounts are not offered on tobacco, film, collectibles, sundry items, videos, and CDs.

Rugrats Magic Adventure

Ages 2–4:	★★★
Ages 5–10:	★★★
Ages 11–15:	★★★
Ages 16–Adult:	★
Senior Citizens:	★

SHOW LENGTH: twenty-five minutes (weekends only)

Presented on weekends (during the nonpeak season) and more often during peak summer and holiday times, this live kid-oriented show features all of the popular characters from *The Rugrats* cartoon in a fun-filled, colorful, musical extravaganza.

This show is presented in a large, air-conditioned theater, so it's the perfect way to break up a day and give young people a chance to relax as they're entertained. Due to the popularity of this show, arrive at the theater at least twenty to thirty minutes before the posted show time. Rugrats Magic Adventure is ideal for kids, between the ages of three and fifteen, or anyone who enjoys the *Rugrats* cartoon on Nickelodeon.

Terminator 2: 3D

Ages 2–4:	N.S.
Ages 5–10:	N.S.
Ages 11–15:	★★★
Ages 16–Adult:	★★★
Senior Citizens:	★★★

SHOW LENGTH: twenty minutes

If you saw the *Terminator 2* motion picture, you know it was jam-packed with nonstop special effects and plenty of action. Well, imagine experiencing this movie in 3-D, in a theater custom-built with interactive special effects that enhance your viewing experience. That's just a preview of what you can expect from this totally incredible 3-D movie that continues the *Terminator 2* storyline. This attraction cost over $60 million to produce, and you'll see why from the moment you're seated in the massive indoor theater. Combining 3-D movie technology with lasers, live actors, robots, indoor pyrotechnics, and state-of-the-art sound effects, you'll experience an attraction the likes of which are not available at any other theme park (except Universal Studios Florida).

Your adventure begins with a visit to Cyberdyne's corporate headquarters, where Kimberly (the director of corporate affairs) provides a brief presentation about the new Skynet system. The movie portion of this attraction transports guests to the year 2029 and reunites Arnold Schwarzenegger, Linda Hamilton, Edward Furlong, and director James Cameron for a thrilling almost-fifteen-minute adventure that's presented in 3-D on a massive 23-foot high by 50-foot wide screen.

Prior to this, there's a nine-minute preshow in a standup waiting room area. For the preshow, stand toward the middle of the room. Make sure you can see the Cyberdyne logos on the large video monitors overhead. The entire attraction takes place in an air-conditioned building. The waiting area to enter the ride, however, is outdoors (but covered).

Due to the violent nature of this attraction (and the loud explosions), it's not suitable for young kids. If it were shown in traditional theaters, it would have a PG-13 rating. For everyone else, however, don't miss it.

Shows are presented throughout the day. As you exit, you'll find yourself in the T2 Gear Supply Company, a gift shop offering T2 souvenirs.

 This is a must-see attraction.

WaterWorld

Ages 2–4:	N.S.
Ages 5–10:	★
Ages 11–15:	★★
Ages 16–Adult:	★★
Senior Citizens:	★★

SHOW LENGTH: fifteen minutes

Based very loosely on the *WaterWorld* motion picture, this is a high-energy live show featuring exciting motorboat stunts and extreme Jet Ski action, all combined with pyrotechnics and other special effects that create realistic explosions designed to keep you at the edge of your seat. The loud explosions may frighten young children. Kids (ages five and older), teens, and adults alike will enjoy this wet and wild show. When the park is crowded, be sure to arrive at the theater at least fifteen minutes before the posted show time to ensure a seat for the desired performance.

The Wild, Wild, Wild West Stunt Show

Ages 2–4:	N.S.
Ages 5–10:	★
Ages 11–15:	★★
Ages 16–Adult:	★★
Senior Citizens:	★★

SHOW LENGTH: twenty minutes

Presented in a specially designed outdoor theater, the Wild, Wild, Wild West Stunt Show offers an exciting, sometimes humorous look at Hollywood's stunt people. It features plenty of demonstrations, so you see how those realistic fight scenes and other stunts are performed in the movies, without anyone getting hurt. More than 100 stunts are performed. The show is suitable for people of all ages.

🧳 TRAVEL TIP

Welcome to Southern California magazine, offered free of charge at many Southern California hotels, motels, and inns, typically offers a coupon good for $4 off per person for up to six admission passes to Universal Studios Hollywood. You can also purchase discounted admission passes online for this and many other California-area attractions from *www.WelcomeMagazine.com.*

The Lower Lot

 The Lower Lot is separated from the Upper Lot by a series of escalators. Like the Upper Lot, the Lower Lot offers several attractions and rides that are enjoyable for the entire family.

Backdraft

Ages 2–4:	N.S.
Ages 5–10:	N.S.
Ages 11–15:	★★
Ages 16–Adult:	★★
Senior Citizens:	★★

SHOW LENGTH: twenty minutes

Based on the movie directed by Ron Howard (who also narrates this attraction), Backdraft offers a behind-the-scenes look at how this film was created. It combines a documentary-style movie with live demonstrations. The theme, of course, is fire, and in the finale, the theater heats up as live (but controlled) explosions happen just a few feet in front of you. Although this attraction is entertaining, you'll learn a lot about the nature of fire and develop a newfound respect for the work of firefighters and the many challenges they face as they enter burning buildings.

This attraction is not suitable for young children. It's presented in a motion picture soundstage that's been designed to present the live demonstrations and movie-based features. Each group is directed through this walk-through attraction by a tour guide.

E.T. Adventure

Ages 2–4:	★★★
Ages 5–10:	★★★
Ages 11–15:	★★★
Ages 16–Adult:	★★★
Senior Citizens:	★★★

RIDE RESTRICTION: Children under 42 inches must be accompanied by an adult.

With the twentieth anniversary rerelease of the *E.T. – The Extraterrestrial* motion picture March 2002, millions of kids and teens had the opportunity to see this timeless classic on the big screen for the first time. At Universal Studios Hollywood, people of all ages can relive the magic of this movie in a way that only Steven Spielberg himself could have created.

E.T. Adventure allows guests to sit on moving bicycle-shaped vehicles that roll and eventually fly while being piloted by E.T. himself. The visuals throughout this ride experience are stunning and realistic. Your adventure begins here on Earth, but with a bit of help from E.T., you'll soon find yourself visiting E.T.'s colorful and charming home planet where you come face-to-face with his family and friends.

At the very end of your adventure, E.T. will even offer a personalized good-bye message to you as he waves. This is something that young kids absolutely love. As you'd probably guess, E.T. Adventure is an extremely popular attraction—and not just among kids—so be prepared for a wait. As you weave your way through the indoor waiting area before you board the ride, you'll have a chance to explore a re-created forest and see some of E.T.'s friends. Just like the movie, E.T. Adventure is innovative, charming, and magical.

👍 This is a must-see attraction.

GameWorks

Ages 2–4:	N.S.
Ages 5–10:	★
Ages 11–15:	★
Ages 16–Adult:	★
Senior Citizens:	★

GameWorks is a small indoor arcade featuring about fifteen coin-operated video games, which you pay for as you play. The cost is $1 per play for most of the games.

Jurassic Park: The Ride

Ages 2–4:	N.S.
Ages 5–10:	N.S.
Ages 11–15:	★★★
Ages 16–Adult:	★★★
Senior Citizens:	★★

RIDE RESTRICTION: Guests must be at least 46 inches tall.

Showcasing a cast of life-size and extremely lifelike robotic dinosaurs, this attraction includes a boat ride through Jurassic Park, which is the prehistoric theme park from the *Jurassic Park* motion picture series. As you pass through the grand gates of this prehistoric theme park, you'll quickly discover that the dinosaurs have gotten loose, and they are hunting humans!

The initial part of your river journey will be quiet, peaceful, and rather beautiful. That is, until an angry T-Rex starts coming close. Then, things start getting a little hairy. Just when you think you're safe, grab onto your personal belongings and prepare for an 85-foot plunge into total darkness for the conclusion of your adventure. This exciting and somewhat scary ride ultimately ends with a splash, so be prepared to get wet! (Also, be sure to protect your valuables, such as cameras and camcorders, from the water.)

For a small fee, waterproof ponchos are sold in the nearby gift shop, so you can enjoy Jurassic Park: The Ride without getting too wet. As you experience the massive drop at the end of the ride, your photo will be taken and can be purchased as a souvenir within the gift shop.

 This is a must-see attraction.

TRAVEL TIP

Throughout the Upper Lot, you'll find props from popular motion pictures on display. Standing with these props typically makes for amazing, personalized souvenir photos. You'll also find characters and celebrity impersonators anxious to take photos with guests.

Lucy: A Tribute

Ages 2–4:	N.S.
Ages 5–10:	N.S.
Ages 11–15:	N.S.
Ages 16–Adult:	★★
Senior Citizens:	★★★

This minimuseum chronicles the life of actress/comedian Lucile Ball. It's a self-paced walk-through attraction that features props, costumes, and countless photos from Lucy's career. This up close and personal look at a Hollywood legend is most suited for adults. In the neighboring Backlot store, you can purchase your own Lucy collectibles. You can easily spend between ten and fifteen minutes looking around this small museumlike area. There's also an interactive Lucy trivia quiz you can participate in.

≡FAST FACT

Guests of Universal Studios Hollywood who are celebrating their birthday on the day of their visit to the park are invited to a special birthday celebration bash, held every afternoon in the Lower Lot (near Jurassic Park: The Ride). Meet the Universal characters for a very special photo-taking opportunity.

Dining Options

 In addition to the various dining options within the theme park (most of which can be classified as fast-food or snack options), there are many full-service restaurants located in CityWalk, a two-minute walk from the main entrance of the Universal Studios Hollywood theme park.

To help you find a restaurant that fits within your dining budget, the following symbols are used to describe the price range for an overall one-person meal. Don't forget to use your discount if you're an annual pass holder in order to save 20 percent on all food and beverages purchased in the park.

THE EVERYTHING GUIDE TO THE DISNEYLAND RESORT

> **$:** Under $10 per person
> **$$:** Under $20 per person
> **$$$:** Over $20 per person

Chilly Willy Ice Cream Co. ($). Also found in the Lower Lot area, this is a great place to stop and chill out with some soft-serve ice cream or a sundae.

Deli Variety ($). Grab a quick burger, sandwich, or pizza at this dining location located in the Upper Lot area.

Doc Brown's Fancy Fried Chicken ($/$$). Fried and grilled chicken entrées are primarily what's offered here. You'll find this fast-food option in the Upper Lot area, near the escalators that lead to the Lower Lot. Outdoor seating is provided.

Flintstone's Drive-In ($/$$). Offering mostly snack items and quick meals, this is a great place for families to grab a fast, relatively inexpensive lunch. It's located in the Upper Lot area but offers no dedicated indoor or outdoor seating. To sit down and enjoy your meal, you'll need to find nearby outdoor seating.

Hollywood Cantina ($/$$). Open seasonally, Hollywood Cantina serves Mexican fast food. It's a great place to stop for a quick lunch, but no indoor seating is available.

Jurassic Cove Café ($/$$). This is the only indoor sit-down dining establishment in the Lower Lot area of the park. The specialty of the house is Teriyaki bowls; however, you'll also find burgers and chicken dishes.

Louie's Pizza & Pasta ($). Pizza is the specialty of this fast-food dining establishment. It's located in the Upper Lot area but offers no indoor or outdoor seating.

Melligan's Pub ($). Found in the Upper Lot area, this pub offers snacks and a good selection of beer and alcohol. It's most suited for adults and offers sit-down service.

Mel's Diner ($/$$). This full-service 1950s-style diner offers a good-size menu that includes burgers, hot dogs, chicken, and other fast-food–type options. Mel's Diner is best known for its milkshakes and offers indoor and outdoor seating.

Studio Commissary ($$). Located in the Lower Lot area, you'll find burgers, chicken, drinks, and other fast-food items. Indoor and outdoor seating is available.

Sweet Liberty ($). To satisfy your sweet tooth, this is a great place to stop for a quick snack. Here you'll find a wide range of freshly made and prepackaged candies and chocolates, along with other sweets.

▐ TRAVEL TIP

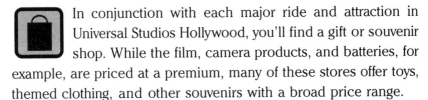

Don't be surprised if you run into Charlie Chaplin, the Phantom of the Opera, Woody Woodpecker, Frankenstein, Groucho Marx, Hercules, Xena, Laurel and Hardy, Marilyn Monroe, Dracula, the Blues Brothers, the Wolfman, the Mummy, or any of the Nickelodeon characters as they wonder throughout the theme park taking pictures and interacting with guests.

Shopping

 In conjunction with each major ride and attraction in Universal Studios Hollywood, you'll find a gift or souvenir shop. While the film, camera products, and batteries, for example, are priced at a premium, many of these stores offer toys, themed clothing, and other souvenirs with a broad price range.

Animal Stars. Located near the Animal Planet Live theater, a wide range of animal-themed products and souvenirs are sold here. You'll find a large selection of adorable animal plush toys. What's special about this shop is that at prescheduled times throughout the day, several animal stars from the Animal Planet Live show make appearances just outside the shop. This provides for an excellent photo opportunity.

Backlot. Hollywood souvenirs and a large selection of Lucy collectibles are sold. You'll find this store in the Lower Lot area.

Cartooniversal. If you're a fan of classic cartoons and cartoon characters, like Woody Woodpecker and Betty Boop, this is the shop for you!

E.T. Toy Closet. Get your picture taken with E.T. or check out the wide range of E.T.-themed toys, clothing items, and souvenirs. This shop is located near the exit of the E.T. Adventure ride.

Film Kiosk. Film, batteries, onetime use cameras, and other photo/camera supplies are sold.

Hollywood Photographs. Throughout the park, you'll find roving photographers who will offer to take your picture. This is the pickup location for those souvenir pictures. Prices vary for each picture. Once you have your picture taken, make sure you hang onto your receipt from the photographer in order to preview and claim your photo later at this location.

Jurassic Outfitters. Located in the Lower Lot, you'll automatically walk through this shop as you exit Jurassic Park: The Ride. Featured here are a wide range of dinosaur-related toys and items, plus other souvenirs. Here, you can also purchase the souvenir photo taken during the final splash of the ride.

Mode Extreme. Trendy clothing and fashion accessories are what's available in this shop.

Nick Stuff. Toys, clothing, and souvenirs from Nickelodeon's top T.V. shows and cartoons are sold here. It's a great place to pick up a gift for a child.

Silver Screen Collectibles. Photos of your favorite celebrities along with life-size cardboard cutouts of Hollywood's biggest stars are sold.

Studio Styles. A wide range of Hollywood and Universal Studios clothing is sold.

Surf Shack. This clothing shop features stylish fashions for the entire family.

T2 Gear & Supply. Located near the Terminator 2: 3D attraction, this shop offers a selection of merchandise based on both the movie and the theme park attraction.

Take One. A wide selection of Hollywood and Universal Studios souvenirs can be found.

Time Travelers Depot. You'll find this shop near the exit of Back to the Future: The Ride. As you'd expect, you'll discover an assortment of products, clothing items, and toys based on the attraction and the *Back to the Future* movies.

≡FAST FACT

In several locations inside the theme park, you'll find digital park maps that list all of the shows and attractions, along with accurate current wait times. One of these digital boards is located adjacent to the Blues Brothers Stage in the Upper Lot area. Another is located in the Lower Lot area, in front of the E.T. Adventure ride.

Tram Central. Souvenirs from the Backlot Tram Tour are sold here, including posters from the theme park's top attractions.

Universal Film Co. This is one of several shops that offer a wide range of photographic products, including film, batteries, and one-time use cameras. You can also rent a digital camera here and have your traditional film developed within an hour.

Universal Studios Store. This store offers the largest selection of Universal Studios merchandise, including logo clothing, that you'll find within the park.

Exploring CityWalk

Hours of operation are 11:00 A.M. to 10:00 P.M. Sunday through Thursday and 11:00 A.M. to midnight Friday and Saturday. During peak holiday seasons, extended hours apply.

When you're ready to break for lunch or have a nice sit-down dinner, check out the places to eat in CityWalk. Many of the restaurants here offer theme-dining experiences, such as the **Hard Rock Café.** There's also **Wizards,** a wonderful dinner theater experience featuring an impressive magic show. **Gladstones** (seafood), the **Wolfgang Puck Café** (gourmet pizza), and **Tony Roma's** are among the other full-service dining options.

In addition, once the theme park closes, eight nightclubs open in the CityWalk area. These adults-only clubs offer full-service bars, music, and plenty of dancing and entertainment. **B. B. King's Blues Club, The Howl at the Moon** dueling piano bar, and the **Rumba Room** are just some of the clubs that require a separate admission ticket to enter in the evenings.

TRAVEL TIP

Universal Studios Hollywood, along with all of the other nearby studios and T.V. networks, offers free tickets to see tapings of popular T.V. sitcoms, game shows, and other programs. Special free T.V. Show Tickets kiosks can be found in CityWalk as well as in the Upper Lot of the Universal Studios Hollywood theme park (near the Wild, Wild, Wild West Stunt Show).

In addition to offering great places to eat, CityWalk also features more than thirty one-of-a-kind stores, plus a lineup of kiosks that sell a variety of items for kids and adults alike. A family can easily spend at least two hours exploring the many shops in CityWalk. You'll also find ongoing live entertainment, talented street performers, and other attractions in this lively outdoor area.

Finally, CityWalk offers a huge, state-of-the-art, eighteen-screen movie theater complex where you can see all of Hollywood's latest blockbusters. There's also a **3D IMAX theater** that features a six-story screen. For movie show times, call ✆ (818) 508-0588.

The Universal Amphitheater

 The **Universal Amphitheater** is one of Hollywood's largest indoor entertainment venues for concerts. Although this theater is located adjacent to Universal Studios Hollywood, it's not considered part of the theme park. Big-name recording artists perform here regularly. Call the phone number for a show/event schedule during the time of your visit. For more information, call ✆ (818) 622-4440, or to order tickets, visit the **Advance Tickets** Web site at ⌨ *www.advancetickets.com*. There's also a box office located in CityWalk.

CHAPTER 19

The Stars Shine in Los Angeles County

MUCH OF THIS BOOK is dedicated to the theme parks located in California; however, there's a lot more to see and do in the Los Angeles County area. Although it would take an entire book to describe all of the activities this city and nearby areas have to offer, this chapter highlights some of the family-oriented favorites.

A Quick Geography Lesson

 Los Angeles County, one of California's original twenty-seven counties, was established February 18, 1850. Originally, the county occupied the area along the coast between Santa Barbara and San Diego, but within a year its boundaries were enlarged from 4,340 square miles to 34,520 square miles.

During subsequent years, Los Angeles County went through additional transitions. The last major detachment occurred in 1889 when Orange County (where The Disneyland Resort and Knott's Berry Farm are located) was established. Los Angeles County remains one of the nation's largest counties, encompassing 4,081 square miles.

Los Angeles County includes the islands of San Clemente and Santa Catalina. It is bordered on the east by Orange and San Bernardino Counties, on the north by Kern County, on the west by

Ventura County, and on the south by the Pacific Ocean. Its coastline is 76 miles long. It has the largest population (9,802,800 as of January 1, 2001) of any county in the nation and is exceeded by only eight states. Approximately 29 percent of California's residents live in Los Angeles County.

≡FAST FACT

Many of the most popular attractions in the Los Angeles area can be found in Hollywood, which continues to be the top visitor destination in Los Angeles County, according to a study commissioned by the Hollywood Chamber of Commerce. Of the 23.9 million visitors to Los Angeles in 1998, 42 percent came to Hollywood.

Los Angeles Sightseeing Tours

 If you have a few hours to spend and want to ensure that you'll see all of the sights Los Angeles (including Hollywood and surrounding areas) is famous for, consider participating in a sightseeing tour.

Starline Tours
📞 (800) 959-3131

🖱 *www.starlinetours.com*

Starline Tours has a fleet of vans, mini-coaches, and motor coaches and offers over eighteen different types of Los Angeles tours. The two-hour tour of movie stars' homes ($29 for adults/$20 for children) is a favorite among tourists, as is the 5½-hour Grand Tour of Los Angeles. You'll find the Starline Tours' guides to be extremely knowledgeable. If you're staying in the Los Angeles area, Starline Tours will pick you up at your hotel at no additional charge.

VIP Tours

☏ (800) 438-1814

🖱 *www.viptoursandcharacters.com*

VIP Tours offers a handful of different tours, using fourteen-passenger vans and a fleet of mini-buses and motor coaches. The Los Angeles City Tour and Movie Stars Homes, for example, is a 4½-hour tour that takes you to key L.A. destinations—including Beverly Hills, Rodeo Drive, Mann's Chinese Theater, and the Walk of Fame—past a handful of T.V. and movie studios, and to many celebrity homes. They offer morning, midmorning, afternoon, and midafternoon departures seven days a week. The cost of this tour is $41 (adults) and $28 (kids). Call the company directly or visit the Web site for information about its other tours. Be sure to bring along your camera. Although these tours don't require too much walking (since you're riding in a bus with a tour guide), it's important to dress comfortable, keeping in mind the bus/van is air-conditioned.

Sunbelt Limousine Tours

☏ (800) 337-6662

In addition to offering private airport limo service in luxury stretch and super-stretch limousines, this company is one of several that offer private tours of numerous different Los Angeles County tourist attractions. Special rates are available on 4-hour tours. Tours can be customized to depart at your convenience. You can also pick and choose destinations.

▐█▌ TRAVEL TIP

You can purchase detailed maps of the stars' homes. For the most part, these maps are accurate; however, they seldom list the home addresses of current stars. In most cases, you'll see a home that was originally built by a celebrity or that was once lived in by someone famous.

The Major Tourist Attractions

 The following is a sampling of the tourist attractions in the Los Angeles County area. Each of these attractions will provide anywhere from one hour's to a full day's worth of entertainment.

Beverly Center

▭ 8500 Beverly Boulevard #501,
Los Angeles 90048

✎ *www.beverlycenter.com*

This relatively upscale indoor mall is located at the edge of Beverly Hills and Hollywood (on Beverly Boulevard, between La Cienega and San Vicente Boulevards). In addition to multiple department stores such as Macy's, Bloomingdale's, Macy's Men's Store, and the country's first Hard Rock Café, the Beverly Center features more than 160 specialty stores and restaurants, plus a thirteen-screen movie theater. The mall has its own indoor parking facility (with self-parking and valet parking available). While this mall does have a somewhat small food court, the dining options are limited. If you want to visit the Hard Rock Café and there's a wait, take a stroll through the mall.

The Comedy Clubs

The world's most famous comedy clubs, where virtually all of the biggest names in comedy have gotten their start, can be found in and around the Los Angeles County area. For example, the **Comedy Store**—☎ (323) 650-6268, ✎ *www.thecomedystore.com*—on Sunset Boulevard has been launching the careers of top comics since 1972. There's also the **Improv** ☎ (323) 651-2583, the **Laugh Factory** ☎ (323) 656-1336, the **Comedy Underground** ☎ (310) 451-1800, and more than twenty-five other comedy clubs in the area. Most have shows every night of the week and cater to an adult (18+ or 21+) crowd.

💼 TRAVEL TIP

For a complete list of comedy clubs in the L.A. area, visit **Digital City Los Angeles** (✍*www.digitalcity.com/losangeles*) and do a search for comedy clubs.

Hollywood Boulevard

Located along Hollywood Boulevard, you'll find an abundance of family-oriented attractions, the newest of which is Hollywood & Highland. You'll also find the **Hollywood Wax Museum** ✆ (213) 462-5991, the **Guinness Book of World Records Museum** ✆ (323) 462-5991, the **Hollywood Entertainment Museum** ✆ (323) 465-7900, and the **Ripley's Believe It or Not! Museum** ✆ (323) 466-6335, all of which have a separate admission fee (although discounted combo admission tickets are available at any of the museum box offices).

Hollywood & Highland (named after its address) opened in the fall of 2001. This $615 million family-entertainment destination occupies 1.3 million square feet. The complex includes the following:

- The 640-room Renaissance Hollywood Hotel
- More than seventy upscale retail shops and restaurants, including Louis Vuitton, Celine, Ann Taylor Loft, Aveda, Banana Republic, bebe, Café Med, Gap, MAC Cosmetics, Sephora, Tommy Hilfiger, DFS Galleria, the Grill on Hollywood, Sisley, Bice, Mercato, Dejaun Jewelers, Victoria's Secret, Limited Express, and Trastevere
- A 30,000-square foot ballroom that will seat 2,200 people
- A multiplex cinema
- The central plaza that overlooks the Hollywood sign
- A 3,300-seat, live-broadcast performing arts theatre.

The Kodak Theater is destined, beginning in 2002, to become the new home for the Academy Awards ceremonies. The remainder of the year, it will be programmed with an eclectic mix of Broadway shows, music, and live nationally televised specials. Adjacent to Mann's Chinese Theater, and located above the new MetroRail subway station, **Hollywood & Highland** offers 3,000 underground parking spaces. For more information, visit ✎ *www.hollywoodandhighland.com.*

≡FAST FACT

The Hollywood & Highland complex boasts two giant electronic signs that you can't miss: a Zipper Sign, which updates the public about the latest entertainment happenings; and the Marquee Sign, which functions primarily as a marquee for the Kodak Theater (located within the complex).

The Hollywood Sign

Hollywood is filled with signs and billboards, but the largest is the world-famous Hollywood sign, which stands 50 feet tall and 450 feet across. This has been a landmark in Hollywood for more than seventy-five years. The sign was originally built as an advertisement for Hollywoodland, a 1920s Beachwood Canyon real estate development. It can be seen from many locations in the Hollywood area and makes an excellent backdrop for a family photo.

The Lion King: The Broadway Musical
The Pantages Theatre
🖼 Hollywood Boulevard and Vine, Hollywood

📞 (213) 365-5555

✎ *www.lionkingla.com*

Straight from the Broadway (New York City) stage, Disney's theatrical presentation of *The Lion King*, which is based on the animated motion picture, has set new standards for musical theater. This award-winning, family-oriented show is spectacular. The costumes are amazing, the music is memorable, and the story is truly a classic.

The Lion King is the winner of twenty-five major awards: six Tonys, including Best Musical; eight Drama Desk Awards; six Outer Critics Circle Awards; the New York Drama Critics Circle Award for Best Musical; a 1998 Theatre World Award; the Astaire Award for Outstanding Choreography; a Drama League Award; and a Grammy for Best Musical Show Album. In addition, director Julie Taymor made Broadway history by becoming the first woman in theatrical history to win the Tony Award for Best Director of a Musical.

The score features Elton John and Tim Rice's music from the animated film, with additional numbers from South African Lebo M and Mark Mancina, as well as three new songs written by John and Rice with contributions from Julie Taymor and Hans Zimmer, along with Jay Rifkin. The resulting sound of *The Lion King* score is a fusion of Western popular music and the distinctive sounds and rhythms of Africa, embracing the Academy Award–winning "Can You Feel the Love Tonight" and the haunting "Shadowland."

Performances for the Los Angeles production are Tuesdays through Fridays at 8:00 P.M., Saturdays at 2:00 P.M. and 8:00 P.M., and Sundays at 1:00 P.M. and 6:30 P.M. (there are also occasional Wednesday matinees). Tickets are available at the Pantages Box Office or by calling **Ticketmaster** at ✆ (213) 365-5555 or ✆ (714) 703-2510. Ticket prices range from $15 to $125 each. You can also obtain tickets online at ✍ *www.lionkingla.com.*

Los Angeles Zoo
Located in **Griffith Park,** at the junction of the Ventura (134) and Golden State (5) Freeways

✆ (323) 644-6400

✍ *www.lazoo.org*

The Los Angeles Zoo is open from 10 A.M. to 5 P.M. daily, with extended summer hours (July 1 to September 3) from 10 A.M. to 6 P.M. Admission costs $8.25 for adults, $3.25 for children, and $5.25 for senior citizens. AAA members and Entertainment Book coupon holders receive a discounted admission.

This 113-acre zoo receives over 1.4 million visitors per year. You may remember it from the opening sequence from the television sitcom *Three's Company*. Although it can't be compared at all to the zoos in San Diego, the Los Angeles Zoo will provide several hours' worth of entertainment. From crocodiles to elephants, exotic birds to primates, and bears to lions, this traditional zoo showcases more than 1,000 animals and features a special children's zoo with educational programs throughout the year.

Mann's Chinese Theater and the Walk of Fame

⊞ 6925 Hollywood Boulevard,
   Hollywood 90028

☎ (323) 464-6266

Built in 1927 as the Grauman's Chinese Theater, this motion picture theater is a famous landmark for a multitude of reasons. Many of Hollywood's biggest motion pictures have and continue to have their premieres here. What's now the Mann's Chinese Theater is a true Hollywood landmark.

When a gala "red carpet" movie premiere event isn't taking place, this theater is open to the public. In front of this theater, along Hollywood Boulevard, you'll find the cement handprints and footprints of more than 200 Hollywood legends, including Clint Eastwood, Clark Gable, Whoopi Goldberg, Tom Hanks, Jack Lemmon, Walter Matthau, Marilyn Monroe, Jane Russell, Eddie Murphy, Paul Newman, Joanne Woodward, and Sylvester Stallone.

Directly in front of the Mann's Chinese Theater (and along Hollywood Boulevard on both sides of the street), is the Walk of Fame. More than 2,000 stars from T.V., motion pictures, and the recording industry have been immortalized with a star on this world-famous sidewalk. At the Mann's Chinese Theater, as well as all along Hollywood Boulevard, there are an abundance of excellent photo opportunities, so bring your camera.

According to the Hollywood Chamber of Commerce, "The Walk of Fame lines both sides of Hollywood Boulevard from Gower to La Brea, and both sides of Vine Street, from Yucca to Sunset. Official groundbreaking ceremonies were conducted February 9,

1960. In sixteen months, when construction was completed, 1,558 luminaries were forever immortalized in the sidewalk. Since then, approximately one to two stars per month have been added. Stars dedicated in 1994 pushed the total over the 2,000 mark. However, even at this rate, it will be many years before the stars in the famed Walk will be completely occupied, assuring the continued presence of Hollywood in the world's media, and remaining a highly visible and lasting tribute to a unique city."

═FAST FACT

Each time a new celebrity is immortalized with a star on the Walk of Fame, a special dedication ceremony is held. To determine if one of these events will take place during the time of your visit, check out *http://hollywoodchamber.net/ walkoffame/frameset.html*.

Melrose Avenue

Melrose Avenue is one of Los Angeles County's more famous streets. It contains many "ultra trendy" boutiques and clothing stores, as well as an abundance of cafés and restaurants. It's easy to spend between one and three hours walking along this popular street and exploring the one-of-a-kind shops. For example, there are several secondhand clothing stores that sell clothing worn by famous celebrities. For a directory of shops, visit *www.mel roseguide.com*. From this Web site, you can print out discount coupons for several of the shops and restaurants.

If you're driving to Melrose Avenue, finding a parking spot can be a bit of a challenge, especially on weekends. You'll find parking meters (two-hour maximum) along Melrose Avenue. There's also an enclosed parking structure on Melrose Avenue and Gardener that offers flat rate parking. You may also find curbside parking on the side streets.

Rodeo Drive

Located in the heart of Beverly Hills, where the rich and famous live, **Rodeo Drive** (✑ *www.rodeodrive.com*) is known for its extremely upscale shops, boutiques, galleries, and restaurants. It's not uncommon to see multiple expensive cars, like Rolls Royce, Mercedes, and BMWs parked at the metered spots along Rodeo.

Many of the world's most-famous clothing designers have their flagship stores here. This stretch of shops is only about three blocks long, but it's a tourist destination worth checking out. Unless you're pretty wealthy, you'll probably need to stick to window shopping, unless you plan on maxing out your credit cards.

For an elegant, but not too expensive breakfast or lunch, drop into Café Rodeo, located at 360 Rodeo Drive. In addition to street (metered) parking, there are a variety of inexpensive parking structures located along and near Rodeo Drive.

≡FAST FACT

Bijan (located at 420 Rodeo Drive), which prides itself on being one of the most expensive stores in the world, requires an appointment to shop there. During a typical visit, a customer will spend upward of $100,000, on items like a $15,000 suit or a $50 pair of socks.

The Santa Monica Pier/Third Street Promenade

▣ 200 Santa Monica Pier,
  Santa Monica 90401

☎ (310) 458-8900 or ☎ (310) 451-5133

✑ *www.santamonicapier.org*

Located along the water in Santa Monica is the Santa Monica Pier, which offers a lovely array of shops, a few carnival rides (including a carousel), and a handful of fast-food and fine-dining establishments. The view is awesome and the area is well worth exploring for an hour or so, especially if the weather is nice. There's a nearby beach and parking is available. Admission is free, and the pier is open all year.

The pier is located a short walk from the Third Street Promenade, which offers an incredible shopping opportunity—both indoors and outdoors. There's the outdoor, pedestrian mall setting, offering a wide range of stores, boutiques, and restaurants, and then there's a nearby indoor mall. Two hours of free parking are provided before 6:00 P.M. at city parking garages on 2nd Street, 4th Street, and Broadway. If you're in the mood for shopping, this is a great area to walk around and explore. Some of the shops in the area include Abercrombie & Fitch, bebe, Diesel USA, The Gap, Guess, Restoration Hardware, Lucky Brand Dundarees, Sketchers USA, Urban Outfitters, and Pyramid Music.

⊕ HOT SPOT

For kids, teens, and adults alike, the **UCLA Ocean Discovery Center** at the Santa Monica Pier—☎ (310) 393-6149, ✉ *www.odc.ucla.edu*—is a marine science learning center and aquarium. Admission for adults is $3. Kids are admitted free of charge. The center opens daily at 11:00 A.M. and closes at 5:00 P.M. or 6:00 P.M., depending on the day of the week and season.

The Staples Center

⌨ 1111 South Figueroa Street
Los Angeles, CA 90015

☎ (877) 305-1111 General Information

☎ (213) 742-7340 Box Office

✉ *www.staplescenter.com*

This indoor stadium is the home to many of L.A.'s professional sports teams, including the Los Angeles Lakers, Los Angeles Kings, Los Angeles Clippers, Los Angeles Avengers, and Los Angeles Galaxy. It's also one of the city's most popular concert arenas. For details about upcoming events, call Ticketmaster or the box office.

The Staples Center is a 900,000-square foot sports and entertainment facility, with a 20,000-seat capacity. The complex hosts over 230 sports, entertainment, and family-oriented events annually. The arena features 160 suites, 32 party suites, and 2,500 club seats. It has 5 concourses and 22 concession stands.

⊕ HOT SPOT

Located in the heart of downtown Los Angeles, the Staples Center is immediately adjacent to the Los Angeles Convention Center, and is easily accessible from the 110 (Harbor) and 10 (Santa Monica) Freeways.

Venice Beach and Boardwalk

Located along the water in Venice, this outdoor area offers street performers, shops, kiosks selling a wide range of souvenir merchandise, and a beautiful beach area. This is definitely a tourist destination that's worth visiting during the summer months and during the daylight hours. This is a great place for walking, in-line skating, or bike riding. In-line skates and bike rentals are available. There are also numerous cafés and fast-food places along the beachfront. In addition to shopping, the main activity here is sunbathing and people-watching. You're destined to see an extremely interesting mix of people here, in addition to tourists. Bring your camera and leave valuables locked in your car's trunk or hotel room.

West Hollywood

West Hollywood has long been a gathering place for gays, lesbians, and some of L.A.'s trendiest people. Here you'll find countless boutiques, restaurants, cafés, bookstores, and nightclubs. For information about West Hollywood, visit ✍ *www.westhollywood.com.*

If you're in the area, check out the **Abbey** on 🖃 692 North Robertson. It is an upscale café, serving breakfast and lunch in a lovely indoor/outdoor setting. The food and home-baked goods are delicious. At night, the Abbey transforms into an upscale "mixed" club, serving the best apple martinis you'll find anywhere. (You have to be at least twenty-one to get in.) Operating hours are from 7:00 A.M. to 2:00 A.M.

 TRAVEL TIP

For a listing of museums in the Los Angeles County area, visit *www.latourist.com/museums-links.htm*.

Westwood Village

Westwood is where UCLA (the University of California at Los Angeles) is located. It's a rather pleasant "college town" with a large selection of shops, movie theaters, galleries, and restaurants. Located about twenty minutes from Hollywood and ten minutes from Beverly Hills (depending on traffic), this is a nice area to explore. For a listing of events and other information about Westwood, visit *www.westwoodonline.com*.

Studio Tours

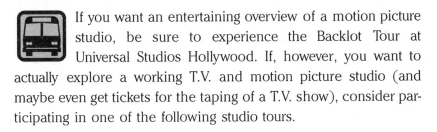 If you want an entertaining overview of a motion picture studio, be sure to experience the Backlot Tour at Universal Studios Hollywood. If, however, you want to actually explore a working T.V. and motion picture studio (and maybe even get tickets for the taping of a T.V. show), consider participating in one of the following studio tours.

NBC Studios Tour

3000 West Alameda Avenue
Burbank, CA

(818) 840-3537

www.nbc.com

See the set of NBC-T.V.'s *Tonight Show* (and maybe see an actual taping). This is a seventy-minute walking tour of a working T.V. studio complex. You'll see a special effects demonstration and actual T.V. show sets, and walk through makeup, wardrobe, and dressing room facilities. There's also a souvenir shop where NBC show merchandise is available. Admission is $7 for adults, $3.75 for children, and $6.25 for senior citizens.

Paramount Studios Tour

⌨ 860 North Gower Street
Los Angeles, CA

✆ (323) 956-1777

✍ www.paramount.com/studio_tour.html

See where shows such as *Star Trek Enterprise* (as well as all of the other *Star Trek* T.V. shows and movies), *Entertainment Tonight*, and movies are produced. Tickets are also available to see the taping of various sitcoms. The tour is $15 per person. Kids under ten are not permitted. This is a two-hour walking tour presented on weekdays only.

Sony Pictures Studio Tour

⌨ 10202 West Washington Boulevard
Culver City, CA

✆ (323) 520-TOUR or ✆ (310) 280-8000

See where T.V. game shows such as *Jeopardy!* and *Wheel of Fortune* are filmed, plus walk past the sets of other popular T.V. shows and movies. On this two-hour walking tour, you'll also see sets from *The Wizard of Oz*. Tickets are $20 per person.

Warner Bros. Studios Tour

⌨ 4000 Warner Boulevard
Burbank, CA

✆ (818) 954-1744

This tour operates on weekdays only (9:00 A.M. to 3:00 P.M.). Admission is $30 and reservations should be made in advance. Children under the age of ten are not permitted on the tour. Of all the studio tours, this one is the most informative and includes the most "behind-the-scenes" activity in terms of working soundstages where T.V. shows (like NBC-T.V.'s *ER*) and movies are made.

▓ TRAVEL TIP

For free tickets to the taping of a T.V. sitcom or game show, call **ABC Television** ☏ (310) 520-1ABC; **Audience Associates** ☏ (323) 467-4697; **Audiences Unlimited** ☏ (818) 506-0067; **CBS Studio Center** ☏ (818) 760-5000; **CBS Television City** ☏ (323) 852-2624; **NBC Television** ☏ (818) 840-3537; or **Paramount Pictures** ☏ (213) 956-5575.

L.A.'s Infamous Nightlife

Located along Sunset Boulevard, Wilshire Boulevard, Hollywood Boulevard, and various other locations throughout Hollywood and the Los Angeles area, you'll find some of the trendiest nightclubs in the world. As with any trend, the hot place to be seen in L.A. changes quickly, so ask your hotel's concierge for recommendations for the best clubs to visit. Most of the L.A. clubs have a specific dress code, and you must be over eighteen or over twenty-one to get in. Some offer live entertainment, while others feature some of the country's best-known DJs.

No matter what type of music you enjoy or what type of crowd you like to party with, chances are there's an L.A. club to satisfy your desires. **Digital City Los Angeles** *(✑ www.digitalcity.com)* offers a detailed listing of nightclubs in the L.A. area. You can also pick up a free copy of *LA Weekly (✑ www.laweekly.com)* at any hotel or newsstand for information about the L.A. club scene. This weekly newspaper also publishes a detailed calendar of events for the entire Los Angeles County area.

The Hollywood area is where you'll find many of the hottest clubs. Be sure to call the club directly for hours, special event information, and dress codes. Here's a partial listing of L.A. County's most popular nightspots:

Aftershock: 11345 Ventura Boulevard, Studio City,
(818) 752-9833

Arena: 6655 Santa Monica Boulevard, Hollywood,
(323) 462-0714

Axis: 652 N. La Peer Drive, Hollywood, (310) 659-0472

Century Club: 10131 Constellation Boulevard, Century City,
(310) 553-6000

Circus Disco: 6655 Santa Monica Boulevard, Hollywood,
(323) 462-1291

Crush Bar: 1743 N. Cahuenga Boulevard, Hollywood,
(323) 461-9017

Dragonfly: 6510 Santa Monica Boulevard, Hollywood,
(323) 466-6111

Florentine Gardens: 5951 Hollywood Boulevard, Hollywood,
(323) 464-0706

FM Station: 11700 Victory Boulevard, Hollywood,
(818) 769-2220

The Forge: 617 S. Brand Boulevard, Glendale,
(818) 246-1717

The Gate: 643 N. La Cienega Boulevard, Hollywood,
(310) 289-8808

Hollywood Athletic Club: 6525 Sunset Boulevard, Hollywood,
(323) 962-6600

Klub Banshee: 8512 Santa Monica Boulevard, Hollywood,
(310) 288-1601

Martini Lounge: 5657 Melrose Avenue, Hollywood,
(213) 467-4068

Moguls: 1650 North Schrader Boulevard, Hollywood,
(213) 465-7449

The Move: 1624 Cahuenga Boulevard, Hollywood,
(213) 356-9313

Nightwatch: 6290 Sunset Boulevard, Hollywood,
(213) 871-2995

The Palace: 1735 North Vine Street, Hollywood,
(213) 462-3000

The Palms: 🖼 8572 Santa Monica Boulevard, Hollywood,
📞(310) 652-6188

The Pink: 🖼 2810 Main Street, Santa Monica, 📞(310) 392-1077

Rage: 🖼 8911 Santa Monica Boulevard, Hollywood,
📞(310) 652-7055

Roxbury: 🖼 8225 Sunset Boulevard, Hollywood, 📞(213) 656-1750

The Star Lounge: 🖼 1413 Fifth Street, Santa Monica,
📞(310) 236-0028

Sunset Room: 🖼 1430 North Cahuenga Boulevard, Hollywood,
📞(323) 463-0004

Trench Town: 🖼 234 W. Manchester Boulevard, Inglewood,
📞(310) 205-2668

Villa Wahnsinn: 🖼 8751 Van Nuys Boulevard, San Fernando Valley,
📞(818) 894-2876

The Viper Room: 🖼 8852 Sunset Boulevard, Hollywood,
📞(310) 358-1881

The West End: 🖼 1301 Fifth Street, Santa Monica,
📞(213) 656-3905

The World: 🖼 7070 Hollywood Boulevard, Hollywood,
📞(323) 467-7070

Need a Taxi?

In the Los Angeles area, the following taxi companies are available. You can also hire a taxi through the front desk/concierge of any hotel.

Bell Cab: 📞(800) 666-6664

Checker Cab: 📞(800) 300-5007

Independent Taxi Owners Association (ITOA): 📞(800) 521-8294

L.A. Taxi: 📞(213) 627-7000

United Independent Taxi Drivers (UITD): 📞(800) 822-8294

Yellow Cab: 📞(800) 272-8294

💼 TRAVEL TIP

You can find out where movies are currently filming on location by picking up a copy of *Shoot Sheet*, a daily list of filming locations at exterior sites around the city of Los Angeles. This publication is provided every weekday by the County and City of Los Angeles's Entertainment Industry Development Corporation.

CHAPTER 20

Exploring San Diego

SAN DIEGO IS HOME to more than 2.7 million people and has become a rich, vibrant cultural center, as well as California's second-largest city after Los Angeles. It's also a wonderful tourist destination for a multitude of reasons. In addition to the sheer beauty of San Diego, this city offers nearly perfect weather throughout the year.

Overview of San Diego

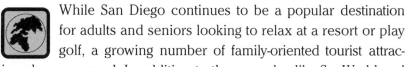 While San Diego continues to be a popular destination for adults and seniors looking to relax at a resort or play golf, a growing number of family-oriented tourist attractions have emerged. In addition to theme parks, like SeaWorld and LegoLand, San Diego is the home to two of the most popular zoos in the world. You'll also find many beautiful beaches, plus museums, shopping, and countless other indoor and outdoor activities suitable for the entire family.

San Diego is located less than 90 miles away from The Disneyland Resort in Anaheim; however, the drive is an easy one. You can also take a bus or train between Anaheim or Los Angeles to San Diego. Once you're in San Diego, however, having a car will certainly be helpful.

It's easy to plan a several-day vacation in San Diego if this city is your only destination. If, however, you're already planning a trip to The Disneyland Resort and/or the Los Angeles area, you might consider taking a one-, two-, or three-day road trip to explore just some of what San Diego has to offer.

If you're looking to stay at a world-class resort, you'll have several to choose from in the San Diego area. There are, however, many more affordable hotels and motels suitable for families. Determine your accommodation needs using the information in Chapter 4; then for assistance in finding and booking hotel/motel accommodations, contact any of the following tourism/travel organizations:

Carlsbad Convention & Visitors Bureau: ☎(800) 227-5722, 🖰 www.carlsbadca.org

San Diego Convention and Visitors Bureau: ☎(619) 239-1212, 🖰 www.sandiego.org

Sights of San Diego Hotel Reservations: ☎(619) 239-0900, 🖰 www.sightsofsandiego.com

Several free publications are available from the **San Diego Convention & Visitors Bureau,** ☎(619) 236-1212). These publications include:

The Rediscover San Diego Activity Coupon Book: This coupon book offers savings of over $3,000 on San Diego activities, including special offers from San Diego's major attractions, such as the San Diego Zoo, the Wild Animal Park, SeaWorld Adventure Park, and LEGOLAND. Also included are savings on other activities, dining, shopping, golf, tours, and transportation.

Visitor Guide: Published annually, this four-color, 128-page magazine-format guide provides detailed information on accommodations, arts and culture, attractions, and transportation services, as well as a major calendar of events listings and maps.

▐▊ TRAVEL TIP

As you plan your trip to San Diego, if you're traveling with kids, be sure to visit the following two Web sites: **San Diego Adventures** (✍ *www.sandiegoadventures.com*) and **San Diego KidsNet** (✍ *www.sandiegokidsnet.com*) for tips on kid-oriented activities.

San Diego Trolley Tours

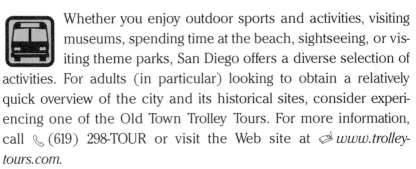 Whether you enjoy outdoor sports and activities, visiting museums, spending time at the beach, sightseeing, or visiting theme parks, San Diego offers a diverse selection of activities. For adults (in particular) looking to obtain a relatively quick overview of the city and its historical sites, consider experiencing one of the Old Town Trolley Tours. For more information, call ✆ (619) 298-TOUR or visit the Web site at ✍ *www.trolleytours.com*.

You'll experience a two-hour tour showcasing over 100 local points of interest. With multiple stops, you can select a few of your favorite destinations and leave the trolley tour to experience attractions, shopping, and dining at your own pace—and then get back on again.

Throughout the trolley ride portion of your tour, you'll enjoy colorful anecdotes, humorous stories, and historical information, all combined in a fast-paced two-hour narrative that will both entertain and educate. The company's trolleys travel through San Diego and Coronado on a continuous loop.

You can start the tour at any one of nine stops throughout the day. Stay onboard the trolley and get a fascinating narrative and overview of San Diego until you return to your starting point (in about two hours). Or, you can hop off at a few of your favorite sights (the trolleys depart at least every thirty minutes), and then reboard and continue with the tour until you return to your starting point. The earlier you start, the more time you will have for visiting attractions, shopping, or dining.

If you're limited in the amount of time you have in San Diego, yet you want to see as much as possible, consider taking an organized tour. Tours operate daily, between 9:00 A.M. and 5:00 P.M. Tickets range from $12 to $22 per person.

 TRAVEL TIP

> One benefit to this tour is that you don't need a car and you don't have to worry about getting lost. Once you get the overview of what's available in San Diego, you can explore on your own and at your own pace, revisiting the attractions that were the most interesting.

The San Diego Beaches

 With over 70 miles of beaches in San Diego, each beach has its own distinct look and appeal. Some of the beaches attract surfers and divers, while others are remote getaways.

To discover the various beach conditions during your visit, call ☎ (619) 221-8884. For details on the specific beaches, visit ✑ *www.ci.san-diego.ca.us/lifeguards/beaches/index.shtml.*

Golf Courses

 No matter what your skill, San Diego offers golf courses that are ideal, plus most offer spectacular views. From seaside settings to desert mountains, there are public and private golf courses in San Diego to meet everyone's needs.

San Diego contains ninety diverse courses and is the home to two PGA tour events that tee off yearly. With year-round sunny skies and 70 degree weather, this is the perfect place to enjoy the game of golf.

≡FAST FACT

To find a course that best suits your needs, visit ✎ *www.sandiego.org/sdgolf.asp*. From this Web site, you can order a free copy of the San Diego Golf Guide—a four-color, forty-page magazine-format guide that provides detailed information on San Diego golf courses, resorts, golf schools, and golf specialty services.

Shopping

 If you're looking to take home souvenirs or just enjoy the sport of shopping, your options are plentiful in the San Diego area. The following are some of the shopping centers and malls you'll find in San Diego. Most are open seven days a week. Call the individual mall/shopping center for hours, or ask your hotel's front desk clerk or concierge.

Bazaar Del Mundo, ▦ 2754 Calhoun Street, San Diego, ✆ (619) 298-1141. Set in Old Town State Historic Park, this area features twenty shops, many selling items from Mexico and other international locations, as well as five international restaurants, and year-round cultural activities.

Belmont Park Shopping Center, ▦ 3146 Mission Boulevard, #F, San Diego, ✆ (619) 491-2988. In addition to offering shops, this shopping center contains a carousel, health club, and roller coaster.

Chula Vista Center, ▦ 555 Broadway, Chula Vista, ✆ (619) 427-6700. Contains over 100 stores, a multiplex movie theater, and several restaurants.

Coast Walk ▦ 1298 Prospect Street, La Jolla, ✆ (858) 454-3031. This shopping area features many one-of-a-kind shops, plus a beautiful ocean view.

College Grove Center, ⌨ California Highway 94 and College Avenue, San Diego, ✆ (619) 583-5313. In addition to shopping at Mervyn's, Wal-Mart, and a handful of other stores, there's also a multiplex movie theater and the Grove Bowling Center.

Del Mar Plaza, ⌨ 1555 Camino Del Mar, Del Mar, ✆ (858) 792-1555. Over forty shops, galleries, and restaurants overlooking the ocean can be found here.

Fashion Valley Shopping Center, ⌨ 452 Fashion Valley, San Diego, ✆ (619) 297-3381. This is an outdoor shopping center, with 150 stores, restaurants, and theaters.

Ferry Landing Marketplace, ⌨ 1201 First Street, Coronado, ✆ (619) 435-8895. Specialty shops, galleries, and restaurants over-looking the bay is what you'll find here.

Flower Hill Mall, ⌨ 27110 Via De La Valley, #B270, Del Mar, ✆ (858) 481-7131. This shopping area features about fifty specialty shops and is located near the Del Mar Racetrack.

Grossmont Center, ⌨ 5500 Grossmont Center Dr., La Mesa, ✆ (619) 461-0630. Shop at over 150 stores, including Macy's, Target, Pier 1 Imports, and Barnes & Noble.

Hazard Center, ⌨ 7676 Hazard Center Drive, #500, San Diego, ✆ (619) 497-2674. Here you'll find a relatively upscale shopping environment, plus a handful of fine restaurants.

Horton Plaza, ⌨ 324 Horton Plaza, San Diego, ✆ (619) 238-1596. This is a multilevel mall that spans seven blocks. It contains 150 stores, a food court, a movie theater, and a repertory theater.

Hotel del Coronado, ⌨ 1500 Orange Avenue, Coronado, ✆ (619) 522-8177. This world-famous resort hotel also offers an upscale shopping experience. You'll find thirty shops on the first floor.

Marketplace at the Grove, ⌨ 3450 College Avenue, San Diego, ✆ (619) 583-5313. Fifty stores, a multiplex movie theater, and a bowling alley are offered at this marketplace.

Mission Valley Center, ⌨ 1640 Camino del Rio N., #1290, San Diego, ✆ (619) 296-6375. This is one of San Diego's largest open-air shopping centers. It contains upward of 150 stores, including Robinson's-May, Bullock's, Loehmann's, and an AMC 20-plex movie theater.

Newport Avenue. Along this stretch, you'll find many specialty shops. Enjoy the walk along Newport Avenue, from Sunset Cliffs Boulevard to the beach.

North County Fair, ⌨ 272 E. Via Rancho Parkway, Escondido, ✆ (760) 489-2332. This is the largest enclosed mall in San Diego.

Plaza Camino Real, ⌨ 2525 El Camino Real, Carlsbad ✆ (760) 729-7927. This shopping center contains more than 150 stores and a multiplex movie theater.

Seaport Village, ⌨ 849 W. Harbor Drive, San Diego, ✆ (619) 235-4014. With its waterfront dining and shopping, this San Diego landmark has something for every member of the family. Dine at one of four award-winning restaurants or select something from one of thirteen sidewalk eateries. Ride on the carousel, walk along the waterfront, or browse through the fifty-seven one-of-a-kind shops. Check out ✍ *www.spvillage.com* for information on special events such as blues and bluegrass concerts.

University Towne Centre: ⌨ 4545 La Jolla Village Drive, ✆ (858) 546-8858. UTC offers 155 stores and a multiplex movie theater, as well as an ice-skating rink and food court.

Major Tourist Attractions

 When it comes to zoos and wildlife, San Diego offers two of the most incredible zoos in the world, as well as SeaWorld. Each of these attractions will provide at least one full day's worth of entertainment that's suitable for the entire family.

If you're traveling with young children (ages three to twelve), LegoLand should also be a scheduled stop during your vacation. Based on the popular toy products, LegoLand is a kid-oriented theme park with over forty rides and attractions.

The San Diego Zoo

⊡ 2920 Zoo Drive
Balboa Park, CA

✆ (619) 234-3153

✍ *www.sandiegozoo.org*

This traditional zoo (where animals are on display, primarily in cages) is the home to more than 4,000 animals. Some of the most popular here include the largest collection of koalas outside of Australia. This zoo also houses a family of panda bears on loan from the People's Republic of China. Polar bears, gorillas, tigers, exotic birds, and many other animals are also on display. For kids, the zoo offers an interactive petting zoo, plus ongoing educational programs and tours. Seeing the pandas up close definitely makes a visit to this zoo worthwhile.

 TRAVEL TIP

While this zoo allows you to get close to many exotic animals not found in other zoos, it's not as spectacular as the nearby San Diego Wild Animal Park. If you have time to visit both zoos, check out this one first. If time is limited, focus on the Wild Animal Park and you won't be disappointed.

The 100-acre San Diego Zoo definitely provides at least a half-day's worth of entertainment. Plenty of walking is required and almost all of the exhibits are outdoors.

The San Diego Wild Animal Park

15500 San Pasqual Valley Road
Escondido, CA

(619) 234-6541 or (760) 747-8702

www.sandiegozoo.org

Of all the zoos in America, this one is among the most spectacular in terms of interaction with the animals and visual appeal. If your time is limited, your entire group will definitely enjoy the San Diego Wild Animal Park, which allows guests to enter into each animal's natural habitat while riding in a monorail.

This is a nontraditional zoo, in that the animals don't live in cages. Habitats have been set up where the animals roam freely. Guests, on the other hand, travel throughout the park's 1,800 acres on an enclosed monorail with a tour guide. The 55-minute tour brings you through much of the park and definitely should not be missed! There are more than 3,200 animals to see both on the monorail tour and in walk-through exhibits. The best time to see the animals is in the late afternoon or on cooler days.

The Wild Animal Park is located about 30 miles north of San Diego, so plan on making this a full day's activity, especially if you're using public transportation to get to the park.

SeaWorld San Diego

500 SeaWorld Drive
Mission Bay, CA

(619) 226-3815 or (800) 325-3150

www.seaworld.com

Killer whales, dolphins, sea lions, walruses, and other sea creatures are all on display at SeaWorld San Diego. The most popular attraction here, especially for kids, is the killer whale show presented within the world-famous Shamu Stadium (an outdoor 7,000-

seat arena). If you're traveling with kids and the weather is nice, consider sitting in one of the front rows where you're guaranteed to get splashed by the whales.

In addition to providing a variety of exhibits, guests can interact with many of the sea creatures. In recent years SeaWorld has expanded to become more of a traditional theme park. Along with the incredible animals, you'll find a wide range of rides and attractions, most of which are suitable for the entire family.

SeaWorld also presents a wide range of live entertainment aside from the killer whale show. There's Cirque de la Mer, a live acrobatic circus presented on the water (somewhat similar to Cirque du Soleil) and the World Rhythms on Ice show (featuring world-class ice skaters, music, and colorful costumes). Throughout the summer, SeaWorld also hosts live concerts for kids and teens, featuring national recording artists, and fireworks displays.

For younger kids, Shamu's Happy Harbor is a large, interactive play area. For people of all ages, there's the Pirate's 4-D attraction and the Wild Arctic ride (a helicopter simulator which takes you face-to-face with polar bears, walruses, and beluga whales). Be sure to bring your camera as you explore SeaWorld!

 **TRAVEL TIP**

Present your AAA membership card when purchasing SeaWorld tickets to receive a special discount. Discount coupons can also be found in the Entertainment Book, as well as in various San Diego area tourist brochures and publications.

Plan on spending a full day at SeaWorld, whether you're traveling with kids, teens, or just adults. For a unique opportunity to swim and interact with dolphins, SeaWorld offers the Dolphin Interaction Program (for a fee of $125 per person). For a separate fee, families can also **"Dine with Shamu."** To enjoy a poolside meal, call ✆ (619) 226-3601 for reservations.

SeaWorld is open daily, starting at 8:00 a.m. or 9:00 a.m. (depending on the season). Closing times vary. In addition to the shows, exhibits and rides, SeaWorld offers more than twenty shops, plus a handful of fine-dining and fast-food restaurants. Public transportation to SeaWorld is available from San Diego, Anaheim, and Los Angeles.

LEGOLAND

One LEGOLAND Drive
Carlsbad, CA

(760) 918-5346

www.LegoLandca.com

Located one hour south of Disneyland in Anaheim and a half-hour north of Sea World in San Diego, LEGOLAND is a kid-oriented theme park, based on the immensely popular LEGO building block toy products. All rides within this park look as if they've been created from LEGO blocks. What makes this park special for people of all ages, however, are the LEGO statues found throughout the park.

The rides, live shows, and special events are designed for kids, between the ages of three and twelve. The park is open daily, starting at 10:00 a.m., June through August. LegoLand is closed on Tuesdays and Wednesdays from September through May, except during the holiday season. (Please check the Web site for this revised schedule.) Closing time varies based on the season, but it is typically between 5:00 p.m. and 9:00 p.m. To see everything, be prepared to spend one full day at this park, but be sure to pace yourself so your kids don't get too tired too quickly.

LEGOLAND covers 128 acres and expertly mixes education, adventure, and fun in this first park of its kind in the United States. There are only two other LEGOLAND parks in the world: LEGOLAND Billund in Denmark marked its thirtieth anniversary in 1998 and LEGOLAND Windsor outside of London opened in 1996 and was recently awarded the British government's top honor for excellence in academic programs.

This park successfully combines forty hands-on interactive attractions, family rides, and shows, with restaurants, shopping, and landscape features. Unique LEGO themes dominate the entire park. Thirty million LEGO bricks were used to create the 5,000 Lego models that decorate the park, adding to its charm and delight. For kids who enjoy building with these blocks, this park will be a life-size inspiration.

The Beginning

This is where your day begins. The Beginning is the main entrance plaza to the Park. Here are some of the things you'll find there:

The Big Shop: An 8,000–square foot store packed with the biggest selection of Lego merchandise in America

Guest Services: Friendly "Model Citizens" (LEGOLAND employees on-hand to answer questions and offer assistance

The Market: Freshly baked muffins, croissants, brownies, and cookies, along with gourmet coffees, espresso, soda, and juices for a quick snack before exploring the park

Market Place: A convenience store selling items such as aspirin and sunblock

Welcoming Dinosaur: A bright red Lego brick dinosaur that stands 9 feet tall and 34 feet from his nose to the tip of his tail stretching over the Lake.

Village Green

The Village Green is a whimsical garden setting that uses Lego Duplo bricks as its primary thematic inspiration. Here, you'll find:

DUPLO Playtown: A play area geared for the park's youngest guests (preschoolers).

Corner Shop: A shop that sells a range of clothing and sportswear with LEGO themes and logos.

Fairy Tale Brook: A lovely (kid-oriented) boat ride through favorite childhood fairy tales, recreated with LEGO bricks.

Magic Theater: Live entertainment.

Ristorante Brickolini's: Hand-tossed wood-fired pizza is the specialty of the house (A pasta machine lets youngsters watch how flour and eggs are transformed into spaghetti and linguini right before their eyes. And a LEGO Chef Brickolini welcomes guests.)

Safari Trek: The wilds of Africa where you'll see life-size giraffes, zebras, lions, and more all made from LEGO bricks.

The Village Theater: Live entertainment.

Water Works: An interactive water play area.

The Ridge

The Ridge is an overlook orientation point in the center of LEGOLAND. In this area, you'll find several rides and attractions, including the following:

Amazing Maze: A traditional labyrinth that takes guests through an elaborate LEGO-inspired course.

Kid Power Tower: See the entire park, even the ocean, from this self-propelled ride to the top of a tower, capped with an exhilarating free-fall to the bottom. This kid-oriented thrill ride is suitable for kids over the age of six.

Sky Cycle: Cycle around the Ridge in people-powered pedal cars.

The Lake

This 1.73-acre man-made body of water is located in the heart of the theme park. It's the home to many real-life fish and aquatic plants. This lake is only from 3 to 8 feet deep and is filled with 2.5 million gallons of water. Within this area of the park, you'll find a handful of water-based rides and activities, including the following:

Coast Cruise: A floating tour through the heart of the park that provides a prime viewing opportunity for many of the Lego models such as the Eiffel Tower, the Sydney Opera House, Mt. Rushmore, the Taj Mahal, and the Statue of Liberty in front of the New York City skyline.

Lion's Bridge: Connects Miniland to the Ridge. (Be sure to listen for the roar of the LEGO lion that is guarding the bridge's gate.)

Fun Town

Here's a chance for youngsters to explore a scaled-down town created just for them. This interactive area includes the following attractions:

Adventurers' Club: Search for the Seven Keys as you travel on a mysterious journey featuring inhabitants of the Amazon rain forest, ancient Egypt, and the Arctic. These areas are all created from LEGO bricks.

Driving School: A "real-life" driving experience for children, ages six through twelve. The cars are created to look as if they're made from LEGOS. Junior Driving School offers a scaled-down version for three- to five-year-olds.

Flight Squadron: Fly in LEGO-inspired airplanes.

Fun Town Stage: Daily live entertainment.

The LEGO Factory: A walk-through tour that shows how Lego bricks are manufactured; a fun, self-paced attraction for guests of all ages.

LEGO Sky Patrol: Maneuver your own LEGO helicopter; a semi-thrill ride for pint-size pilots.

Skipper School: Learn boating skills as you navigate through the "skipper's" watery course.

Castle Hill

This area creates an illusion of a time when kings and queens reigned supreme. The main structure in this area is a castle.

The Dragon: A kid-oriented roller coaster housed in the castle. Merlin the Magician is the host on the fully animated ride that leads down to a cave where a fire-breathing dragon is guarding the crown jewels.

Castle Courtyard Theater: Live entertainment daily.

Enchanted Walk: A nature stroll through a landscaped setting, exhibiting LEGO models of animals native to the area.

The Hideaways: An outdoor playground area that contains rope climbs, cargo nets, and slides.

The Royal Joust: Ride LEGO-themed horses through a number of medieval scenes.

Miniland

This is the one area that will appeal to guests of all ages. Here, dozens of LEGO Master Builders express their art with the replication of five areas of the United States, constructed with 20 million LEGO bricks in 1:20 scale. Miniland presents famous landmarks built entirely from LEGO elements, including landmarks from Washington D.C., New Orleans, New York, and the California coastline. There's also an animated, interactive New England harbor scene and current events area.

Imagination Zone

Some of the most impressive "educational" elements of the park can be found here. In addition to more life-size LEGO models, the LEGO **Mind Storms** area uses technology to introduce participants to the world of robotics using the new "intelligent" LEGO brick, the RCX.

The RCX contains a computer that allows players to create behavioral programs for their robotic creations. This workshop is targeted to children, ages eight and older, who will use cutting edge

LEGO Technic models and control them via computer. Other attractions include the following:

Build & Test: Build a car and test it against competition on a race track.

Duplo Play: A free-play area for young people.

LEGO Show Place: Offers a unique interactive movie where guests decide the ending.

Maniac Challenge: A learning center featuring a computer-equipped workshop that uses LEGO software and interface programs.

═FAST FACT

The LEGO building blocks are one of the most successful toy products in history. LEGOS are currently sold in more than 138 countries throughout the world. Thus far, over 300 million children and adults have bought LEGO bricks, resulting in several billion hours of creative play.

Other Tourist Attractions

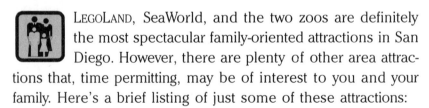 LEGOLAND, SeaWorld, and the two zoos are definitely the most spectacular family-oriented attractions in San Diego. However, there are plenty of other area attractions that, time permitting, may be of interest to you and your family. Here's a brief listing of just some of these attractions:

Balboa Park: ✆ (619) 239-0512. This cultural heart of San Diego is set on 1,200 acres of land, located just north of downtown. In a short walk, you'll find several museums, theaters, gardens, a carousel, and the famous San Diego Zoo.

Belmont Park: ▢ 3146 Mission Boulevard, #F, San Diego, ✆ (619) 491-2988. This outdoor park and recreation area contains a selection of shops, restaurants, a wooden roller coaster, and the Plunge swimming pool.

Cabrillo National Monument: ☎(619) 557-5450. This location, which overlooks the water, is an excellent location for whale watching from land. You'll also find a monument that honors Juan Cabrillo's landing in San Diego back in 1542.

Del Mar Fairgrounds: ✉ 2260 Jimmy Durante Boulevard, Del Mar, ☎(858) 793-5555. For adults, thoroughbred horse racing is presented throughout the summer. This is also the location where the annual San Diego County Fair is held.

Embarcadero/Harbor Drive: Adults especially will enjoy taking a leisurely stroll through this lovely bayfront area that features Seaport Village and a lovely harbor. You'll find a selection of fine shops along Harbor Drive.

Gaslamp Quarter: ✉ 410 Island Avenue, San Diego, ☎(619) 233-5227. The historic downtown district features restaurants, galleries, shops, and jazz bars. This is a wonderful place to walk around in the evening before catching a bite to eat.

Horton Plaza: ✉ 324 Horton Plaza, San Diego, ☎(619) 238-1596. If you're in the mood to walk, shop, enjoy live entertainment and maybe a fine-dining experience, then check out this seven-block area.

Hotel del Coronado: ✉ 1500 Orange Avenue, Coronado, ☎(619) 435-6611. Even if you can't afford to stay in San Diego's most prestigious and well-known hotel/resort, you'll probably enjoy visiting. This is an internationally renowned Victorian resort hotel that has hosted twelve U.S. presidents and countless celebrities. In addition to sightseeing and shopping, a self-guided tour is available.

Mission Basilica San Diego de Alcala: ✉ 10818 San Diego Mission Road, San Diego, ☎(619) 281-8449. This mission was founded back in 1769. The area now contains a museum, working archaeological site, and landscaped gardens that are open to the general public.

Mission Bay: In addition to providing a home to SeaWorld, this 4,600-acre park offers picnic areas, 17 miles of oceanfront beaches and trails, plus areas for boating and swimming.

Old Town State Historical Park: San Diego &(619) 220-5422. A favorite of tourists and locals alike, Old Town commemorates the area's earliest European settlement. Five original adobes, such as La Casa de Estudillo, reflect ordinary life in San Diego from 1821 to 1872. Old Town is also the site of the Whaley House (one of the best-known haunted houses in America), and home to Bazaar del Mundo, with its strolling mariachis, splashing fountains, specialty boutiques offering unique international collectibles, and international restaurants.

Palomar Observatory: Highway of Stars, Palomar Mountain, &(626) 395-4033. For astronomy buffs, this observatory houses America's largest telescope. Free tours are offered daily.

Quail Botanical Gardens: 230 Quail Gardens Drive, Encinitas, &(760) 436-3036. Stroll through the lush gardens and view exotic plants from all over the world. This is a 30-acre botanical garden located just north of San Diego County.

San Diego Convention Center: 111 West Harbor Drive, San Diego, &(619) 525-5000. In addition to being a popular tourist destination, San Diego is also the host city for hundreds of conventions and trade shows throughout the year. Many of these events are held within the 760,000–square foot convention center.

⊕ HOT SPOT

If you're traveling with kids, one museum in particular that's worth visiting is the **Children's Museum of San Diego,** ✉200 West Island Avenue, San Diego, &(619) 233-KIDS.

Useful Phone Numbers

THE FOLLOWING USEFUL PHONE NUMBERS will help you plan the ultimate vacation to Disneyland or to any of the tourist attractions and theme parks described in this book.

AARP (American Association for Retired Persons):
&(800) 424-3410

The Abbey: &(310) 855-9977

ABC Television Show Tickets: &(310) 520-1ABC

Adventure City: &(714) 236-9300

Air Canada: &(800) 776-3000

The Airport Bus: &(800) 772-5299

Alamo Rent-A-Car: &(800) 327-9633

All Los Angeles Hotels: &(800) 663-4680

AMC Theaters: &(714) 769-4AMC

American Airlines: &(800) 433-7300

American Automobile Association (AAA): &(800) 222-4357

American Automobile Association's Travel Department:
&(800) 222-7448

American Eagle: &(800) 433-7300

American Express Travel: &(800) 346-3607

American Taxi (servicing John Wayne Airport): &(888) 482-9466

AmericaWest Airlines: &(800) 2-FLY-AWA

Amtrak: &(800) USA-RAIL

Anaheim Chamber of Commerce: ☎(714) 758-0222

Anaheim Hills Golf Course: ☎(714) 998-3041

Anaheim Hotels Online: ☎(800) 826-0533

Anaheim Indoor Marketplace: ☎(714) 999-0952

Anaheim Museum: ☎(714) 778-3301

Anaheim/Orange County Visitor & Convention Bureau:
  ☎(714) 765-8888

Anaheim Plaza Shopping Center: ☎(714) 635-3431

Anaheim Reservations: ☎(619) 578-7820

Anaheim Visitor Center: ☎(714) 239-1340

Animal Inns of America: ☎(714) 636-4455

Arrowhead Pond of Anaheim: ☎(714) 704-2500

Audience Associates T.V. Show Tickets: ☎(323) 467-4697

Audiences Unlimited T.V. Show Tickets: ☎(818) 506-0067

Avis Rent-A-Car: ☎(800) 230-4898

Bed & Breakfast International of California: ☎(800) 872-4500

Bell Cab (Los Angeles): ☎(800) 666-6664

The Block at Orange (Anaheim): ☎(714) 769-4000

Bowers Museum of Cultural Art and Kidseum: ☎(714) 567-3600

Budget Rent-A-Car: ☎(800) 221-1203

Buena Park Mall: ☎(714) 828-7722

Burke Williams Day Spa: ☎(714) 769-1360

Carlsbad Convention & Visitors Bureau: ☎(800) 227-5722

CBS Studio Center Show Tickets: ☎(818) 760-5000

CBS Television City Show Tickets: ☎(323) 852-2624

Checker Cab (Los Angeles): ☎(800) 300-5007

The Comedy Underground: ☎(310) 451-1800

Continental: ☎(800) 525-0280

Dad Miller Golf Course (Anaheim): ☎(714) 765-3481

Delta Airlines/Delta Express: ☎(800) 221-1212

Discovery Science Center (Anaheim): ☎(714) 542-2823

Disney Club: ☎(800) 654-6347

Disney Ice Arena: ☎(714) 735-7465

Disneyana Convention: ☎(407) 827-7600

Disneyland Admission Ticket Information: ☎(714) 781-4043

Disneyland Child Services: ☎(714) 781-4210

Disneyland/DCA Guest Relations: ☎(714) 781-4560

Disneyland Hotel: ☎(714) 956-MICKEY

Disneyland Operating Hours Information: ☎(714) 781-4565

Disneyland Pet Care Kennel: ☎(714) 781-4565

Disneyland Resort Wedding Planning: ☎(714) 956-6527

Disneyland Tours: ☎(714) 781-7290

Disneyland Traffic Advisory Hotline: ☎(714) 781-4400

Disneyland's Lost Child Department: ☎(714) 781-4210

Disney's Grand Californian Hotel: ☎(714) /300-7170

Disney's Paradise Pier Hotel: ☎(714) 956-MICKEY

Disney's Walk of Magical Memories: ☎(800) 760-3566

Doll & Toy Museum (Anaheim): ☎(714) 527-2323

Downtown Disney Dining Reservations: ☎(714) 300-7800

East Hills Animal Hospital: ☎(714) 921-2500

Edison International Field: ☎(714) 634-2000

Enterprise Rent-A-Car: ☎(800) 736-8222

Entertainment Book: ☎(800) 933-2605

ESPN Zone: ☎(714) 300-3776

Frontier Airlines: ☎(800) 432-1359

Glacial Garden Ice Arena in Anaheim: ☎(714) 502-9023

Glen Ivy Hot Springs Spa: ☎(909) 277-3529

Greyhound Bus: ☎(714) 999-1256, ☎(800) 231-2222

Guinness World of Records Museum: ☎(323) 462-5991

Hawaiian Air: ☎(800) 367-5320

Hertz: ☎(800) 654-3131

The Hilton Anaheim: ☎(714) 750-4321

Hilton Sports & Fitness Center: ☎(714) 750-4321

Hollywood Entertainment Museum: ☎(323) 465-7900

Hollywood Wax Museum: ☎(213) 462-5991

Horizon Air/Alaska Air: ☎(800) 547-9308

Hotel Reservations Network: ☎(800) 964-6835

House Call Physicians: ☎(800) DOCS-911

House of Blues: ☎(714) 781-4560

The Improv: ☎(323) 651-2583

Independent Taxi Owners Assoc. (Los Angeles): ☎(800) 521-8294

Islands Golf Center (Anaheim): ☎(714) 630-7888

Joey & Maria's Comedy Italian Wedding: ☎(800) 944-5639

John Wayne Airport Information: ☎(949) 252-5200

KinderCare Learning Centers: ☎(714) 774-5141, ☎ (714) 991-5443

Knott's Berry Farm: ☎(714) 220-5200

Knott's Soak City: ☎(714) 220-5200

Knott's Southern California Resort: ☎(800) 333-3333

Kodak Customer Information: ☎(800) 242-2424

L.A. Taxi (Los Angeles): ☎(213) 627-7000

The Laugh Factory: ☎(323) 656-1336

LEGOLAND California: ☎(760) 918-LEGO

The Lion King: Broadway Musical: ☎(213) 365-5555

Los Angeles Famous Hotels Directory: ☎(800) 984-4878

Los Angeles Visitor & Convention Bureau: ☎(213) 624-7300

Los Angeles Zoo: ☎(323) 644-6400

Mann's Chinese Theater & the Walk of Fame: ☎(323) 464-6266

Medieval Times Dinner & Tournament: ☎(714) 521-4740,
  ☎(800) 899-6600

Miami Air: ☎(305) 871-8001

Midwest Express: ☎(800) 452-2022

Movieland Wax Museum: ☎(714) 522-1154

National Car Rental: ☎(800) 227-7368

NBC Studios Tour: ☎(818) 840-3537

NBC Television Show Tickets: ☎(818) 840-3537

Northwest Airlines: ☎(800) 225-2525

Old Town Trolley Tours (San Diego): ☎(619) 298-TOUR

Orange County Tourism Council: ☎(714) 278-7491

Paramount Pictures T.V. Show Tickets: ☎(213) 956-5575

Paramount Studios Tour: ☎(323) 956-1777

Pet's Choice: ☎(714) 701-1717

Pinocchio's Workshop (Grand Californian Hotel): ☎ (714) 956-6755

Priceline.com: ☎(800) 774-2354

Rainforest Café: ☎(714) 772-0413

Rib Trader Merlin's Magic Dinner Show: ☎(714) 744-9288

Ripley's Believe It or Not! (Buena Park): ☎(714) 522-1152

Ripley's Believe It or Not! Museum: ☎(323) 466-6335

San Diego Beach Information: ☎(619) 221-8884

San Diego Zoo: ☎(619) 234-3153

San Diego Wild Animal Park: ☎(760) 747-8702

Santa Monica Pier/Third Street Promenade: ☎(310) 458-8900, ☎(310) 451-5133

Sav-On Drugs: ☎(714) 530-0500, ☎(714) 530-5280

SeaWorld San Diego: ☎(619) 226-3901

Six Flags Hurricane Harbor: ☎(661) 225-0208

Six Flags Magic Mountain: ☎(619) 255-4111, ☎(818) 367-5965

Sony Pictures Studio Tour: ☎(323) 520-TOUR

Soprano's Last Supper: ☎(800) 944-5639

Southwest: ☎(800) I-FLY-SWA

Spa & Fitness Club: ☎(714) 850-0050

Spirit Airlines: ☎(800) 772-7117

Staples Center: ☎(877) 305-1111, ☎(213) 742-7340

Starline Tours: ☎(800) 959-3131

Sun County Airlines: ☎(800) 359-5786

Sunbelt Limousine Tours: ☎(800) 337-6662

SuperShuttle: ☎(800) 554-3146, ☎(310) 782-6600

Ticketmaster: ☎(213) 365-5555, ☎(714) 703-2510

TWA: ☎(800) 892-2746

Traveler.com: ☎(800) 610-5749

Tumi Luggage: ☎(800) 322-TUMI

UCLA Ocean Discovery Center: ☎(310) 393-6149

United: ☎(800) 241-6522

United Express: ☎(800) 453-9417

United Independent Taxi Drivers (Los Angeles): ☎(800) 822-8294

United Shuttle: ☎(800) 748-8853

Universal Amphitheater: ☎(818) 622-4440

Universal Studios Celebrity Annual Passes: ☎(888) 309-9625

Universal Studios Hollywood: ☎(800) UNIVERSAL

Universal Studios Vacations: ☎(800) 711-0080

US Airways: ☎(800) 428-4322

US Airways Trip Packages: ☎(800) 455-0123

Vanguard Airlines: ☎(800) 826-4827

VIP Tours: ☎(800) 438-1814

Virgin Atlantic: ☎(800) 862-8621

Walt Disney Travel Company: ☎(800) 225-2024, ☎(714) 520-5050

Warner Bros. Studios Tour: ☎(818) 954-1744

West Coast Taxi Cab: ☎(714) 547-8000

Wild Bill's Wild West Dinner Extravaganza: ☎(800) 883-1546

Yellow Cab (Los Angeles): ☎(800) 272-8294

Yellow Cab of Orange County: ☎(714) 535-2211

Attraction Selection Worksheet

THE FOLLOWING WORKSHEETS will help you choose which rides, shows, and attractions you and your traveling companions will want to experience once you arrive at each of the Disney theme parks. Place a checkmark in the appropriate column next to each listed ride, shows, and attraction.

Disneyland

Rides, shows, and attractions are listed in alphabetical order.

1=Must see	2=Experience if time permits
3=Already experienced	4=No interest

Attraction Name	1	2	3	4
Alice in Wonderland	☐	☐	☐	☐
The American Space Experience	☐	☐	☐	☐
Astro Orbitor	☐	☐	☐	☐
Autopia	☐	☐	☐	☐
Believe: There's Magic in the Stars fireworks spectacular	☐	☐	☐	☐
Big Thunder Mountain Railroad	☐	☐	☐	☐
Calling All Space Scouts . . . A Buzz Lightyear Adventure	☐	☐	☐	☐
Casey Jr. Circus Train	☐	☐	☐	☐
Chip 'n Dale Treehouse	☐	☐	☐	☐
Cosmic Waves	☐	☐	☐	☐
Davy Crockett's Explorer Canoes	☐	☐	☐	☐
The Disney Gallery	☐	☐	☐	☐
Disneyland Monorail	☐	☐	☐	☐
Disneyland Parade of the Stars	☐	☐	☐	☐
Disneyland Presents Animazement–The Musical	☐	☐	☐	☐
Disneyland Railroad	☐	☐	☐	☐
Donald's Boat	☐	☐	☐	☐
Dumbo the Flying Elephant	☐	☐	☐	☐
Enchanted Tiki Room	☐	☐	☐	☐
Fantasmic!	☐	☐	☐	☐
Fantasyland Theatre	☐	☐	☐	☐
Frontierland Shootin' Exposition	☐	☐	☐	☐
Gadget's Go Coaster	☐	☐	☐	☐
The Golden Horseshoe Stage	☐	☐	☐	☐

Attraction Name	1	2	3	4
Goofy's Bounce House	☐	☐	☐	☐
Haunted Mansion	☐	☐	☐	☐
Honey, I Shrunk the Audience	☐	☐	☐	☐
Indiana Jones Adventure	☐	☐	☐	☐
Innoventions	☐	☐	☐	☐
"It's a Small World"	☐	☐	☐	☐
Jolly Trolley	☐	☐	☐	☐
Jungle Cruise	☐	☐	☐	☐
King Arthur Carrousel	☐	☐	☐	☐
Mad Tea Party	☐	☐	☐	☐
Main Street Cinema	☐	☐	☐	☐
Main Street Vehicles	☐	☐	☐	☐
Mark Twain Riverboat	☐	☐	☐	☐
Matterhorn Bobsleds	☐	☐	☐	☐
Mickey's House	☐	☐	☐	☐
Minnie's House	☐	☐	☐	☐
Mr. Toad's Wild Ride	☐	☐	☐	☐
Peter Pan's Flight	☐	☐	☐	☐
Pinocchio's Daring Journey	☐	☐	☐	☐
Pirates of the Caribbean	☐	☐	☐	☐
Rafts to Tom Sawyer Island	☐	☐	☐	☐
Roger Rabbit's Car Toon Spin	☐	☐	☐	☐
Sailing Ship *Columbia*	☐	☐	☐	☐
Sleeping Beauty Castle	☐	☐	☐	☐
Snow White's Scary Adventure	☐	☐	☐	☐
Splash Mountain	☐	☐	☐	☐
Star Tours	☐	☐	☐	☐
Starcade	☐	☐	☐	☐
Storybook Land Canal Boats	☐	☐	☐	☐
Sword in the Stone Ceremony	☐	☐	☐	☐
Tarzan's Treehouse	☐	☐	☐	☐
Teddi Barra's Swingin' Arcade	☐	☐	☐	☐
The Walt Disney Story	☐	☐	☐	☐
Other:_____	☐	☐	☐	☐
Other:_____	☐	☐	☐	☐

Disney's California Adventure

Rides, shows, and attractions are listed in alphabetical order.

Attraction Name	1	2	3	4
The Backlot Stage–Goofy's Beach Party Bash	☐	☐	☐	☐
Boudin Bakery	☐	☐	☐	☐
Bountiful Valley Farm	☐	☐	☐	☐
California Screamin'	☐	☐	☐	☐
Disney Animation	☐	☐	☐	☐
Disney's Electrical Parade	☐	☐	☐	☐
Disney's Eureka! A California Parade	☐	☐	☐	☐
Games of the Boardwalk	☐	☐	☐	☐
Golden Dreams	☐	☐	☐	☐
Golden Vine Winery	☐	☐	☐	☐
Golden Zephyr	☐	☐	☐	☐
Grizzly River Run	☐	☐	☐	☐
Hyperion Theater	☐	☐	☐	☐
It's Tough to Be a Bug	☐	☐	☐	☐
Jim Henson's Muppet-Vision 3D	☐	☐	☐	☐
Jumpin' Jellyfish	☐	☐	☐	☐
King Triton's Carousel	☐	☐	☐	☐
Maliboomer	☐	☐	☐	☐
Mission Tortilla Factory	☐	☐	☐	☐
Mulholland Madness	☐	☐	☐	☐
Orange Stinger	☐	☐	☐	☐
Redwood Creek Challenge Trail	☐	☐	☐	☐
S.S. Rustworthy	☐	☐	☐	☐
Soarin' over California	☐	☐	☐	☐
Sun Wheel	☐	☐	☐	☐
Superstar Limo	☐	☐	☐	☐
Who Wants to Be a Millionaire–Play It!	☐	☐	☐	☐
Other: _____	☐	☐	☐	☐
Other: _____	☐	☐	☐	☐
Other: _____	☐	☐	☐	☐

Budget Checklist

USE THIS FORM to help you approximate the cost of your trip to The Disneyland Resort and Southern California in advance. Planning your itinerary before you leave and setting budgetary spending limits will help you enjoy your vacation without going into unexpected debt or spending outside of your budget.

BUDGET CHECKLIST

Expense	Calculation	Totals
Adult airfare	$ _____ per ticket × $ _____ (# of adults)	$ _____
Child airfare	$ _____ per ticket × $ _____ (# of children)	$ _____
Rental car	$ _____ per day/week × $ _____ (# of days/weeks)	$ _____
Insurance/gas	$ _____ per day × $ _____ (# of days)	$ _____
Transportation (taxi, bus, etc.)	$ _____ per trip × $ _____ (# of people) × $ _____ (# of trips)	$ _____
Hotel/motel	$ _____ per night × $ _____ (# of rooms) × $ _____ (# of nights)	$ _____
Adult Disney ticket	$ _____ per ticket × $ _____ (# of people) × $ _____ (# of days)	$ _____
Child Disney ticket	$ _____ per ticket × $ _____ (# of people) × $ _____ (# of days)	$ _____
Adult Universal Studios ticket	$ _____ per ticket × $ _____ (# of people) × $ _____ (# of days)	$ _____
Child Universal Studios ticket	$ _____ per ticket × $ _____ (# of people) × $ _____ (# of days)	$ _____
Other attraction	$ _____ per ticket × $ _____ (# of people) × $ _____ (# of days)	$ _____
Other attraction	$ _____ per ticket × $ _____ (# of people) × $ _____ (# of days)	$ _____

BUDGET CHECKLIST (continued)

Expense	Calculation	Totals
Adult nighttime entertainment	$ _____ per person × $ _____ (# of nights)	$ _____
Child nighttime entertainment	$ _____ per person × $ _____ (# of nights)	$ _____
Show/movie	$ _____ per person × $ _____ (# of shows)	$ _____
Total meal budget	$ _____ per person × $ _____ (# of meals) × $ _____ (# of days)	$ _____
Snack/drink budget	$ _____ per person × $ _____ (# of days)	$ _____
Souvenir budget	$ _____ per person	$ _____
Child care	$ _____ per hour × $ _____ (# of hours) × $ _____ (# of children)	$ _____
Kennel costs	$ _____ per day × $ _____ (# of days) × $ _____ (# of pets)	$ _____
Airport parking	$ _____ per day × $ _____ (# of days)	$ _____
Other	_____	$ _____
Other	_____	$ _____
Other	_____	$ _____

Approximate Vacation Expenses Total: $ _____

Planning Your Itinerary

YOU'VE JUST READ about the majority of activities, theme parks, tourist attractions, and ways of spending your time in the Southern California area. Now that you know all that there is to see and do, before leaving on vacation, do a bit of preplanning to help ensure you make the most of your vacation and stay within your allocated budget.

Plan Accordingly

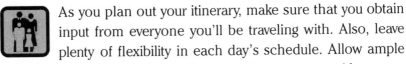 As you plan out your itinerary, make sure that you obtain input from everyone you'll be traveling with. Also, leave plenty of flexibility in each day's schedule. Allow ample time to explore and enjoy experiences as they happen, without worrying too much about staying on a timetable and getting to the next activity. In most cases, creating an itinerary with plans down to the hour or minute might make you more organized, but it will also create a tremendous level of stress during your vacation as you try to stick to your schedule. Be sure to leave time in your schedule for travel (between destinations, such as theme parks), meals, rest/relaxation, waiting in line, and so on.

For the purposes of preplanning your itinerary and visiting theme parks, it's best to divide your day into three chunks of time: morning, afternoon, and nighttime. Use this itinerary planning worksheet to help preplan your itinerary, keeping in mind that you'll most likely be altering this itinerary once you arrive in the Los Angeles area and start vacationing. Make a copy of this worksheet for each day of your vacation, and then use the completed worksheet as a guide for scheduling the things you believe you (and the people you're traveling with) will most enjoy based on the time you have available.

 # Airline Information

Departing date:

Departing time:

Airline:

Flight number(s)/connecting cities:

Departing airport:

Arriving airport:

Arrival time:

Seat assignment(s):

Returning date (to go home):

Departing time:

Airline:

Flight number(s)/connecting cities:

Departing airport:

Arrival time (to home city):

Seat assignment(s):

Travel agency used:

Travel agent/airline phone number(s):

Parking lot name/number at airport:

Location/aisle:

Airport Ground Transportation Information

Getting to the airport: _____

Taxi/limo service name: _____

Phone number: _____

Reservation number: _____

Pickup date/time: _____

Pickup location: _____

Getting home from the airport: _____

Taxi/limo service name: _____

Phone number: _____

Reservation number: _____

Pickup date/time: _____

Pickup location: _____

Rental Car Information

Rental car company: _____

Confirmation number: _____

Daily rate: _____

Pickup location: _____

Rental car company phone number: _____

Type of car reserved: _____

Accommodation
Information

Hotel/resort name:

Phone number:

Reservation number:

Check-in date:

Checkout date:

Type of accommodations reserved:

Daily Itinerary

Travel Itinerary

Make a copy of this worksheet for each day of your vacation; then use the completed worksheet as a guide for scheduling the things you believe you (and the people you're traveling with) will most enjoy based on the time you have available.

DAY 1

Date: _____

Day of week: _____

Morning Activities

Time	Location	Activity Description

Breakfast restaurant: _____

Reservation time: _____

Restaurant phone number: _____

Afternoon Activities

Time	Location	Activity Description

Lunch restaurant: _____

Reservation time: _____

Restaurant phone number: _____

DAY 1

Evening/Nighttime Activities

Time	Location	Activity Description

Dinner restaurant:

Reservation time:

Restaurant phone number:

Other

DAY 2

Date: _____

Day of week: _____

Morning Activities

Time	Location	Activity Description

Breakfast restaurant: _____

Reservation time: _____

Restaurant phone number: _____

Afternoon Activities

Time	Location	Activity Description

Lunch restaurant: _____

Reservation time: _____

Restaurant phone number: _____

DAY 2

Evening/Nighttime Activities

Time	Location	Activity Description

Dinner restaurant: _____

Reservation time: _____

Restaurant phone number: _____

Other

_____

_____

_____

_____

_____

_____

_____

_____

_____

_____

DAY 3

Date: _____

Day of week: _____

Morning Activities

Time	Location	Activity Description

Breakfast restaurant: _____

Reservation time: _____

Restaurant phone number: _____

Afternoon Activities

Time	Location	Activity Description

Lunch restaurant: _____

Reservation time: _____

Restaurant phone number: _____

DAY 3

Evening/Nighttime Activities

Time	Location	Activity Description

Dinner restaurant: _____

Reservation time: _____

Restaurant phone number: _____

Other

_____

_____

_____

_____

_____

_____

_____

_____

_____

_____

DAY 4

Date: _____

Day of week: _____

Morning Activities

Time	Location	Activity Description

Breakfast restaurant: _____

Reservation time: _____

Restaurant phone number: _____

Afternoon Activities

Time	Location	Activity Description

Lunch restaurant: _____

Reservation time: _____

Restaurant phone number: _____

DAY 4

Evening/Nighttime Activities

Time	Location	Activity Description

Dinner restaurant: _____

Reservation time: _____

Restaurant phone number: _____

Other

_____

_____

_____

_____

_____

_____

_____

_____

_____

_____

_____

_____

DAY 5

Date: _____

Day of week: _____

Morning Activities

Time	Location	Activity Description

Breakfast restaurant: _____

Reservation time: _____

Restaurant phone number: _____

Afternoon Activities

Time	Location	Activity Description

Lunch restaurant: _____

Reservation time: _____

Restaurant phone number: _____

DAY 5

Evening/Nighttime Activities

Time	Location	Activity Description

Dinner restaurant:

Reservation time:

Restaurant phone number:

Other

DAY 6

Date: _____

Day of week: _____

Morning Activities

Time	Location	Activity Description

Breakfast restaurant: _____

Reservation time: _____

Restaurant phone number: _____

Afternoon Activities

Time	Location	Activity Description

Lunch restaurant: _____

Reservation time: _____

Restaurant phone number: _____

DAY 6

Evening/Nighttime Activities

Time	Location	Activity Description

Dinner restaurant: _____

Reservation time: _____

Restaurant phone number: _____

Other

_____

_____

_____

_____

_____

_____

_____

_____

_____

_____

_____

DAY 7

Date: _____

Day of week: _____

Morning Activities

Time	Location	Activity Description

Breakfast restaurant: _____

Reservation time: _____

Restaurant phone number: _____

Afternoon Activities

Time	Location	Activity Description

Lunch restaurant: _____

Reservation time: _____

Restaurant phone number: _____

DAY 7

Evening/Nighttime Activities

Time	Location	Activity Description

Dinner restaurant: _____

Reservation time: _____

Restaurant phone number: _____

Other

_____

_____

_____

_____

_____

_____

_____

_____

_____

_____

_____

Index

We Have

EVERYTHING!

The Everything® Guide to Las Vegas

Jason Rich

1-58062-438-3,
$14.95 ($22.95 CAN)

Las Vegas is fast becoming America's choice for family vacations. With fabulous weather, great restaurants, and unbelievable attractions, there is something for everyone, all day, and all night. *The Everything® Guide to Las Vegas* is the one resource you need to help you with your vacation planning, and to guarantee that you won't miss a thing. It includes shows and attractions for every member of the family, restaurant listings in and out of the casinos, the best shopping and day trips, and much more!

The Everything® Guide to New England

Kimberly Knox Beckius

Whether it's "leaf-peeping" in the fall, skiing in the winter, taking historical tours in the spring, or spending leisure time at seaside resorts in the summer, New England is the perfect year-round travel destination. This comprehensive book offers many exciting places to go and things to see, from tracing the footsteps of our country's beginnings on Boston's historic Freedom Trail, to sampling local wines at one of Connecticut's vineyards, to enjoying the scenery at Maine's Acadia National Park.

1-58062-589-4,
$14.95 ($22.95 CAN)

Available wherever books are sold!

Everything® and everything.com® are registered trademarks of F+W Publications, Inc.

For Travel!

The Everything® Family Guide to Hawaii
Donald P. Ryan, Ph.D.

The Hawaiian islands have long been known as a premier travel destination. This island paradise is also gaining recognition for its family-friendly sites, high-quality accommodations, and exciting activities. *The Everything® Family Guide to Hawaii* provides readers with an easy-to-use guide to all the best hotels, shops, restaurants, and attractions in the Aloha State. This book features tips for finding the cheapest fares, traveling between islands, avoiding the tourist traps, and enjoying the unique culture and heritage of the Hawaiian people.

1-59337-054-7,
$14.95($22.95 CAN)

The Everything® Guide to New York City, 2nd Edition
Lori Perkins

1-59337-136-5,
$14.95 ($22.95 CAN)

The Everything® Guide to New York City, 2nd Ed. features all of New York's best-loved attractions, from Battery Park to Museum Mile. Starting with the must-see landmarks—the Statue of Liberty and Empire State Building—to surprising secret treasures that are off the beaten path, this book includes information on where to stay and eat, neighborhood explorations, shows and attractions, New York after dark, and more.

To order, call 800-872-5627 or visit *ww.everything.com*

The Everything® Family Guide to The Walt Disney World Resort®, Universal Studios®, and Greater Orlando, 4th Edition
Jason Rich

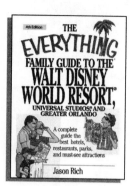

1-59337-179-9,
$14.95 ($22.95 CAN)

Packed with fun things to see and do, the Orlando area is the number one family vacation destination in the country. In this newest edition, travel expert Jason Rich shares his latest tips on how the whole family can have a great time—without breaking the bank. In addition to the helpful ride, show, and attractions rating system, the revised fourth edition contains a fully updated hotel/motel resource guide, rated restaurant listings, and the inside scoop on all the new additions.

The Everything® Family Guide to Washington D.C., 2nd Edition
Lori Perkins

The Everything® Guide to Washington D.C., 2nd Ed. captures the spirit and excitement of this unique city, from important historical showpieces such as the White House and the Smithsonian, to the best museums, galleries, and family activities. You'll find up-to-date reviews for tons of hotels and restaurants, guided tours, loads of attractions and activities, museums for every interest, and more!

1-59337-137-3,
$14.95 ($22.95 CAN)